ENDORSEMENTS

PLAN A

"Dwight Robertson's book *Plan A* is powerful! It hits a chord in every one of us, no matter where we are in life. In the end, the only important question will be, "What difference did my life make?" And the only appraisal that matters is what God thinks. This book is a Spirit-anointed guide that will assist you in your personal journey."

C. Kemmons Wilson, Jr.
Founding Family
Holiday Inns
Memphis, Tennessee

"Dwight Robertson and Mark Vermilion have produced a page-turner, Kingdom-advancing, great read. *Plan A* is filled with "chance encounters," "God's little coincidences," "divine appointments," "holy disturbances." These define Dwight's life and they describe a life committed to God's Plan A. Are they occurring in your life?"

Joyce Godwin
President
Godwin Resources
Albuquerque, New Mexico

"If you have ever wrestled with questions like, 'Can God use me?' or 'Could I really make an eternal difference?'—and all of us have—this practical and powerfully illustrated book gives a resounding YES! Dwight Robertson makes a compelling case answering both why and how every believer should get 'off the sidelines and in the game.' It is on my 'must read' list; I highly commend it to you!"

Steve Moore
President and CEO
Evangelical Fellowship of Mission Agencies
Atlanta, Georgia

"*Plan A* is an absolute encouragement to me because it loudly declares that everyday people are the ones God will use to transform the planet. We just have to look at life through God's lens. This book is a reminder that changing the world is not about having a position, but a disposition... to give away our lives. Get ready to be challenged by the stories in this book."

Dr. Tim Elmore
Founder and President
Growing Leaders
Duluth, Georgia

"The call of *Plan A* is clear and concise. In the mind of God, there is only one option and that option is us! As a pastor, I can only imagine what would happen if the people of God lived out the words of this book. If we answer the call, we will see the Lord transform the way we view our lives and the people around us."

Robert Gelinas
Lead Pastor
Colorado Community Church
Aurora, Colorado

"*Plan A* is filled with fresh, thought-provoking life experiences that will help you find and connect with the purpose God has shaped for you. More than ever, I've been encouraged to "get off the sidelines" and get involved in God's *Plan A* for reaching the world."

Georg Andersen
Architectural/Interior Designer
New York, New York
Conway, Arkansas

"God is waiting to bless you and challenge you through the prayerful reading of this book. Let Him speak to you, guide you, and use you mightily. God wants to fill you with Himself, and to make you a vital part of His *Plan A*."

Dr. Wesley L. Duewel
President Emeritus
OMS International, Inc.
Greenwood, Indiana

"CAUTION: DO NOT READ THIS BOOK IF YOUR DESIRE IS TO BE A SPECTATOR IN THE KINGDOM OF GOD. This book will challenge and change you...but equally important, it will leave you encourged.

Tobin Cassels III
President
Southeastern Freight Lines
Columbia, South Carolina

"Dwight Robertson expresses on paper what overflows out of his heart: an intense passion for the vehicle God uses to draw people into His Kingdom—laborers! By the time you complete this book, you'll have caught the same zeal to use your ordinary gifts and abilities, while allowing and expecting God to come through in extraordinary ways."

Bay Forest
Founder
Focus Ministries
Pagosa Springs, Colorado

"Dwight Robertson's book *Plan A* masterfully shows that every life matters. It proves that God gives all of us (who are ordinary people) the opportunity to impact the world beyond our imagination."

Ryan DeVoe
Founding Family
JD Byrider Corporation
Indianapolis, Indiana

"I highly recommend this book to anyone who wants to live a life that's full of purpose."

Scott Porter
President
Formula Boats
Decatur, Indiana

"This is a book of encouragement that every Christian needs to read. Read it, then pass it on."

Bill English
Author and Consultant
Mindsharp
Maple Grove, Minnesota

PLAN A

AND THERE'S NO PLAN B

DWIGHT ROBERTSON
W/ MARK VERMILION

Published by Kingdom Building Ministries,
14485 E. Evans Ave., Aurora, Colorado, 80014.

Unless otherwise indicated, Scripture references from the Holy Bible,
New International Version (NIV). Copyright © 1973, 1978, 1984,
International Bible Society. Used by permission of Zondervan Bible Publishers.
Bold lettering indicates emphasis added by the author.

Front Cover Design: Kristian Andersen + Associates, Indianapolis, Indiana.
Layout: Gary Bell Design Associates, National City, California
Printing: EP Graphics, Berne, Indiana

ISBN: 0-9788142-0-7

CONTENTS

INTRO

JAMES THE ROOFER

It wasn't what I wanted to find after a weekend of travel. But it wasn't something I could ignore either.

I'd just returned from speaking at a conference, where I'd had a very full schedule. My return flight had been full of delays, missed connections, and some pretty rough turbulence.

I was ready to relax.

But as I settled into my favorite recliner, I looked up and saw it—a big dark spot on the entryway ceiling of my home, clear evidence that the roof was leaking. My wife, Dawn, told me it had been an intense weekend of stormy weather while I was away and that more thunderstorms were on the way. I had to do something right away about the leak.

I didn't know any roofers who lived in the area, so I pulled out the Yellow Pages. I was a little nervous about hiring someone I knew nothing about, but I didn't have much of a choice. I needed the work done right away—before the next round of storms set in.

I made seven calls before I found someone who could quickly respond to my need. His name was James.

When James answered the phone, he immediately put me at ease with his pleasant voice and polite manner. He at least *sounded* like he was a man of his word. He told me when he could come and assured me he'd be on time. He was.

When James arrived, I was surprised to find a rugged guy with long hair in a ponytail—it just wasn't the image I had in my mind from our phone conversation. He introduced himself, asked me a few questions about the roof, and then climbed up on it to check out the damage.

He soon crawled back down and quoted me a price for the work. It seemed like a very fair price. He said the job would take him only two or three hours, and he could do it right away. I agreed to the price, and, before I knew it, he was back up on the roof making the repair.

About ninety minutes later, he knocked on the door again. I cringed. I thought he was going to tell me the damage was worse than he thought—and that it was going to cost me more than he quoted.

"All done!" he said when I opened the door. "It shouldn't give you any more problems now. If it does, just give me call." He then handed me a bill for a price that was *not* what he quoted. It was for less.

"I got it done quicker than I thought I would," he explained. "It wouldn't be fair to charge you for all the time I quoted since I didn't need it to complete your job."

I was amazed by his honesty!

As I was writing the check, he excused himself to take an incoming call on his cell phone. I listened as he interacted with a prospective customer on the other end of the line. He treated her with just as much professionalism and courtesy as he had me.

"You really do a great job with the way you treat your customers on the phone," I said as I handed him the check. "You're so polite and professional. I've really enjoyed working with you."

That's when something very unexpected happened.

James humbly looked down at the ground for a moment as I affirmed him, and then he looked up at me: "Thank you for your kind words, but, you know, I haven't always been this way. I don't know if you've ever heard of this term or not, but thirteen years ago, I was 'born again.' I became a Christian, and I'm not the same person I used to be."

As he continued to tell me about some of the changes in his life, he occasionally shook his head, as if he were *still* amazed.

He told me how he wants to love and serve God every day by serving his customers with kindness and respect. He said he sees each one of his jobs as God's entrusted daily assignment for him.

He was talking so openly about his desire to serve God that I began to glance out of the corner of my eye to see if there was a Bible or something lying around our entryway that would clue him in that I was also a Christian. I couldn't see anything that would tip him off.

"James, I'm a Christian, too," I finally told him.

VALIDATION

James got pretty excited about our shared faith in Jesus, and our conversation turned to deeper spiritual things. I encouraged him that God was obviously using him in the everyday places where he showed up to work.

"Do you realize you're going places where few pastors can go and reaching people with God's love that few pastors can reach?" I asked.

"I've thought about that a lot," he replied, "but I've never heard anyone else talk about it in that way."

"James, God has really positioned you for ministry to others!" I continued with a growing sense of excitement. "In fact, it reminds me of how Jesus did ministry when He was on earth. He went where needy people were and served them in the places where they lived, worked, and went about their daily lives.

"That's really what you're doing!"

I then asked if I could pray for him and his daily ministry before he left.

By time time, Dawn and our two children, Dara and Dreyson, had entered the room. They joined me in placing hands on James the Roofer. We prayed a blessing and commissioning over his ministry—just like the elders at a church often pray over missionaries before sending them out to their fields of service.

His body trembled under our hands as we prayed. I soon realized he was sobbing. (It wasn't what I expected from such a rugged-looking guy.) After we prayed, it took awhile for him to gain his composure.

"I'm sorry for crying," he said. "I don't do this very often. It's just no one has ever treated my ministry like it's important. For thirteen years now, I've believed in my heart that this is how God has chosen for me to represent Him to others—and, in all that time, no one has ever validated that what I do is important to God."

He went on to tell me that he prays that God will send him customers who need to hear the Good News about Jesus. He then prays for each of his customers by name and asks God to give him opportunities to minister to them. James then told me about one of those opportunities.

A few years ago, he said, he was working on the roof of a home in the inner city of Denver. He was startled when he heard a gunshot and screaming from inside the house.

He scrambled off the roof and ran inside to find a man lying on the floor with the back of his head blown open. The man's family had already called 911, but it was clear to everyone in the room that he wasn't going to make it.

James knelt next to the man and told him he didn't have long to live. The man locked eyes with him.

"God loves you very much. Do you want to know that you're going to heaven to be with Him when you die?" James asked him—unsure of whether the dying man could hear him. The man nodded his eyes up and down, because he couldn't talk or move his body. James then led the man into a relationship with Christ by asking him questions and allowing him to continue answering with his eyes.

The man died a few moments later.

By this time, I was nearly in tears myself. I asked James for his business card, and I told him I'd place it on our refrigerator next to the other prayer magnets for missionaries and pastors. Then our whole family promised James that we would pray for him. (And although we haven't seen him since, we still do.)

He thanked us repeatedly as he walked out the door.

OVERLOOKED AND UNDERVALUED

As I returned to my recliner, I thanked God for that "chance encounter" with James the Roofer. God used it to deeply stir my heart and reaffirm my own calling to help ordinary Christians like James know the joy and purpose of living their lives for the one-and-only cause that counts for eternity.

But I was deeply grieved that James felt so overlooked and undervalued in his ministry service to God. Especially when the Bible shows us how often God chooses *ordinary* people like him to do His *extraordinary* Kingdom work.

Some find that hard to believe because we live in a day when "professional" ministers (those who make their living from their ministry work) and "Christian celebrities" (those who minister from platforms and in media spotlights) are held up as standards for what it looks like to do something important for God.

But the day-to-day ministry of faithful servants like James the Roofer is at the heart of God's plan for reaching the world.

It's time to take another look at what God has to say in His Word about the nature of ministry and who's qualified to do it. God chose ordinary vessels. He validated weak and imperfect people who served Him in hidden places. He honored the poor in spirit. He sought out the humble. And He called them all to significant places of influence.

And you know what? He still does.

If you feel like you're too ordinary to contribute to the work of God's Kingdom, this book could powerfully reshape your thinking about the importance of *your* ministry service.

If you've ever felt like the kind of work you do in God's Kingdom is overlooked, underappreciated, and maybe even unimportant—then this book may be a source of hope and encouragement for you. It may propel you forward in your ministry service with a greater passion and sense of purpose.

And if you're in a place of influence in the Body of Christ, this book could help you challenge, inspire, encourage, and equip other ordinary Christians like James the Roofer to put their faith into action through ministry service.

THE PLAN FOR THIS BOOK

This book is laid out in four sections: The Plan, The Problem, The Power, and The Possibilities. Some sections have multiple chapters; others have just one.

The first and longest section—The Plan—lays out each of the countercultural pieces of God's Plan A for reaching the world. Its insights will surprise and challenge you.

Chapter one ("Rewind") is an introduction to the plan.

Chapter two ("All-Inclusive") deals with the WHO of ministry. It answers the quesion, "WHO does God choose when He has a high-impact ministry assignment?"

Chapters three and four ("Out of the Box" and "Camouflage") cover the WHAT of ministry. They answer the question, "WHAT does high-impact ministry look like?" Be ready. It may not look like what you expect. It may look a whole lot more appealing!

Chapters five and six ("In the Moment" and "Little Do We Know") examine the WHEN of ministry. They answer the question, "WHEN does high-impact ministry take place?" Sounds like too basic and simple of a question, doesn't it? Let me assure you, the answers to it have profound implications for your life.

Chapters seven and eight ("Up Close" and "Meal Tables") focus on the WHERE of ministry. They answer the question, "Where does high-impact ministry happen?" I'll give you a hint on this one: It doesn't just happen inside the four walls of a church building.

Chapters nine and ten ("One Life at a Time" and "Your Story") deal with the HOW of ministry. They answer the question, "HOW did Jesus do ministry and HOW does He want us to do it?" .

That's Part I—the who, what, when, where, and how of God's Plan A.

In Part II—The Problem—we'll look at one of the most pervasive threats to Plan A and its accomplishment. Chapter eleven ("Spectators") deals head on with the issue and calls you to do something about it.

In Part III—The Power—we'll focus on the Power Source behind Plan A. In Chapters twelve ("40,000 Volts"), thirteen ("Connectors"), and fourteen ("Letting Go"), we'll discover how God expresses His unconditional love and transformational power through His followers—who act as His connectors to the world.

In Part IV—The Potential—we'll examine how the simple actions and words of one person can powerfully impact all of eternity. Chapter fifteen ("Ripples") examines the eternal impact of a single person's life, and chapter sixteen ("Imagine") asks us to think about what could happen if more Christians committed themselves to God's Plan A for the world.

KEEP IN MIND

Here are some additional things to keep in mind as you're reading this book...

As you'll soon find out, I love to tell stories. The pages ahead are full of them. In most cases, the stories are personal ones, and they include details about other people's lives—especially family, friends, and neighbors. It's important for you to know that I've changed the names of people in many of my stories in order to protect their identities. In some cases, I've even changed details that might also give away who they are.

I also want you to know that Kingdom Building Ministries has created a website to accompany this book. It has additional applications, resources, and practical tools that can support you as you apply the concepts in this book to your life—or teach them to others. To access the website, go to *www.kbm.org*, and click on the "Plan A Connection" link.

Finally, there's a team of people praying for you as you read this book and apply it to your life. We're praying that God will use it to encourage you, challenge you, equip you, and fan into flame your passion for Him and desire to become an active participant in His Plan A.

PART ONE

THE PLAN

*God has a Plan A for
reaching the world,
and it includes the
involvement of every Christian.*

REWIND

In his book *What's So Amazing About Grace?*, Philip Yancey tells a story about evangelist Billy Graham and a historic trip he made to the former Soviet Union.

> During the Brezhnev era at the height of the Cold War, Billy Graham visited Russia and met with government and church leaders. Conservatives back home reproached him for treating the Russians with such courtesy and respect. He should have taken a more prophetic role, they said, by condemning the abuses of human rights and religious liberty. One of his critics accused him of setting the church back *fifty* years. Graham listened, lowered his head, and replied, "I am deeply ashamed. I have been trying very hard to set the church back *two thousand* years" (emphasis added).

TWO THOUSAND YEARS AGO

God's Plan A for redeeming the world is a two thousand-year-old plan. But don't let that scare you away. It's as relevant, powerful, and important today as it was when Jesus first put it into action.

oblem is, somewhere along the way, parts of it got watered down, istorted, and even forgotten. In order to understand it, then, we have to hit the "rewind" button and go back two thousand years to the time when Jesus walked the earth.

When I read the gospel accounts of Jesus' life and try to picture in my mind how He lived and went about His ministry, I'm struck by how differently most of us live our lives and approach ministry today.

When Jesus traveled from place to place, He was keenly aware of the needs of people around Him. He didn't race from one place to another. He didn't hurry past the poor and needy—without even noticing them—so He could get to the synagogue. He slowed down and *saw* their needs.

> "...Jesus went about all the cities and villages, teaching in their synagogues and preaching the gospel of the kingdom, and healing every disease and every infirmity. When he **saw** the crowds, he had compassion for them, because they were harassed and helpless, like sheep without a shepherd" (Matthew 9:35-36, RSV, emphasis added).

He *saw* the people around Him as He traveled. He really *saw* them! We struggle with seeing the needs of others around us. We're caught up in our own lives—our own needs and interests. And usually, we're in too much of a hurry to take the time to truly see others.

When's the last time you really saw the waitress who serves you at your favorite restaurant? I'm not talking about just seeing her with your eyes. I'm talking about seeing her with a fully engaged mind and heart as well.

When's the last time you really saw the checkout girl at the grocery store? The teller at the bank? The guy at work who seems so self absorbed? The kid down the street whose parents work all the time?

Jesus saw those sorts of people. Every direction He looked, I saw how directionless people were. They were turning every direction, but had no direction. They were harassed and helpless—wandering aimlessly through life without hope and purpose.

And Jesus saw them.

Now, that may not seem like a big deal to you, but it is. Have you ever personally felt like you were unseen and overlooked by others around you? How did it make you feel? Unimportant? Forgotten? If you've ever been unseen by others, then you'll understand why it was so important that Jesus saw people and their needs.

Not long ago, my son, Dreyson, started the school year at a new elementary school. When he got home from school on the first day, I asked him how it went.

"It was awful, Dad," he moaned. "I was invisible."

I wasn't exactly sure what he meant by "invisible." Was his imagination running wild? (I thought maybe it was time to cut out some of his video-game privileges. Maybe they were having a negative effect on his thinking!)

But he knew "invisible" was the perfect word for what he was feeling.

"All the other kids already have their friends, and they wouldn't pay any attention to me," he continued. "No one would play with me at recess. No one would sit with me at lunch. No one would talk to me in class.

"I was *invisible*, Dad!"

Unfortunately, what Dreyson was feeling that day isn't uncommon. Many others feel the same way as they live out their overlooked, unnoticed, and unseen lives. They feel lonely and unappreciated—like they're not valuable to other people. I think "invisible" is the right word to capture how many people feel.

It's time we slowed down and started seeing people. Like the Zulu people of Southern Africa do.

When two Zulu people see each other, one person greets the other by saying, "I *see* you!" And the other person replies, "I am here!" What a powerful greeting!

Could the actions of our lives speak the same message—"I see you!"—to others around us? I don't think it would be that difficult. Next time someone serves you at a restaurant, bank, or store, speak to them as if you truly see them. Don't just treat them like impersonal servants. Treat them like real people.

And don't just view your time with them as *transactions*—view them as *interactions*.

Greet your servers by name (it's usually clearly marked on a nametag) and ask them about how their day is going. Encourage them. Tell them what you appreciate about their service. If you do, you'll be among the very few who truly sees them.

BEYOND SEEING

Seeing is important. But it's only the first step in Jesus' ministry model. He not only saw people, but He also *stopped* and served them—right where they were.

Most of us don't do a very good job at *stopping* to serve others. But Jesus did. In fact, *seeing* and *stopping* were two of the recurring expressions of His love.

He looked into the faces of innocent children who weren't highly valued…and He stopped and put them on His lap.

He walked daily among poor beggars and often stumbled across men lying by the roadside with crippling physical illnesses…and He stopped and put His healing hands on their diseased bodies.

He often encountered women who were living sad and hopeless lives of adultery…and He stopped and talked to them about the way of hope.

He sometimes came face to face with those who were oppressed and tormented by evil spirits…and He stopped and delivered them.

Religious people walked past them. Jesus didn't. He slowed down and saw them. He stopped for them.

He met people where they were and got involved in the pressing needs of their lives.

ONE WORD

At one point, He turned to His disciples and shared with them the *one word* that was *His* response to all of the needs they were seeing and stopping for. It was the word that represented His Plan A for reaching the world with His Good News, and He gave no other option for a Plan B. (There's apparently no contingency plan if this one doesn't work.)

It was His word to describe people who would be willing to see the needs of others and stop to serve them. People like James the Roofer.

So, what word did Jesus choose? To be honest, I'm reluctant to say it. Even though it's what this book is about, it's not a very glamorous word—and as important as it is, it may not grab your attention and keep you reading. But it's a word and a concept that will set us back two thousand years to the values and ministry model of Jesus.

It's a word you'll probably never see in a Madison Avenue advertising campaign or in a church's marketing or membership materials.

It's a word that just doesn't have much sizzle.

In fact, when I founded Kingdom Building Ministries (the organization with which I still serve) more than two decades ago, I considered adopting this word in our mission statement and marketing materials. But a consultant urged us to drop it as fast as we could.

"It will never draw people to your ministry," she said.

When I didn't budge, she pleaded with me, "Please let us help you pick a better word to represent your ministry!"

"There's only one problem," I replied. "It's the word *Jesus chose* two thousand years ago to represent His plan for reaching the world. Who are *we* to change *His* word?"

So, what's the word?

*"Then he said to his disciples, 'The harvest is plentiful,
but the **laborers** are few; pray therefore the Lord of the
harvest to send out **laborers** into his harvest'"* (Matthew 9:37-38, RSV, emphasis added).

What the world needs, Jesus said, is *laborers*. Common *laborers*.
Laborers are Jesus' means for reaching the world with His love
and forgiveness. And they aren't just critical to His plan. They *are*
His plan.

His only plan.

EVERYDAY, EVERY-PLACE MINISTERS

But what exactly *is* a laborer? After all, it's not a familiar, "house-
hold" word used to describe most Christians.

As I've examined Scripture, I think there's a clear and simple
definition: *A laborer is a disciple in action.*

The word *disciple* implies one who learns from and follows another. In Jewish tradition, each rabbi had his own disciples, whom
he mentored and taught. And in this same tradition, Jesus gathered
a group of disciples around Himself during His earthly ministry.

But after traveling from village to village, Jesus didn't tell the
twelve that the world needs more *disciples*. He told them the world
needs more *laborers*—disciples who put their love for Him into
action through ministry service.

A laborer is an active minister. Not just the "professional" kind
like pastors and missionaries, but the common, ordinary kind like
my wife (an art teacher) and children (students).

Laborers are "every-day, every-place ministers" like my friend
Don, who works as a major-market radio executive, and leads
some of his seeker friends and coworkers in a regular Bible study
to help them discover God's amazing love and purpose for their
lives.

Or like my friend Tobin, who owns a large trucking company
and deeply cares for the welfare of his employees.

Or like my friends Norm and Becky, who were sent home aft short stint as overseas missionaries. They decided God must ha a different kind of ministry for them. Norm became a salesman and Becky became a full-time mom. And, together, they became "missionaries" in their own suburban Texas neighborhood, caring for and sharing with their neighbors.

Or like James the Roofer, who sees every interaction with his customers as a potential, God-appointed ministry assignment for that day.

Laborers are everyday, ordinary people. They're people who express their love for God through practical, hands-and-feet service. And because they naturally show up on the everyday scenes of life, they can influence people that no professional minister could. Because they have everyday kinds of jobs, they can reach people who'd never step foot in a church building.

Want to know what a laborer looks like? Look in the mirror. God is calling *you* to be one.

And since laborers are God's Plan A for reaching the world, that means *you* are God's Plan A for reaching the world around *you*.

You are God's Plan A to the other soccer moms and dads as you take your kids to practices and games. *You* are God's Plan A to your co-workers, with whom you spend more hours than nearly anyone else in your life. *You* are God's Plan A in your neighborhood, where you have time and opportunities to develop natural and meaningful relationships with your neighbors. *You* are God's Plan A in your high-school classroom or college dorm. *You* are God's Plan A at your favorite restaurant that you visit so often.

Not just your pastor. *You*.

You are God's Plan A. (And did I mention there's no Plan B?)

26

2

ALL-INCLUSIVE

My friend, Grace, was about as ordinary as anyone I've ever known. She didn't seem to be a likely candidate for high-impact ministry.

She lived in an old farmhouse on Strawtown Pike in a rural area of North-Central Indiana. One of her legs was shorter than the other, and she walked around with a signature limp. She was in her seventies, and she wore her wiry gray hair up in a bun. She usually wore a colorful dress and nylon stockings that sometimes bagged a little around her ankles.

Grace and her husband had raised five boys, but by her senior years, they were grown and living with their families in other places. When her husband passed away, she found herself in a strange season of life—with fewer responsibilities and meaningful things to do.

She often prayed that God would give her something significant to do for Him in her final years.

She wanted to sprint to the finish line.

Grace once told me, "I don't know how God could use an old woman like me, but if He'll show me what He wants me to do, I'll do it!"

I got to be a firsthand witness as God answered her prayers.

One day, she was reading a prison-ministry magazine and found an open letter from an inmate named Bobby, who had recently be-me a Christian. Bobby was looking for a "Godly grandmother" who would disciple him. He had just committed his life to Christ at a prison revival service, and he wasn't sure what to do next.

Grace wrote the magazine editor and asked if he could help her get connected with Bobby. She told the editor she had raised five boys and she had it in her to be the spiritual grandmother of another.

She wasn't really sure what to do with her new spiritual grandson, but she found some correspondence Bible studies and began leading him through them. Soon, Bobby led his cellmate to Christ, and Grace became his spiritual grandmother, too.

Not long afterward, I visited her for lunch, and she showed me pictures of her growing group of "seven boys"—each of whom had become a Christian through Bobby's influence.

"I'm having the time of my life!" she exclaimed as she shared with me each of their personal stories.

"Right now, I've got a captive audience," she said with a smile and a twinkle in her eye, "but I figure they won't be in prison for the rest of their lives. Today, they'll impact the lives of their fellow inmates, and some day, they'll get out of prison and impact the world for Christ."

I stopped by her house again a number of months later. She welcomed me into her home, and I went to hang my coat in her closet, but there was no place to put it. The closet was full of filing cabinets and Bible-study lessons. I looked around her living room and was surprised to find that the couch and coffee table had been replaced by work tables and computers.

"Wow! What's going on, Grace? It doesn't take all of this to disciple seven inmates."

"Oh, Dwight, a lot has happened since you were last here," she replied. "God has done more with this ministry than I ever imagined!"

I was eager to hear all about it.

"Did you know that prisoners get transferred?" she continued. "I've had boys get transferred to prisons in Alabama and Texas, and they've been sharing Christ with inmates in those prisons, too. "I'm now leading Bible studies with inmates in three prisons—a from my little farmhouse!"

IN OVER HER HEAD

I continued to make regular trips to Grace's house to check up on her. The last time I went, she had a world map up on her wall with dots all over the Americas.

"Grace, what are all these dots?" I asked in amazement.

"These are my boys and all their 'extras,'" she replied.

"Okay, I know about your boys, but what are their 'extras'?"

"Well, a while back, my boys started getting out of prison, and they'd lead their wives, children, and other family members to Christ. So, they asked me if I'd be a spiritual grandma to their family members as well. Those are the 'extras' that I never expected God to make a part of my spiritual family."

"But what about all these dots in Latin countries?" I asked. "How did they get there?"

She told me that some of the Hispanic inmates had introduced her to their Spanish-speaking friends and family members when they got out of prison. She started receiving letters written in Spanish from people in Cuba, so she prayed that God would send her someone who could translate.

God led her to a retired Spanish teacher named Clara.

"I'm in over my head, Dwight!" she proclaimed. "We're now discipling more than a thousand Spanish-speaking people, and Clara comes over to my house three days a week to translate their correspondence. I've even added seven college students who volunteer with us.

"It started in Cuba, and it's spreading all over Latin America."

A few months later, I called her while I was on the road, speaking at an event on the West Coast.

"How are you doing Grandma Grace? You've been on my mind this week."

You're not the only one," she quipped with her trademark laugh. My kids have been thinking about me this week, too. In fact, they're worried about me, Dwight.

"They checked my bank account, and they found out I have only $14.63 left in it. Apparently, I've spent more than I realized on all my correspondence.

"I told them I may be broke, but more souls are going to heaven!"

I laughed with her for a few minutes, and then I asked her a question I'd wanted to ask her for a long time.

"Grace, how many people are you corresponding with?"

"Oh, that doesn't matter," she said humbly. "I love all of them as if they're my own grandkids."

After some coaxing, I finally got her to give me a number.

"I don't know the exact number. Last I counted, there were more than ten thousand."

I was shocked. I didn't know what to say, so she continued as if it were no big deal. "Last week, the U.S. Postal Service told me I had to get an industrial-size mailbox or they won't deliver all my mail anymore."

Then she started laughing, and she could hardly squeak out her next statement: "Dwight, I have a dream that someday the post office will assign me my own zip code!"

We both laughed together again, and our laughter soon gave way to praise. What an amazing thing to witness! God had chosen to send ripples through all of eternity through an old, gray-haired widow and an odd assortment of her friends out of a farmhouse on Strawtown Pike in the Middle of Nowhere, Indiana.

But it shouldn't have surprised me. He's clearly told us and shown us that that's His plan. Throughout history ("His story"), He's often chosen obscure people who live in small places to accomplish His big eternal plans and purposes.

Writer Richard Exley says it this way: "God has a history of using the insignificant to accomplish the impossible."

SPOTLIGHTS AND PLATFORMS

So, why is it that our plans for high-impact ministry in the American church are so different than Jesus' plan? Why don't we champion the ministry potential of ordinary people who do ordinary things in ordinary places of life? Why have we become so enamored with ministry activities that happen in the spotlight and on the platform—the "celebrity" forms of ministry?

For some time now, it seems that our ministry heroes have been "Christian celebrities"—talented musicians, dynamic speakers, best-selling authors, high-energy televangelists, powerful Christian leaders, and well-known pastors.

But while these well-known people have impacted the Kingdom of God in very significant ways, *"Christian celebrities" aren't the answer to the great harvest need!*

When the vast work of the Kingdom is done, it will have been accomplished by nameless, faceless people who did what they could, where they were—and God added the increase to their labor. That's God's Plan A.

The world needs God's love expressed in and through the lives of countless faithful Kingdom laborers. He's not calling just a few select people to make a difference. Instead, His plan is to mobilize an army of laborers who go into every place of need in every corner of the world.

This idea was at the heart of God's movement in the church during the Protestant Reformation started by Martin Luther five centuries ago.

> "[It is a] false assumption that there is a *special* calling, a vocation, to which superior Christians are invited to observe...while ordinary Christians fulfill only the commands;" said Luther, "...there simply is no *special* religious vocation" (emphasis added).

I believe this is also at the heart of God's movement in our day. In fact, I believe He wants to continue in our day the reformation work He started with Martin Luther. He's fueling a movement of commonplace laborers, and *every one of us* is called to be a part of it.

When Luther referred to "superior Christians," he was talking about those who had taken a monastic vow—the clergy. Perhaps in our day, our idea of the "superior Christian" is one who does ministry on a platform or in a spotlight.

But there's no disqualification of the commonplace in this movement: *Every* Christian has a significant role to play.

I think Jesus was intentional when He chose the word *laborer* to describe His plan for the world.

It's an all-inclusive word.

It's an "everybody" word.

It doesn't describe what kind of gifts or talents a laborer has, or what kind of work a laborer does. Maybe that's because the Kingdom of God needs all kinds of laborers. From those who serve on the platform to those who serve in the hidden places. From those who serve with their mouths and minds to those who serve with their hands and feet.

FIRST-ROUND DRAFT CHOICES

The Bible makes it clear that commonplace laborers aren't the "losers" who get picked last for God's ministry team, while the "Christian celebrities" get picked first.

Laborers are His first-round draft picks!

Just look at the twelve common men Jesus chose to be His disciples. They weren't superstars. They weren't rabbis. They weren't the most brilliant scholars or the most charismatic speakers. They were a cross-section of average people—some fishermen, a tax collector, some businessmen, and the like.

A few years ago, I found a tongue-and-cheek memo that illustrates just how average (and even unqualified) these disciples were to start a movement that's lasted more than two thousand years.

To:
Jesus, Son of Joseph
Woodcrafters Carpenter Shop
Nazareth 35922

From:
Jordan Management Consultants
Jerusalem 26544

Thank you for submitting the resumes of the twelve men you have picked for management positions in your new organization. All of them have now taken our battery of tests, and we have not only run the results through our computer but also arranged personal interviews for each of them with our psychologist and vocational aptitude consultant.

It is the staff's opinion that most of your nominees are lacking in background, education, and vocational aptitude for the type of enterprise you are undertaking.

Simon Peter is emotionally unstable and given to fits of temper. Andrew has no leadership qualities. The two brothers, James and John, Sons of Zebedee, place personal interests above company loyalty. Thomas demonstrates a questioning attitude that could undermine company morale. We feel it our duty to tell you that Matthew has been blacklisted by the Greater Jerusalem Better Business Bureau. James, the son of Alpheus, and Thaddeus definitely have radical leanings, and they both registered a high score on the manic-depressive scale.

One of the candidates, however, shows great potential. He is a man of utility and resourcefulness, meets people well, has a keen business mind, and has contacts in high places. He is highly motivated, ambitious and responsible. We recommend Judas Iscariot as your controller and right-hand man. All the other profiles are self explanatory.

We wish you every success in your new venture.

Yours Truly,
Jordan Management Consultants

Think about it for a moment. In its not-so-serious way, this memo describes some of the serious deficiencies of the men *God chose* to carry forth the most important message in the world. These are the men *He chose* to be the leaders of the most important movement in history!

And yet you and I, if we were in charge, may have easily passed them over as being too flawed and, well, commonplace. We may have felt that their gifts were not the right kinds or at the right level to do an important work in God's Kingdom.

Maybe that's the point.

As He chose weak men and women like Abraham, Jacob, Gideon, David, Mary, Martha, Mark, Peter, and the other eleven disciples, God seemed to be sending an emphatic message from heaven.

He seemed to reinforce the same message when He chose a stable in a small town to be the birthplace of His Son. And He reinforced it again when chose carpentry—not a "religious" position—to be Jesus' vocation.

And later, when Jesus—the King of Kings and Lord of Lords—was at the height of His glory, God chose for Him to ride into Jerusalem on a donkey, not a chariot. This was His triumphal procession, and He did it on a lowly donkey!

Finally, He chose for Jesus to die a criminal's death on a lowly cross.

And in these final events of Jesus' life, it's as if God were putting an exclamation point on the message He'd been communicating all along:

> *God does extraordinary things through ordinary*
> *(and even lowly) people and circumstances.*

He always has, and apparently, He always will.

But for far too long in the American church, we've elevated and exalted the status of certain kinds of highly visible gifts in the Body of Christ. We've said or implied that those who have leadership gifts or dynamic communication skills—or those who stand on a platform in front of large groups of people—are the ones who are doing the *real and important* work of the Kingdom. (Of course, these high-profile ministers are doing important work, but they aren't the *only* ones doing something important in God's Kingdom.)

The One who started this eternal movement, Jesus, gave us an example to follow two thousand years ago. He surrounded Himself with flawed people who had very average gifts. He equipped them during His short time on earth, and then He empowered them by sending His Holy Spirit. The result? They spread a world-changing message and movement in every direction.

GRACE THE GRANDMA'S LEGACY

Grace the Grandma passed away a few years ago. The Kingdom of Darkness was no doubt glad to see her go. But the impact of her life will be felt for decades to come, as each of her "spiritual grandsons" influences the lives of others.

Grace's life was a living sermon to every one of us. It was a reminder that God still wants to use us all in unimaginable ways to reach the world.

Paul Billheimer once wrote, "The fate of the world is in the hands

of nameless saints." Not Christian celebrities. Not up-front personalities. Not "superior Christians."

The fate of the world is in the hands of commonplace laborers
like Grace the Grandma and James the Roofer. It's in the hands of
people like you.

3

OUT OF THE BOX

I was a young pastor when Dawn and I were first married. Like many pastor's wives, she was scrutinized by people in our church to see if she fit their idea of a pastor's wife.

She didn't.

One lady in our congregation asked me, "Does she play the piano?" She didn't.

"Does she sing?" she continued. She didn't do that either.

"Can she lead women's Bible studies?" Sorry, that's just not Dawn.

Finally, she asked in frustration, "Well, what does she do that would make her a good pastor's wife?"

Truth is, Dawn has *many* amazing, unique and wonderful gifts, but they don't fit the mold that some wanted to squeeze her into.

While she can't play the piano, you should see her flair for art and color. She's not a singer, but she's great with hospitality—and wow, can she cook! She doesn't feel comfortable speaking to large groups, but if you get her in a small group or a personal conversation, she shines.

That's how God has designed her.

Early in our marriage, she traveled with me as I spoke at different events, and event coordinators would sometimes mistakenly assume that Dawn could also speak at their events. Without telling us, one coordinator actually scheduled her to speak to a ladies group during a weekend ministry event. By the time we found out, it was too late to cancel.

On the day of the event, I prayed over Dawn. She was terrified. I promised I would pray for her the whole time she spoke. She took a deep breath and walked out the door to face her speaking assignment. And I got on my knees.

Two hours later, she came back to the room where we were staying.

"How did it go?" I excitedly asked as she walked through the door.

"Well," she replied in a resigned tone, "Before this, *I* knew I couldn't speak. And now, *they* know it too. And I hope they tell the world that I'm not a speaker. Public speaking is not *my* ministry!"

GIFTED FOR MINISTRY

God has distinctly and uniquely made Dawn—and every one of us—with a ministry purpose in mind.

There are no clones, copies, or dittos. He's given each of us a unique role to play in carrying out His Plan A.

Psalm 139 tells us that He has "fearfully and wonderfully made" each of us for a unique destiny and purpose. And He's designed us in a way that'll enhance our personal effectiveness in the places where He puts us.

> *"For we are God's workmanship, created in Christ Jesus to do good works, which God prepared in advance for us to do"* (Ephesians 2:10).

There's no exclusivity in God's Kingdom employment plan. Jesus is an "equal opportunity" employer. His desire is to uniquely employ every one of us in His Kingdom—through our careers, our hobbies, our past experiences, and our spiritual gifts.

For Dawn, ministry is not on a stage or behind a microphone. It's often in our home and neighborhood.

A few years ago, shortly after we'd moved into a new neighborhood, Dawn began to build relationships with some of the ladies who lived around us. She soon decided to invite them into our home so they could all get to know each other.

One fall Saturday, she made some of our favorite baked goods and invited a bunch of the ladies over. At her request, I prayed a commissioning prayer over her—like I did with James the Roofer—before I left the house.

Our kitchen and dining room were her place of ministry. Our neighborhood friends would be her congregation.

Soon the house was full. She had a great turnout, and the ladies had a wonderful time—so wonderful that they weren't leaving.

Four hours later, Dawn began to ask them if their families might be looking for them. They finally began trickling out the door of our home—smiling, laughing, and happy they'd been able to spend time together. Dawn assured them it wouldn't be the last time.

They began meeting regularly—always looking forward to Dawn's scrumptious baked goods—and as time went on, they began to share with one another about deeper issues in their lives.

God moved in the times Dawn spent with these women. One committed her life to Him, another worked to put her marriage back together, and several others started going to church for the first time since they were kids.

It was a ministry few professional ministers could've ever had with them. Dawn was their minister, uniquely gifted for building the kind of relational bridges that were needed to reach their hearts.

MINISTRY THAT LOOKS LIKE YOU

What about you? Have you discovered relational ministry opportunities that look like you?

We sometimes have a very narrow view of what "ministry" looks like. We struggle because we just don't fit into a typical "ministry" mold—whether it's a mold we're trying to force ourselves into or a mold somebody else is trying to force on us. Often, our ideas of what ministry looks like just don't look like us.

Maybe the reason they don't look like us is because they weren't meant to. Maybe God has another form of ministry in mind that would feel natural and look just like you. God has, after all, created you with a Kingdom-building purpose in mind, and He's uniquely designed you for that purpose.

> *"'For I know the plans I have for you,' declares the Lord...."* (Jeremiah 29:11a).

> *"For you [God] created my inmost being; you knit me together in my mother's womb. I praise you because I am fearfully and wonderfully made....All the days ordained for me were written in your book before one of them came to be"* (Psalm 139:13-14, 16).

ARCHES, WHORLS, AND LOOPS

In a world of more than six billion people, it would be easy for you to believe that there's nothing unique about you. But there is.

There's something about you that's different from every other person who's ever lived. You've had it from the time you were in your mother's womb, and it'll stay the same throughout your life.

It's your fingerprint.

The arches, whorls, and loops (terms for different skin patterns) on your fingers create a pattern unlike anyone else's. That's why crime investigators have long used fingerprints as a way of identifying people who were present at a crime scene.

If God paid that much attention to making your fingers unique from everyone else's, doesn't it make sense that He intends for you to be different in other ways, too? Doesn't it make sense that He wants your ministry expressions to be unique?

That's why the New Testament spends so much time talking about how God designed us with differences, as one body of believers with many distinct parts (Romans 12, 1 Corinthians 12).

One of the greatest joys you'll ever know is when you live out God's unique-and-distinct ministry purpose for your life. You'll get frustrated if you try to imitate the ministry styles and forms of other people—especially when God hasn't made or called you to serve in the same way.

He's designed you like no other, and His design is perfect for the ministry He's called you to.

That's your *ministry* fingerprint.

BREAKING OUT OF THE BOX

God has given each of us the entrepreneurial freedom to creatively apply our gifts and passions to ministry. But many of us are stuck in a box, believing that ministry has a limited number of expressions.

It's time to break out of the box.

I love seeing people begin to find the distinct-and-unique ministry roles that God has called them to (and designed them for).

They come alive. They begin to find a greater sense of purpose.

Have you found the good works you were created to do?

You can be wildly entrepreneurial and creative as you think about your life's impact. There are so many things about you that God can use to minister to other people. Things that you may have never considered as being a part of your ministry toolbox.

Here's one example: Many people have found that their hobbies and recreational interests—skateboarding, backpacking, fishing, coffee drinking, windsurfing, listening to jazz music, baking, and the like—are all employable for Kingdom service.

I get excited about some of the hobby-based ministries my friends are involved in:

> *Naomi loves to read books,* so she started a book exchange with ladies in her community as a means of building relationships with them over a common interest. It's a natural place for her to share her love for God as well.

41

Steve loves to fly-fish and teach other people how to fly-fish. He also loves to share his faith in Christ with people. So, he decided to mix the two. Steve takes his unbelieving friends on weekend fly-fishing trips into the mountains, where he introduces them to a relationship with Christ while teaching them how to fly-fish. His approach is natural and highly relational. He calls it *Life on the Fly*.

Vonda is a nurse who joined a bowling league with her coworkers so that they could get to know each other better. It has opened up opportunities for them to have spiritual conversations.

Paul is a gourmet coffee lover. A few years ago, he found a creative way to combine his love for coffee with his greater love for God. Paul made a deal with the owner of a struggling coffee shop in his town that he'd bring in paying customers if he could do Bible studies with them. Paul's one-on-one meetings with unsaved friends soon grew into a coffeehouse ministry, and the owner gave him the freedom to preach out loud to those who came. The owner was delighted with the increase in customers and revenue. Paul has since done the same thing in other coffee shops.

Fred is an experienced hunter, and he started a club for his friends who share his love of hunting. Each year, his club hosts a wild-game cook-off night where he arranges for someone to share his testimony as a part of the evening's program.

What things do you enjoy doing?

Allow God to show you ways you can employ those things to build His Kingdom. Get creative and entrepreneurial!

Laborership (a word I've made up) doesn't have to be boring and lifeless. In fact, there's a growing movement of entrepreneurial people who are finding laborership to be joyful and exhilarating because they've smashed the small box that they'd previously placed around "ministry." And they've recognized that just about every aspect of life has relational ministry potential.

They've realized it doesn't have to look like the "same ol' same ol.'"

THE JOY OF BEING A LABORER

There isn't a man, woman, young person, or child who doesn't have a specific role to play in helping build God's Kingdom on earth. His Plan A is all inclusive.

If you haven't already, it's time for you to discover your own ministry fingerprint—the one God gave you--so that you can have a greater eternal impact on the lives of others.

That's when you'll experience the joy of being a laborer in God's Kingdom and a greater sense of purpose in your life. There's nothing like it.

When I'm speaking, I often ask the audience, "Do I look miserable?"

"No!" they reply and laugh as if I've asked something ridiculous.

"Well then, I just want to allay any fears you might have," I continue. "Being an active laborer in God's Kingdom doesn't make you miserable. It brings incredible joy! My life has its pain like everyone else's, but it's also full of joy, energy, passion, and fulfillment."

Welcome to the joy of laborership!

4

CAMOUFLAGE

I've been in vocational ministry for much of my professional life—a fact that, at times, has enhanced my capacity to minister to others and, at other times, has hindered it.

When I'm relating to my non-Christian neighbors, I've found that my ministerial title usually hinders it.

That's why I don't often reveal to them the specifics of what I do for a living...at least at first. When my neighbors ask, I simply (and truthfully) say, "I'm an executive with a nonprofit organization."

This response gives me the chance to build relationships with them as an ordinary guy. When I'm at home—working in my front yard or walking with my kids through the neighborhood—I lose all my other ministerial titles and become Dwight the Neighbor. I really like it.

Ask most pastors or ministry leaders, and they'll tell you the same thing: When non-Christians find out what we do for a living, they often become stiff, self conscious, and guarded around us. They discount our attempts to connect with them—as if we're doing it because we're paid to, not because we want to. They treat what we say as a cliché, as if we're saying some rehearsed line that all pastors are supposed to say, instead of authentically sharing from our hearts.

"DON'T TALK LIKE THAT!"

I've experienced this dynamic many times over the past two decades, but perhaps never so clearly as I did one summer evening a few years ago when my next-door neighbors Chad and Julie came over for a cookout.

Dawn and I had been building a friendship with them, and we'd even invited them to come to church with us. They hadn't accepted that offer, but they did like doing other things with us.

It was a natural, fun, relaxed, and growing relationship...until that evening.

As we sat around chatting in our backyard—waiting for the burgers to cook on the grill—Chad began to tell a story about a coworker with whom he was having a conflict. He got more and more heated as he told the story. He became more and more animated. And finally, he spewed a string of expletives that gave full expression to his anger.

Julie nearly jumped out of her lawn chair. "Chad, don't talk like that around Dwight!" she said emphatically.

Chad gave her a strange look. "Why? Did I say something wrong?"

Then she looked at me as if she knew something I thought she didn't know. "*You* know," she stated firmly.

I was confused. I really was. I liked Chad a lot. We'd been doing things together for a long time, and I'd heard much worse language than this coming from his mouth.

(Truth is, I was much more concerned about his heart than his mouth. I believed that someday I'd see a change in his heart that would change the way he talked. I guess I've never much believed in trying to "fix people" from the outside-in.)

Still baffled by Julie's emotional outburst at her husband, I said, "I'm sorry, I don't know what you're talking about."

"You *know*!" she said more firmly. But I didn't.

"Your daughter told me that you're a...you know...you're a...a... a preacher," she finally said in a hushed tone—as if she were saying something offensive.

Then she quickly looked back at Chad. "Don't swear anymore around Dwight. You're embarrassing me. He's a preacher!"

I did my best to keep a positive face. I played it off, as if it were no big deal. But my heart sank. I grieved over their sudden discomfort with me—not with me really, but with their image of preachers. I suddenly took on all the baggage from Chad and Julie's past experiences and perceptions of preachers and organized religion. Their comfort with me was suddenly gone.

I was no longer Dwight the Neighbor in their eyes. I was…you know…a…a…a *preacher*.

I wanted so much to be a regular guy around them again and to have a real relationship. My whole family did. We loved them.

But Chad started avoiding me. The next day, we had an awkward moment as I pulled our trash cans out to the road at the same time he was pulling out his.

"Hey, Chad!" I greeted him. "We sure had a great time with you last night."

But he wouldn't look me in the eye.

"Yeah, uh, thanks for having us over," he stuttered, and then he darted back into his house.

Since then, I've worked hard to get our friendship back where it was before I was exposed as a…a…you know…a preacher. I've sought to prove to Chad and Julie in many ways that I *really* care for them and their family. I've also sought to demonstrate to them that my love for God is something more than what I do as a career. It flows from my "twenty four/seven" life's passion.

MINISTRY UNIFORMS

In reflecting on that unfortunate incident in our backyard, I've realized that, as a professional minister, I'm missing something that ordinary ministers like James the Roofer have. I'm missing my *special ministry uniform*.

Now, what I'm saying may sound strange to you if your idea of a ministry uniform is a black suit with a special white "clergy collar." But that's not the kind of uniform I'm talking about. I'm talking about a ministry uniform that's more like what the army gives its troops when they go into combat.

It's called camouflage...or camo, for short.

The purpose of camo is to allow its wearers to *blend in* with their surroundings. It makes them somewhat "invisible" to those who might be scared away by their presence. It actually allows them to go farther into enemy territory and accomplish more of the mission for which they were sent.

In the same way, God has outfitted each of his front-line, "nonprofessional" ministers with camouflage. It's part of the way He's designed and equipped them to carry out His Plan A.

For some, camouflage comes in the form of an ordinary job—in professions like education, healthcare, business, or construction. For others, it comes in the form of their membership in a club or their presence in a particular neighborhood. And for some, the camouflage is that of a student or full-time mother.

Regardless, camo is the thing that allows you to naturally connect with people *in their world*, ministering to them out of the overflow of who you are—in the places where their pain and needs will most naturally emerge.

The purpose for wearing your ministry camo is not to hide your faith or do something covert. Rather, it's to allow people who've been turned off by some aspect of Christianity or "organized religion" to get to know you apart from their spiritual baggage. It allows their "spiritual walls" to stay down until they can see the fruit of God's Spirit in you. It allows them to get to know the true you and to wonder why you're refreshingly different.

Once they've had the chance to sense Christ in you, they'll likely *want* to know more about why you do life the way you do.

I *lack* this wonderful ministry uniform when people find out I work for a ministry organization and "preach" all over the country. But I *gain* it when people see me as Dwight the Neighbor.

If you're a follower of Christ, you've been issued a camo uniform. What does yours look like?

Not sure? Try to think of the thing that allows you to naturally fit in with those who aren't followers of Christ. What is it that places you in a relationship with others who might not otherwise have a way of being close to the love and presence of the living God who abides in you? That's your ministry uniform. It's your camo.

Take notice of it. And let God regularly employ it to bring others closer to Him.

JOE AND MARY'S KID

If you really think about it, Jesus Himself was sent to the earth in camouflage. He didn't come in His full glory as Almighty God, but as a human being (Philippians 2:5-8). Furthermore, He was born into the family of a common tradesman—a construction worker—not a well-known rabbi. (James the Roofer should feel good about that.) And for a while, He was simply known as Joe and Mary's son.

Those who encountered Jesus in everyday settings probably didn't know they were up close to God in the flesh. His human body and His commonplace surroundings were all part of His camouflage.

Perhaps God was telling us something about His primary means of ministering to those in need. Perhaps He was modeling for us how He houses His grace and truth in the camouflage of people's vocations and normal life circumstances. Perhaps He was showing how He wants to express His love to others through the lives of ordinary people, through their natural relationships with others, and through their mundane, daily routines.

Jesus' ministry was able to happen up close with people because they were comfortable with Him. They invited Him to their homes and meal tables, introducing Him to their close friends. They may have even introduced Him as a carpenter. (After all, we often quickly tell *what we do* after we introduce *who we are*.)

Jesus housed the values of the Kingdom in His own camouflage.

Then, He chose to pour out those values into twelve more camouflaged vessels.

He's still doing it today through the specially designed camouflage uniforms He's given us.

Your ministry uniform is one of the most valuable assets you have as you serve others and bring God up close to them. Are you using it?

IN THE MOMENT

In the early nineties, Kingdom Building Ministries organized "city camps" in large urban areas. Their purpose? To equip adults—younger and older—to do ministry in inner-city environments. They lasted for several days and combined classroom training with ministry experiences in different urban settings.

We held one of the camps in Boston, where both students and trainers participated in an outreach experience in Harvard Square. We gave them an assignment to build relational bridges with people hanging out in the square and then share Christ with them.

As I walked around, looking for someone to start a conversation with, I got "distracted" by a really good street musician—a saxophone player who had his case open on the ground to receive whatever change we'd toss his way. I listened for a while and found myself drawn to him and his music. Part of me felt like I should stick around, listen to his music for a while longer, and talk with him when he was done.

But another part of me felt like I was wasting time. I felt like I needed to get back to the ministry assignment at hand. So I did. I moved on to a different part of the square, silently praying that God would orchestrate a divine appointment with someone who needed to know about Him.

To my surprise, God led me right back to that street musician. It took me awhile, but I finally realized that it had been God who was drawing me to him all along. The street musician *was* my ministry assignment, not a distraction from it.

I quickly made my way back to the location where he'd been playing, but I didn't hear his music. I glanced around and didn't see him anywhere either.

My heart sank. I thought he'd left.

I was both surprised and relieved when I finally found him sitting on the ground a stone's throw away from where he'd been playing his music. He was talking with Janelle, one of the participants in our city camp.

Janelle looked up and saw me as I was walking in her direction. "Dwight, come here! I want to introduce you to someone!" she hollered.

Within moments, she was introducing me to Marcus the Sax Player, and she invited me into their conversation.

She explained to me that she'd felt drawn in her spirit to Marcus and his music—in much the same way I had. So, she proactively started a conversation with him between songs. Before long, he asked her what she was doing there. And when she told him, he got a very serious look on his face and asked her if she could sit down and talk with him.

At that point in the story, Janelle turned to Marcus.

"Marcus, tell Dwight what you've been telling me. Tell him why you wanted to talk to me."

Then she quickly turned back to me.

"Dwight, you aren't going to believe this!" she exclaimed.

Marcus then began to tell me his story. He said he'd been fighting a battle with depression and that just the night before, he'd tried to commit suicide.

But something kept him from doing it. It was the thought that there might be a God who could help him find peace.

"Last night, I prayed for the first time in a long time," Marcus said. "I prayed, 'God, if you're there and if you can help me, please let me know in the next twenty four hours. If you're not there, I don't want to live anymore.'"

He then looked me straight in the eye. "I prayed that prayer almost twenty four hours ago. I don't think it's a coincidence that Janelle came to tell me all about God, do you?"

"No, Marcus, it *wasn't* a coincidence," I replied in a hushed voice that matched how I was feeling. (I had started to get the sense that God was doing something powerful there. It was like we were standing on holy ground.)

"Do you remember when I was over there listening to your music a little while ago?" I asked as I pointed to where he'd been playing.

He nodded and replied, "Yes, I *do* remember you."

"God was leading me to talk to you then, just like He led Janelle to talk to you now. That's why I came back. I knew I needed to talk to you! I knew I needed to tell you about how much God loves you.

"Marcus, God is answering the prayer you prayed yesterday!"

For the next hour, we talked and prayed with him and led him into a relationship with Christ. His countenance changed almost immediately after we prayed with him. We then introduced him to some Christians who lived in the area who could help him on his new spiritual journey.

And that was the end of the story, right? Not exactly. God used that experience in a profound way to do a new work in *my* life, too.

More than ever before, I felt the joy of following God's *in-the-moment* leading to minister to someone. But like never before, I also felt a sense of responsibility to hear and obey God's promptings. It was sobering to realize that Janelle's and my obedience to God's leading was a "life and death" matter for Marcus.

And I almost missed it.

I wondered if there were other times that I'd missed God's promptings in the ordinary moments of my daily life. I realized that I needed to make it a habit to listen for them. I prayed that God would help me more actively tune in His voice *throughout* each day—not just in my morning quiet times.

LEARNING TO LISTEN

Jesus, the Good Shepherd, said that His followers—His sheep—know His voice and follow where He leads (John 10:4). It's His job to lead us; it's our responsibility to listen and obey.

God alone knows fully how our obedience to His *in-the-moment* promptings will matter for all of eternity. We may not understand at the time why He's asking us to do something, but *He* knows. And His ways and thoughts are higher than our own (Isaiah 55:9). He's reminded me of that many times.

For example, late one evening, I was driving at about fifty miles an hour down a country road in rural Pennsylvania when I sensed God's leading to stop the car. He didn't lead me to just slow down; He led me to completely stop! It seemed a little strange (actually, it seemed very strange!) but the prompting was so strong and clear that I knew I had to stop as quickly as I could.

There I sat in the middle of the road...waiting for something to happen.

The countryside around me was still and quiet—blanketed in darkness, except for the one hundred feet or so in front of me that was illuminated by my headlights.

I waited for several minutes, and then slowly and cautiously proceeded up the dark road. I was a little confused about why God had asked me to do something so bizarre. And as the moments passed, I began to think I'd imagined hearing His voice. To be honest, I felt *really* foolish and was glad nobody else was there to witness it.

Suddenly, I saw something move in the road ahead as the beams of my headlights shined upon it. I continued to drive cautiously toward it and soon recognized that it was a deer. I flipped on my brights and was startled at what I saw next. There was a *whole herd* of deer standing there—at least twelve to fifteen of them.

Had I not stopped, I would've plowed into the middle of them at fifty miles an hour.

It was a powerful reminder to me that God speaks to us in the mundane moments of our lives—and it's important that we listen for His voice and obey it. It might be a critical situation—physically or spiritually—for ourselves or someone else.

God knows what He's doing, even if we don't. He's the ultimate, always-right life-investment counselor who knows how to best guide our lives and daily moments. He knows how to invest our actions and words in ways that'll have a profound impact in this life—and reap dividends for all of eternity.

John 10:4 says, "...*his sheep follow him because they know his voice*." You are His sheep. The question is: Are you listening for Him?

He's *promised* in His Word to lead you, but you must listen and obey.

> "*The Lord will guide you always...*" (Isaiah 58:11).

> "*I am the Lord your God, who teaches you what is best for you, who directs you in the way you should go*" (Isaiah 48:17).

> "*Whether you turn to the right or to the left, your ears will hear a voice behind you, saying, 'This is the way; walk in it*'" (Isaiah 30:21).

> "*The Lord confides in those who fear Him*" (Psalm 25:14).

Unfortunately, we don't always listen very well. Perhaps we've become like children who, over time, tune out their parents' voices. They find it expedient to not hear their parents' commands, thinking that "not hearing" keeps them from being accountable to obey.

Parents often hear the excuse "I didn't hear you" when confronting their children about disobedience. And how do parents usually reply? "That's because you weren't listening!"

Recently, I jokingly told my son that it may be time to take him to the ear doctor because he's had so much trouble hearing what I've asked him to do. He laughed, but I think he got the point.

Do we do that with God? Are we like the disobedient child who doesn't listen to his father's commands? It sure seems like we are.

Maybe it's because we're so focused on *our own* "important" agendas. Too busy getting other things done. Rushing through life so "on task" that—without realizing it—we miss important Kingdom-advancing moments all along the way.

It seems we've gotten good at *tuning in* the horizontal and *tuning out* the vertical.

For many of us, it's time to change the station we're listening to. It's time to tune in and listen for God's voice throughout the day—even while the background noise of our lives blares and competes for our attention.

God speaks regularly and often to us. But it's easy to miss Him if we're not attentive, because He often speaks with a still, small voice.

Elijah the prophet learned that God wasn't in the mighty wind or the earthquake or the fire. He came in a gentle whisper (1 Kings 19:11-12).

Shhhhhh! Perhaps God is speaking to you in a gentle whisper, too. As you've read this book—this chapter—maybe He's been nudging you in ways that are soft and subtle. Can you hear Him? Or is your mind and life moving too fast to hear a whisper? If so, you may be missing important opportunities to impact others' lives through timely words and deeds.

Martyred missionary Jim Elliot once wrote, "Wherever you are, be all there." It's become one of my favorite quotes.

It's a reminder to me to stay "in the moment"—to not get so caught up in the busyness of life that I can't hear God's voice. And to embrace what I call "Spirit-directed living and laboring."

ALONG THE WAY

Jesus lived a Spirit-directed life. His agenda was the Father's agenda—so rather than become upset or frustrated by interruptions, He embraced them as opportunities for ministry.

Stopping *along the way* to take care of someone's immediate need seemed to be the norm of His life—not the exception.

Time and time again, He noticed what was going on around Him, and He slowed down or completely stopped what He was doing to minister to someone.

For a Type-A personality like me, hearing God's voice *in the moment* and stopping *along the way* is the hardest thing to do. When we Type A's have a stated destination, we don't want to deviate from the most direct and quickest path to get there. We have a plan and a schedule, and we want to stick to it. Maybe you can relate.

But God doesn't always operate according to *our* schedules—He often prompts us to break out of them so we can minister to others in their moment of need. Problem is, we're so attached to our schedules and routines that we often see His promptings as *interruptions* rather than *opportunities*. In truth, it's a selfish way to live our lives.

I have a friend who has this message placed in a prominent place on his desk: "Interruptions *are* the ministry." The first time I saw it, I asked him why it was there.

"I've just noticed over years of doing ministry that it's easy to lose sight of what ministry is really about," he replied. "We get our minds too focused on tasks, when ministry is ultimately about people. I just want to constantly remind myself that people aren't an interruption to my work. They *are* my work."

Likewise, God's promptings aren't interruptions to your life and ministry. They're the ministry of your life...and they're the life of your ministry. They're part of God's Plan A.

That's what Jesus modeled. *He often responded to along-the-way, in-the-moment, interruptive, and Spirit-directed ministry opportunities:*

- One time, He was on His way to heal a young girl who was dying, when He noticed that another woman touched His garment and received healing (Mark 5:21-34). He slowed down, embraced the moment, and invested in an impromptu conversation that changed her life.

♦ Another time, He sat down by a well to rest from His journey. He knew that the woman who joined Him wasn't there by coincidence. She needed so much more than the mere physical water she came to get. She needed water that would quench her spiritual thirst. Jesus took the conversational initiative with her, and His insightful questions and words of truth that day forever impacted her life and eventually spilled over to all those she told about the encounter (John 4:4-42).

♦ Later, Jesus was just "passing through" Jericho—on His way to Jerusalem—when He glanced up in a tree and saw Zacchaeus, who was trying to get a glimpse of Jesus. Jesus saw that Zacchaeus needed more than just a distant glance. He needed an up-close encounter. So, Jesus asked Him to do lunch (Luke 19:1-10).

These weren't "planned" ministry meetings, but they weren't happenstance either—not from God's perspective. They were Spirit-directed ministry moments that brought about God's will in the lives of needy people.

FOLLOWING HIS CUES

Jesus' lifestyle is our ultimate model for life and ministry. So, if He slowed down and did ministry along the way, it's probably safe to say that He wants us to do the same.

He prompts us like an off-stage director giving cues to an on-stage actor. He prompts us when He wants us to slow down, to stop, to listen, or to say something that'll serve as *"a word aptly spoken, like apples of gold in settings of silver"* (Proverbs 25:11).

He prompts us when He wants us to share about Him with someone. When He wants us to pray. When He wants us to do lunch or coffee with someone. When He wants us to place a timely telephone call or write a timely note. When He wants us to place a hand on a shoulder, lend a listening ear, or simply be there without saying anything at all.

I know He's orchestrating one of these moments in my life when something in my spirit goes off—almost like an alarm. Sometimes my heart beats stronger and my breathing gets faster. Sometimes I feel compassion so deeply that I know I *have* to do something. And sometimes I think I hear Him whisper. I'm not always sure, but in the moment, I think I do.

So, in faith, I've learned to step out. I know little about where it'll lead—but I know fully Who is leading me.

In these times, God is brokering a divine appointment—a meaningful ministry moment.

WHAT IF I'M WRONG?

When I speak to different groups about Spirit-directed ministry, I'm often asked the question, "What if I get it wrong?" or "What if I do something that God didn't really prompt me to do?"

While these are legitimate concerns, a far more important concern should be that we'll miss critical (and possibly urgent) in-the-moment ministry opportunities. In most cases, the worst that can happen if you get it wrong is that you'll look foolish to others.

I'm willing to take that chance, aren't you?

A dear friend of mine used to say, "God can steer a car in motion far better than He can a car that's stuck in park."

I've learned to respond to God's in-the-moment, along-the-way promptings by taking action steps of obedience, rather than getting paralyzed by endless internal debates that might cause me to miss critical Kingdom opportunities.

Jesus wants more opportunities to minister to others in the everyday arenas of our lives, but we're not affording Him nearly enough chances!

When He came in the flesh, He ministered to people *as He went*, and now He wants to minister through you—*as you go*. He'll never stop seeking to maximize the ministry opportunities of each moment.

I encourage you to listen for God's voice and obey it. You may get it wrong from time to time, but practice is the only way to get better at hearing His voice.

Don't remain parked in your spiritual driveway because you're afraid to get it wrong. It's time to get out there and drive...and let Him lead where you go.

6

LITTLE DO WE KNOW

My kids and I love to listen together to the music of Denver & The Mile High Orchestra, a Christian big band with great talent and an even greater heart for God. It's one of the few groups we *all* like to listen to. Their music—and especially their concerts—appeal to seven-year-old kids and seventy-year-old seniors alike!

In the late spring of 2004, they held a concert in our area, and my whole family went to it.

In the middle of the concert, they took a freewill offering, giving us the opportunity to support a summer ministry tour they were planning in Athens, Greece, during the 2004 Olympic Games.

The band's lead singer, Denver Bierman (the "Denver" part of Denver & The Mile High Orchestra), shared that they were nearly $50,000 short of making the trip to Athens, where they'd perform free, open-air, evangelistic concerts near Olympic venues.

I quickly gained a vision for what they'd be doing in Athens. I knew their high-energy, twelve-piece band would be perfect for drawing and keeping crowds.

What I didn't know was that my daughter, Dara (who was twelve at the time), was getting a vision for it, too. More than that, God was speaking to her about giving money from her savings to help the band go on the trip. This was money she'd been saving for over a year to buy a small motor scooter.

During the concert, she approached her mom and me, and

shared what she believed God was asking her to do.

"Would you be willing to write a check for the amount of money I have in my savings account?" she asked. "I promise to pay you back tomorrow."

We questioned Dara to make sure *she* was certain. She was. Then we questioned her two more times so that *we* could be certain.

"I'm very sure this is what God wants me to do," she assured us.

So, we wrote the check.

After the concert, Denver learned how God had moved in Dara's heart and how she'd responded. He was encouraged and deeply moved by her generosity. He was convinced that it would be the "loaves and fishes" that God would use to provide further for their trip.

A few months later, Denver & The Mile High Orchestra traveled to Greece and shared their music with thousands from all over the world who'd come to the Olympic Games. After the concerts, they built relationships with people who were drawn in by their music and shared Christ with them.

They also had a chance to encourage some Christians from Islamic countries who'd fled from religious persecution in their homeland.

And Dara? She started saving for that scooter again. She knew it would be more than a year before she could save enough, and that was okay by her. She was thrilled that she got to play a role in sending the Gospel to another nation through one of her favorite groups.

And I was thrilled that Dara had gotten her first taste of Spirit-directed living and laboring—and it was a good taste. Even as a young girl, she was discovering that God *wants* to speak to her and guide her—not just in her set-aside quiet times with Him, but throughout her everyday life.

THE REST OF THE STORY

A few months after Dara gave her sacrificial gift, I felt prompted to share about it in a message I was giving at a church in Indianapolis. I had never told the story in public, and I hadn't planned on telling it in this message.

But midway through, God began prompting me, and He continued to prompt me. So, I told the story at a fitting place in the message and went on preaching.

At the close of the service, a distinguished-looking businessman named Bruce approached me. He'd been deeply moved by Dara's example of obedience.

"God spoke to me about *my own* personal obedience through her example," Bruce the Businessman said.

He went on to tell me that one of the multiple businesses he owned was a motorcycle shop. "Dwight, God has prompted me to give your daughter the scooter she was saving for. I think this is a test of *my* obedience. Maybe it's the first of many."

I didn't think much about it until he called me two weeks later and asked me to go to a website and choose the scooter she wanted.

We followed his instructions, and a few weeks after that, the scooter arrived at my office!

I know God doesn't always fully reward us in this life for our small acts of obedience. (My wife and I made that perfectly clear to Dara.) But I can't tell you how much it meant to her to feel the smile of God's approval on her obedience.

She knew He was proud of her for putting Him and His Kingdom ahead of her own personal gain. And she'll know for the rest of her life that God speaks to her in unexpected moments and in unexpected ways, and that He wants her to obey.

THE CHAIN OF EVENTS

A year later, I was in the Indianapolis area again, and I asked Bruce the Businessman to join me for lunch.

That's when the rest of the story unfolded.

When we sat down at the lunch table, I could tell Bruce had a lot on his heart to share with me.

"Dwight," he began, "I was really moved when I heard how your daughter had listened to the voice of God at that concert. In fact, that's when I made a commitment to God to listen for His voice, too.

"And over the past year, it's set forth a God-led chain of events that has radically altered my life, my personal ministry, and my future.

"One by one, I've acted on God's promptings . . . and the results have been amazing!"

Bruce then introduced me to the young man he'd asked to join us for lunch. The young man beamed as he told me how he came to know Christ through Bruce's living testimony.

They went on to tell me that Bruce had started holding Bible studies for his employees, and a number of them had made decisions to follow Jesus. He began holding baptism services in swimming pools to baptize all the employees, friends, and family members who were making spiritual commitments through his influence.

As all of this was happening, Bruce had begun to sense God calling him to redeem the time he'd lost—years of living out his own agenda. God was calling him to venture into things well beyond what he'd previously imagined.

Bruce couldn't hold it in any longer. "God has called me into overseas missions work!" he finally exclaimed. "And it all started that morning when I took a first step of obedience to God's in-the-moment prompting to give a scooter to your daughter."

As Bruce was sharing all of this, I thought about the chain of events God had set in motion through ordinary laborers who were obedient to His in-the-moment leadings. God had taken each of our simple acts of obedience and made something bigger out of them.

Denver & The Mile High Orchestra had answered God's call to go to Greece. My daughter had obeyed God by giving sacrificially to help them go. I obeyed God's prompting to tell her story in the middle of a message. Bruce the Businessman obeyed God, giving Dara the scooter she'd been saving for.

And God took the chain of events from there, using Bruce to

spiritually impact his family, friends, and company—and eventually leading him into overseas missions work.

Today, Bruce the Businessman is Bruce the Missionary, serving an "unreached people" halfway around the world.

WHAT GOD SETS IN MOTION

What could God set in motion through your daily acts of obedience? Are you missing the chance to set off a chain of events because you're not listening for His voice?

Do you ignore His leading because you can't see far enough down the road to what He ultimately wants to accomplish through your obedience?

Remember, you may not understand why He's asked you to do something at the time you're doing it. For a time, Dara didn't know. A few weeks after she gave her savings, she asked me how much it would cost to get a group the size of Denver & The Mile Orchestra across the ocean on a plane.

I simply replied, "A lot." I didn't want her to think her gift was small when she compared it to their great need.

But she kept asking, "How much, Dad?"

"Oh, I don't know exactly," I said, thinking she'd let it go. She didn't.

When she found out how much all of their airfares would cost, she said, "How embarrassing! My gift didn't do much."

I quickly replied, "Honey, it wasn't the size of your gift that captured God's attention. It was the amount left over. You gave it *all*!

"He measures the size of your obedience, He sees your heart of willing sacrifice, and He adds His immeasurable blessings. *God will use what you gave to change lives!*"

Little did I know. The ripples of Dara's obedience are now being felt halfway around the world! That's what God can do when His laborers commit themselves in obedience to follow His lead—*in the moment* and *along the way*.

Are you listening for His voice? Are you following it?

UP CLOSE

You can probably remember where you were and what you were doing the morning of September 11, 2001, when you first heard the news of the terrorist attacks on New York and Washington D.C. It was a defining moment in our country's history.

You may also remember the horror you felt while watching those first television images of the airliners crashing into the World Trade Center. Do you remember them? The news played them over and over until they were all we could think of!

For the first twenty four to forty eight hours, those horrific images were all we saw. And all we heard about was the rising death toll, and speculations about who was behind the attacks and where they might strike next. There wasn't much security or hope to hang on to.

Then, we began to see some more positive images on our TV screens, and we began to hear more hopeful stories of survivors and heroes.

We heard about people who'd sacrificed their own lives to bring down one of the planes before it could crash into another building and kill others. We heard about volunteers all over America who were donating blood and money, and doing whatever they could to help with the rescue and recovery efforts.

And then we heard the stories about common police officers and firefighters who'd taken tremendous risks—some even giving their lives to save others at the scene of the World Trade Center attack. These heroic stories started the healing process in us. And they did something else for us as well. Something unexpected. They helped us understand how important ordinary laborers are when our need is desperate.

Prior to September 11, most of our cultural heroes were celebrities. But the events following September 11 seemed to change all that—at least for a while. They altered our definition of a hero.

Of course, celebrities helped in the days after the attacks. Actors and athletes helped raise money to support recovery and clean-up efforts. And politicians made sure that the front-line workers were mobilized and supported. They did what they could, and their efforts were important. But for the most part, their work was done from a distance.

And there's only so much you can do from a distance.

When people are desperate, they're not looking for the closest celebrity. They need laborers. They're looking for people who can meet them where they are with what they need in that moment.

They need people who can get *up close*.

The men and women trapped beneath the rubble at Ground Zero didn't need help from a distance. More than anything, they needed immediate and highly committed help up close. They needed firefighters. They needed police officers. They needed all forms of emergency workers.

They needed people on the scene.

ON-THE-SCENE HEROES

The same kind of on-the-scene heroes are needed in the Kingdom of God.

Jesus called them *laborers*.

Average Christians must see themselves as crucially needed, daily dispensers of God's grace—enabling Jesus in them to be up close, wherever their work and personal lives take them.

We impress people from a distance, but we impact them up close.

People need laborers up close because they need God up close to them. And while many have tried to keep God at a distance, they may find it more difficult to keep His laborers at a distance.

What might happen if Christians slowed down and genuinely listened to those around them who have few others to share their pain with?

What if we opened up our lunch hours for relational meetings and our homes for loving hospitality?

What if we got out of our comfort zones and met our neighbors?

What if we traveled off the beaten paths of our lives and got up close to the poor and marginalized—often in inner-city areas?

What if we looked around for the mud puddles of human need and waded in?

Imagine how we'd usher God's presence—up close—into the lives of others!

Several years ago, I was speaking to a group of college students in an intense summer laborer-training program that our ministry hosts called *The Laborer's Institute*. After I spoke about up-close ministry, a young man named Tanner approached me and gave me his summary of what being a laborer is all about.

"I've figured out what it means to be a laborer," he said. "It's just hanging out with people, loving them, and sharing truth when you get the chance. *Everyone* can do that!"

Getting up close to people.

Hanging out with them.

Loving them in practical ways.

And sharing truth with them.

I'm not big on formulas, but that's pretty close to what Jesus did. And Tanner was right. It's a model that *anyone and everyone* can follow.

No wonder his denomination now says he's one of the most successful missionaries they've ever seen—and he's still in his twenties!

He's just been following the up-close ministry strategy that Jesus modeled.

UP-CLOSE IMPACT

Tanner's description of a laborer reminds me of the up-close work God did through a fifteen-year-old kid named Lance, whom I met in the early days of my speaking ministry. I got to know Lance when I was speaking in the Dominican Republic, on the campus of a ministry for American kids with behavioral problems.

On the third day of my week of ministry there, Lance asked if he could talk with me. We met in his dormitory, where he shared all that God had been doing in his life that week. It was clear that God had begun to light a fire in his heart.

He then explained that he was not in the program for behavioral reasons like the rest of the kids. His parents had asked him to enter it to help put more structure and discipline in his life.

"I've gotten a lot out of my time here," Lance said, "but now I'm thinking maybe it's time for me to go home."

"You may be right," I replied. "But is it possible that, while you're still here, God is giving you a temporary assignment? Is it possible that He wants to use *you* to minister to the kids here while you're with them? Is it possible God has you here to pray for them while you're up close to them?"

Lance's eyes lit up as I continued sharing the possibilities.

"That's it!" he said. "That's something I can do for God while I'm still here! I know things about their lives that their parents don't know—that not even the staff here knows. I'll pray for them and talk with them about how much they need God."

Over the next few days, Lance and I talked about his new sense of purpose for the rest of his time in the Dominican Republic. I gave him a book on prayer, and we prayed together for some of the other kids from his dorm I'd met that week—including a kid named Chris, who professed to be an atheist.

After I left the campus, Lance and I continued to write over the next few weeks. In one letter, he wrote:

> "The other day, Chris announced at the dinner

table that he is no longer an atheist. I have now changed my prayer from, 'Lord, please show Chris that you're real' to 'Lord, Chris needs to know you personally. Please help him make a decision for you.'

"The power of prayer is *really strong*!!!"

Little did I know that I wouldn't receive another letter from Lance.

A few weeks later, I received a phone call from one of the program administrators in the Dominican Republic.

"I'm afraid I have some bad news," she said. "There's been a terrible tragedy here this week.

"A group of boys from one of our dormitories was swimming in the river. A flash flood came quickly from upstream and washed three of the boys away—including Lance. We were able to rescue two of them, but we couldn't get to Lance. . . . Dwight, I'm sorry to tell you that Lance is dead."

I was stunned.

As I sat in silence, trying to figure out how to respond, she continued.

"Dwight, as we were cleaning out his locker and sorting through his belongings, we came across some things you'd given him—encouraging letters and a book about prayer. The book had highlights and notes all through it.

"We also found his prayer journal, and we were surprised to see how many kids and situations he'd been praying for. It's amazing what we've been piecing together from his prayer list."

She went on to tell me that they'd been noticing some big changes on campus in the weeks since I'd been there. People were experiencing personal victories where they'd been struggling for years.

Staff members who'd been dealing with discouragement and depression were finding a renewed sense of joy and purpose. And some of the hardest kids were experiencing major breakthroughs, and their attitudes were changing.

"We now realize that Lance had been praying for those things," she said. "God has been answering Lance's prayers!"

I spoke with Lance's parents after his funeral. They shared with me that five kids gave their lives to Christ at the funeral. One of them was Chris—the former atheist.

All because of a fifteen-year-old kid who caught a vision for the role he could play in others' lives as one who was *up close* to them.

Perhaps, right now, God wants to give you a vision for the role *you* can play in the lives of people you're up close to—in your neighborhood, your office, your assembly line, your dormitory, or your algebra class. Perhaps He wants you to pray for the needs you see in their lives or be the vessel through which He can meet those needs.

God is looking for active laborers who will pray and love in *up-close* spheres of influence. Will He find that—like Lance—you're available?

8

MEAL TABLES

When we were first married, Dawn and I developed a close friendship with Rob and Denise, an unmarried couple who'd been living together for four years. We met them through some mutual friends and really enjoyed hanging out with them.

They were very aware of our Christian faith, and we shared naturally and freely about it with them on a number of occasions. When we felt the time was right, we invited them to go to church with us and then come to our home afterward for dinner.

They said they'd love to, but they'd need to check their schedules and get back with us.

Two weeks passed. Their reply never came.

Finally, Denise called us late on the Saturday night before we were to go to church together. She was very apologetic.

"Dwight, I'm sorry it's taken us so long to get back with you about going to church," she said. "We're not usually like this when someone asks us to do something. But I think I need to be honest with you about why we've been struggling with the decision."

She explained that Rob had had a negative church experience when he was a teenager.

"Some people made him feel like he wasn't welcome in their church because he didn't have his act together. He had long hair, tattoos, and an earring.

"And you know Rob . . . he probably said a few things he shouldn't have about their rules. It may have even been his fault, but it's still hard for him to step back into church again.

"I'm sorry, Dwight. We just can't go with you. But…"

She hesitated and then continued. "We were wondering if we could still come over for dinner—*after* you get home from church."

I assured her that I understood their struggle, and I let her know how deeply sorry I was about Rob's negative church experience. Then I told her how thrilled I was that they were still joining us for dinner.

"Who was that on the phone at this hour?" Dawn asked as I came to bed.

"It was Denise. She finally responded to our invitation."

"Really? Are they coming with us to church?" she excitedly asked.

"Yes, they are," I replied. "But they're not coming to the morning service."

Dawn looked at me, puzzled.

"I don't understand."

"Well, they're coming to our house for dinner *after* the service," I replied. "And if you believe that the church is God's people, then, yes, they're coming to church. *We're it!*"

The next day, they pulled up to our meal table, and we talked more about Rob's past church experience. Dawn and I assured them that his experience wasn't what God would've wanted.

That day, we became the church to Rob and Denise.

Our meal table became their sanctuary. And our lives became their sermon.

MEAL-TABLE MINISTRY

I'm not sure if you've noticed, but Jesus spent a lot of time with people around meal tables. It seems to have been one of His up-close ministry hot spots.

The Gospels record that He ate with, drank with, or fed people many times as a part of His ministry to them. It happened enough times that I think it was a very intentional part of His ministry strategy.

Here are just a few examples:

- After Jesus' encounter with Zacchaeus, He went to Zacchaeus' home for a meal and became the bread of life to him and his "sinner" friends (Luke 19:1-10).

- Another time, He hung out with the Pharisees around a meal table when a "woman who had lived a sinful life" anointed Him with an expensive perfume. He affirmed her actions and held them up as a model for the ages to come (Matthew 26:6-13).

- Jesus' *first miracle* was changing water into wine at a wedding feast (John 2:1-11). And His *last supper* with the disciples left us with a powerful portrait of how much He loved them (John 13:1-17).

- After Peter had denied Jesus three times, Jesus reinstated him over a meal of fresh fish (John 21:1-19). It was a powerful and poignant moment in their relationship.

- On several occasions, when Jesus was ministering to crowds of thousands, He was sure to feed them—in what may have been the first outdoor "festival" gatherings (Mark 6:30-44).

- When He stopped at a well—a place that may be similar to our modern-day Starbucks—to get a drink, He had a life-changing conversation with a woman (John 4:4-26).

- And I love the way Matthew recorded his first encounter with Jesus. After Jesus initially called Matthew to be His disciple, they soon went to his home and ate a meal together.

"As Jesus went on from there, he saw a man named Matthew sitting at the tax collector's booth. 'Follow me,' he told him, and Matthew got up and followed him. While Jesus was having dinner at Matthew's house, many tax collectors and 'sinners' came and ate with him and his disciples" (Matthew 9:9-10).

This passage is full of examples of how Jesus did ministry. It tells us that He went where sinners were, He did ministry as He went, and He did ministry around meal tables.

Jesus hung out and did lunch with Matthew's tax-collector and "sinner" friends. He wanted to be with them, and they seemed to want to be with Him—especially when there was a meal involved. It provided Jesus with one of the most natural, up-close opportunities to get to know them and build relationships with them.

Clearly, Jesus valued the meal table as a rich environment for up-close, relational ministry. I think He still does. Why? Because it's one of the only places where people will pull up close to each other and linger long enough for deep relational transfer of thoughts and feelings.

That's why it's sad that so many families don't eat together around their dinner tables anymore. They lose the power and relational bonding that come in those mealtime moments.

But it's also why many families *do* guard their mealtimes. Some make sure the whole family is around the table for at least the majority of dinner meals each week. They guard it as a time to catch up on what's happening in everyone's lives. And they won't allow the TV or other technology to distract from their mealtimes.

In addition to being a connection place, the meal table is also where family traditions and stories are often passed from one generation to another. Ask most people where they heard their family stories told, and they'll point to those relaxed (often holiday) mealtimes where no one hurried to leave the table.

They'll speak with fond memories about how they laughed and talked for hours. They got up from those times at the table with full stomachs and even fuller hearts.

I'm probably *not* telling you anything you don't already know—you've likely experienced the relational power of moments you've spent around the table with others. But I *am* giving you a new application for the power of this concept: You can use it to effectively minister to others in natural, highly relational, and up-close ways.

Just like Jesus did with Matthew and Zacchaeus. And just like Dawn and I did with Rob and Denise.

TUNA-FISH SANDWICHES

Back in my bachelor days, I lived in a small house in a friendly, blue-collar neighborhood. One of my favorite neighbors was Thelma Vice, a kind, gray-haired widow. She always struck me as being out of place in my neighborhood because she was one of the classiest ladies I knew.

I enjoyed our fleeting moments of conversation as we ran into each other coming or going, and I wanted to get to know her more. So, one day, I invited her over for lunch.

Hospitality is not my greatest gift—which was evident that day—but I scrounged around and made the best use of what I had. It was either tuna-fish or PB&J sandwiches. I chose tuna fish. I couldn't bear making PB&J for such a classy lady!

I cut the sandwiches into diagonal halves to add a little more elegance to my presentation, and I served them with some chips and tea. I settled for dining on TV trays, since I had nothing else that would even function as a meal table. (Did I mention that this happened in my *bachelor* days?)

I whispered a final prayer as the doorbell rang, and soon, Thelma was seated at her TV tray. We began with small talk, but it didn't take long for us to get to deeper things. And then, about the time she finished the first half of her sandwich, she told me that a lot of her friends had been dying lately.

"I'm really scared," she said.

"What are you afraid of?" I asked.

She began to cry as she said, "Because I don't know what's going to happen to me after I die."

In that one conversation around a meal table of TV trays, we went further and deeper in sharing than we'd gone in numerous prior "passing" conversations.

I prayed with Thelma, and that day, she became very clear about what was going to happen to her after she died. She knew she had an eternal destiny in heaven.

She wasn't afraid anymore—at least, not in the same life-crippling way.

And we became very good friends. She eventually became known to my wife and kids as Grandma Vice. More important, she became God's friend, and she loved and served Him to her dying days.

What was the turning point of Thelma's life? It was a mealtime conversation over tuna-fish sandwiches.

Our family has continued to invite our neighbors over for meals ever since. Sometimes, we invite one neighbor family. At other times, we invite several neighbor families at once.

Recently, we organized a block party, and twenty two families from our neighborhood showed up. It was an amazing time of connecting with people we hardly knew—in ways that opened the door for further involvement in their lives.

It affirms something I've witnessed many times: People are usually more willing to fellowship with others when there's a meal table involved. And relationships go deeper and conversations go further at meal tables.

MINISTRY POTENTIAL

As I share the power of meal-table ministry with my speaking audiences, I ask them a simple question: "How many of you like to eat?"

They laugh a little, and nearly everyone raises a hand.

"Well, then," I continue, "most of you have *great* ministry potential!"

We laugh together, but they clearly get the point. There's tremendous power in meeting around a meal table. At home. At your local coffee shop. Or in your favorite restaurant.

Has God been speaking to you about reaching out to specific people in your sphere of influence? Maybe you could invite them over for a meal.

It doesn't have to be anything formal or fancy, and it doesn't require a lot of preparation.

Even some TV trays and a couple of tuna-fish sandwiches will do.

9

ONE LIFE AT A TIME

*Before reading this chapter, grab a pen and write
down the names of five people who've had the greatest
impact on your life. We'll come back to your list later.*

In my early days of ministry, I spent six weeks at a language
school in Honduras. I thought I'd probably be doing a lot of ministry in Spanish-speaking countries, and I was told that attending
a language school would be a great way to quickly improve my
ability to speak Spanish.

As a part of the experience, I lived in a Honduran home for the
whole six weeks and practiced my conversational Spanish skills
with my host family. I also shared a room with Eduardo, the fifteen-year-old son of my host couple.

Having to speak Spanish nearly every moment of every day for
six weeks was pretty intense. But otherwise, the pace was much
slower than what I was used to back in the States.

It gave Eduardo and me plenty of time to hang out—actually,
way too much time for an introvert like me.

I was looking forward to spending lots of time alone, a luxury I
rarely got back at home. Eduardo, on the other hand, was looking
forward to our spending lots of time together. (It think it was a rare
luxury for him to have a "big brother" around.)

I can remember one of the first mornings when I got up very

early to have some time alone with God. I found a chair in the corner of a room and even turned it toward the wall to communicate that I didn't want to be disturbed. I tried to stay very quiet as I read the Bible and prayed. But Eduardo woke up and noticed I wasn't in bed.

"What are you doing?" he asked when he found me.

"I'm having my time *alone* with God," I replied, hoping he'd hear the *alone* part.

"Can I join you?"

He joined me that morning and nearly every morning for the next six weeks. We read the Bible together, and he asked a lot of questions. We prayed together and talked about many aspects of our relationships with God.

As time passed, it became more and more clear to me that God had paired us up for a reason. He was using us in each other's lives in different ways.

Eduardo's relationship with God went much deeper that summer, and the trajectory of his life changed forever. And, in a way, so did mine.

As I lived up close to Eduardo's life and spiritually invested in him in a personal way, I began to more fully understand and appreciate the way Jesus did relational ministry. It's become more of a hallmark of my life and ministry ever since.

At the time, I don't think I fully understood why I was there. I actually thought I was there to learn Spanish—and my time with Eduardo was a side benefit. Now I think it was the other way around. I think God sent me to Honduras to spend six weeks with Eduardo. And, oh yeah, I got better at speaking Spanish while I was there.

To be honest, I really haven't used my Spanish skills as much as I'd planned. But I've stayed in contact with Eduardo ever since. I helped him attend a Christian university in the U.S., and I connected him with peers who could help him continue to grow in his faith.

Not long ago, I got a call from Eduardo. He was excited to tell me that he's now discipling young people in Tegucigalpa, the capital city of Honduras.

He goes into their schools and hangs out with students at lunchtime. He leads them into a relationship with Jesus and then passes into their lives some of the things that others have passed into His. He prays and reads the Bible with them. He talks with them about their daily relationships with God and challenges them to put their faith into action.

Just like I did with him years ago...for a short, but God-appointed time.

At one meaningful moment in our recent conversation, Eduardo said, "Dwight, I'm doing what I remember you did for me, because I don't know what my spiritual condition would be if you hadn't spent those six weeks with me."

It wasn't until that moment that I really understood how much my up-close, relational investment in his life had meant to him. I thought ahead to a time somewhere in the future when he'll hear one of the kids he's working with say the same thing to him.

RELATIONAL MINISTRY

When Jesus walked the earth, He set forth a highly relational model for developing and growing the lives of people. It included calling His disciples "friends."

He ate with His disciples around meal tables, walked and talked with them on long journeys, camped in remote places with them, encouraged them, prayed with them, served with them, and ultimately entrusted His eternal cause to them—*all in highly relational ways.*

If you think about it, Jesus' ministry could easily look like a failure by today's standards. He spent an awful lot of time hanging out with a relatively small number of disciples—teaching them through His words, actions, and life.

His methods didn't seem very time efficient, and His movement didn't sustain much early numerical growth. Maybe that's why His methods aren't often employed today.

But through the life of Jesus, God seemed to be pointing to a different strategy for ministry. He seemed to be saying that the most powerful form of ministry happens in a relational context—up close over time. That's what Jesus did. And it's what Eduardo and I did during my time in Honduras.

I summarize Jesus' ministry model in this way: *More time with fewer people equals a greater Kingdom investment.*

This idea is a critical part of Jesus' Plan A for reaching the world. He's looking for willing laborers who will spend time in close relationship with others, passing on to them the values of His Kingdom.

MASS PRODUCTION

Here's the deal, though. As critical as up-close, relational ministry is to Jesus' Plan A, it runs contrary to the rest of the world's plans. It's not the kind of logic that's been instilled in us since we were young. It's countercultural and even counterintuitive for most of us.

The world's plans run on the logic of efficient and cost-effective mass production. God's Plan A is based on the logic of one-life-at-a-time investing in others—which is a slow, seemingly inefficient, relational process.

I have to tell you, God's ministry strategy can be a tough sell—even among Christians—because mass production is a familiar way of life that's woven into the fabric of our daily living. You can't escape it!

Nearly every product we buy in America is mass-produced in manufacturing plants. Long gone are the days when furniture was artistically handcrafted, clothing was tailor fit and handstitched, and meals were homemade from what was raised and harvested on the family farm. The Industrial Revolution changed all that.

In America, it seems we've come to believe that mass production is the best and most efficient way to do things in nearly every case, nearly all the time.

But as efficient and cost effective as it is for making products, mass production *isn't* the best model for people-oriented activities…like spiritual development.

People's spiritual lives simply cannot be mass-produced.

They're developed *one life at a time* through a slow process of relational transfer that cannot be bypassed through mass-production ministry.

Let me say it again: You cannot mass-produce Kingdom laborers.

Maybe that's why God chose to express His love for the world in the form of *a person*—His own Son, Jesus, "the Word who became flesh." And maybe that's why in Jesus' three short years of recorded ministry, most of it happened in life-on-life encounters and relationships, not in large-venue events.

Still, the mass-production mindset has crept into our modern-day understanding of ministry. We largely believe that speaking to crowds and televising programs to as many people as possible are the best ways to reach the world for Christ.

While these approaches—which work on the rules of addition—may reach more people in the short run, they actually reach fewer people in the long run. And they reach them less effectively than relational ministry.

THE MATH OF SPIRITUAL MULTIPLICATION

Jesus' relational ministry model works on the rules of multiplication. (For that reason, some have called it "spiritual multiplication.") To find out its vast potential, just grab a calculator and do some simple math.

If you were to speak to one hundred thousand people each year for the next twenty five years (an overly ambitious goal for all except the most popular speakers), you would reach two and a half million people. That's simple addition.

But if you were to invest regularly and deeply in the lives of two different people (a very achievable number) each year for the next twenty five years—and you taught each of those people to pour their lives into two more people each year (who would do the same, and so on)—you would, together, reach more than thirty million people in that same twenty five-year period. That's spiritual multiplication.

Year	Public Speaking (Addition)	Life-on-Life Investing (Multiplication)
1	100,000	2
2	200,000	4
5	500,000	32
10	1,000,000	1,024
15	1,500,000	32,768
20	2,000,000	1,048,576
25	2,500,000	33,554,432

Obviously, the math wouldn't play out quite this perfectly in the real world (there will always be attrition), but I think you get the point: Over time, multiplication—an idea that one movie has called "paying it forward"—is a powerful strategy for reaching the world. In fact, it's the only strategy that could possibly reach a world of more than six billion people.

I'm reminded of an ancient legend that better illustrates the power of spiritual multiplication. (This legend has been told in different ways with different details over the years, but the point is always the same.)

It's said that the Emperor of China summoned the man who created the game of checkers to be his special guest for a naval celebration dinner. (The Emperor apparently loved the game of checkers!) At the end of the dinner, the Emperor told the man (in front of other invited guests and dignitaries) that he could have anything he asked for.

The man asked for one grain of wheat, multiplied and compounded for each square on the Emperor's checkerboard. In other words, he asked for one grain of wheat for the first square, two grains for the second square, four for the third square, eight for the fourth square, sixteen for the fifth square, and so on.

The Emperor was insulted by such a small request and had the man thrown out of his presence. What the Emperor didn't realize was that the man had just asked for enough kernels to cover the whole country of India in a foot of grain!

That's the power of multiplication.

And it has the same power when it's applied to one person investing in the life of another. What seems small at first multiplies exponentially over time.

DEEP IMPACT

Spiritual multiplication is clearly a ministry strategy that reaches more people, but it's more than that. It's also a strategy to impact them in a deeper way.

In other words, it's both deep and wide.

At the beginning of this chapter, you were asked to write down the names of the five people who've had the greatest influence on your life. Now take a break for a moment and answer these two questions:

1. How many of the names listed are people with whom you've had close proximity and relationship?

2. How many are speakers, authors, or others with whom you've had little or no relationship?

My experience in having others do this little exercise is that more than eighty percent of the people who've had the greatest influence on our lives are those with whom we've had a meaningful relationship.

Without a doubt, most of us have been greatly impacted by a speaker's message or a book. In fact, the majority of Christians have made a deeper spiritual commitment at a service or event where God used a speaker's message to convict their hearts.

As founder and president of a speaking ministry, I've seen first-hand how God deeply impacts lives through anointed and gifted speakers. I've watched as people have responded to our speakers' invitations by the tens, hundred, and thousands. And they're not just temporary decisions either. We receive calls, letters, and e-mails all the time from people who are still living out their decisions years later.

But as life changing as those decisions are, nothing can replace the power of one life pouring into another over time in a relational context. Nothing.

Jesus Himself preached powerful sermons to "the multitudes," but He spent most of His time investing in the lives of a small group of people. What must it have been like to be up close to Him for three years as one of His first disciples? What would've it been like to hear and see in person all the things the Gospels do *and don't* record?

I think that's part of the deep impact of Jesus' up-close ministry style: The disciples got to see Him in all kinds of settings. They got to see Him model how to love God and people in the context of everyday life—with all of its complications and surprises.

And, if you think about it, God has allowed us to get up close to the life of Jesus as well (though in a limited way) by giving us access to the historic accounts of His life in the Gospels. Notice that God didn't just give us the teachings of Jesus—the "red letters." He also gave us the stories of Jesus' life—the "black letters"—so that we, too, can see how He lived.

The truly unforgettable lessons in your life are likely the ones you've gotten to see lived out. That's why the people who've had the most indelible impact on your life are those who've lived in close proximity to you for at least a short time.

Likewise, your life will have its greatest impact on those who live, work, play, and do life in close proximity to yours. That seems to be how God designed it. And it's how Jesus modeled it. It's Plan A.

VALID CONCERNS

If you're like some I've talked to about life-on-life spiritual multiplication, you may have some concerns. You may be uneasy about multiplying yourself, because you don't want to pass on your frailties to others. But spiritual multiplication is not about multiplying *yourself*. It's about multiplying *followers of Jesus*.

Your role is to come alongside others in their spiritual journey and help them to set (and keep) their gaze upon Jesus—the author and perfecter of their faith (Hebrews 12:2a).

Some have concerns that they don't know enough answers to help other laborers mature in their faith. Well, on the one hand, that's a good reason to spend more time in the Word. But on the other hand, you don't have to know all the answers. You know the One who does. Instead of giving others "pat" answers, join them in the journey to find out the answers to their questions.

It's okay to let yourself off the hook. You don't have to be a spiritual "know it all" to walk with them…pray with them…seek with them…encourage them. Just don't let yourself off the hook to invest in their lives—even if you think you don't have a lot of answers.

When you embrace God's Plan A for reaching the world, you're embracing a relational ministry style. You impress people from a distance, but you impact them at the deepest levels when you're up close to them—walking with them in their spiritual journeys.

Jesus did ministry one life at a time. And He's calling you to do the same. Are you answering His call?

10

YOUR STORY

The pain of Dawn's third miscarriage was still fresh in our lives when our neighbor, Diana, showed up at our door.

Diana handed Dawn a meal and shared how sorry she was for our loss. As she turned to go, she stopped and began to cry. Soon, she was convulsively weeping right there on our front porch. Dawn invited her in.

As they sat down in our living room, Dawn quickly recognized that Diana's level of emotion was connected with a personal loss of her own.

Dawn was fresh home from the hospital and still feeling the pain of her own loss, which gave her a powerful ability to empathize with her friend as she listened and cared for her.

Diana shared that Dawn's loss had uncovered the pain of an earlier tragic loss in her own life that she'd never dealt with.

Her pain had been bottled up for years, and few people knew about it. But like lava bubbling up from a deep place within her, it had found its way to the surface, and Dawn was God's laborer in that moment to bring comfort and healing to Diana.

Dawn was God's Plan A in that moment for her.

She was able to share with Diana out of the pain of her own loss and the comfort God had been giving her. They cried together and shared words of hope.

In that life-on-life moment, few things could've ministered more to Diana than the credibility, compassion, and understanding that flowed from Dawn's own painful circumstance—from her personal story.

As Dawn and I talked later that evening about her time with Diana, I told her, "Honey, no one else could've ministered to Diana like you did tonight. She needed *you*. She needed the comfort of *your* established relationship. She needed the hope of *your* story."

A POWERFUL MINISTRY TOOL

I'm convinced that, along with your ministry camouflage, your story is quite possibly the greatest tool you have in your ministry toolbox. When it's authentically shared in an up-close, relational way, it's perhaps the most gripping and irrefutable evidence of God's love that you can present to anyone.

It's not information. It's not a sermon. It's a story.

And it's not about a historical figure who lived in another time and another place. It's about *you*—someone they're close to and someone they feel safe and comfortable with.

You and I can be God's best advertisements.

We can be like those "before and after" TV commercials that show a real and verifiable change—except the change in our lives isn't caused by a product that a company wants to sell. It's caused by the real and living God, and it was paid for by His supreme sacrifice on the cross.

Our testimonials make it clear to the world that His love and grace are powerful and transformational—able to turn our worst frailties into trophies of His faithfulness.

Furthermore, they show the world that, despite our present weaknesses (and we all have them), God has never given up on us. We're making progress, and we're confident that *"he who began a good work in [us] will carry it on to completion"* (Philippians 1:6).

Your story is one powerful example of how much God loves us all. And it's an example of how life changing His grace and forgiveness are.

In reality, then, your story is powerful because it's an expression of His story.

People can argue with logic and information. They're quite comfortable doing so. They can get very heated, and say this or that isn't true—regardless of how much you personally believe it.

But no one can argue with your story!

They can't say the change in your life isn't true—especially if they've been around you long enough to see it themselves. It gives you the opportunity to tell them *why* it's true.

In addition, your story helps you establish common ground with others—especially when there's an overlap between your story and their own. These overlaps become the *starting places* for you to better serve them—for you to more sensitively tailor-fit your presentation of God's story in a way that's more meaningful and relevant to their situation.

And you know what's great about telling your story? You're an expert on the subject! You don't have to be a theology scholar to recognize God's love and work in your own life. You've experienced it!

A HOLY DISTURBANCE

One summer Saturday morning in 1982, I hung out with a new friend named Gary. That morning, I got to see his life and listen to his story—and it forever changed my own.

I actually went to his home that day to swim in his swimming pool. But God used the allure of his pool to get me close to Gary's living testimony—his life story—and I saw for the first time in him a guy my own age who loved God deeply, intimately, and passionately.

Gary's life stirred in me a hunger for the living and relational God—a hunger that has characterized my life ever since.

Up to that time, I'd been "churched" and knew information *about* God. But that day, I encountered someone who actually *knew* God. I'd never seen such a vibrant relationship with God before in one of my peers.

Gary talked about Jesus the way my other friends talked about their girlfriends. His love for Jesus was that real and exciting to Him. Whenever He would talk about His relationship with God, his face would light up.

At one point, I said to him, "Gary, you talk about Jesus like you're dating Him or something. It's like you're in love with Him!"

"Isn't that how our relationship with Jesus was meant to be?" he replied. "Didn't God tell us to love Him with all our heart, mind, soul, and strength? Why would I talk any other way?"

Wow! I'd never heard someone my own age talk about God like that.

Gary went on to share with me the story of how he came into such a close relationship with God. And it changed my life. I left that day on a life quest to find what he'd found with God.

His story changed my story.

I've since referred to what happened in me on that day as a *holy disturbance. Holy* because it was all God's doing. *Disturbance* because my heart, my life, and my story were stirred and forever changed.

That's the power of one person's story when it's told at a God-appointed time to another person He's prepared to hear it.

QUILTING BEES

When I was a kid, I loved to hear my grandmother's stories about the quilting bees she participated in decades ago.

Occasionally, women of all ages in her community would bring bags of their fabric scraps and gather together at someone's home to collectively sew one quilt. The resulting masterpiece was a patchwork of every participant's work and fabric.

I was a very small child when I actually witnessed one of her quilting bees and realized what made those quilts so special. I saw how many hands and how much time it took to make one. I watched each person lovingly and laboriously apply her hand-sewn details to something that *one person* would eventually possess.

One person would take home the quilt, along with "a piece" of each person whose loving hands had helped make it.

In the same way, each of us is a patchwork quilt of others' stories. We're a collage made by all the people who've brought a piece of the fabric of their own lives to weave into ours. They've woven the fabric of their own stories into ours.

Think of the people over the years who've pulled up to your life (like they were pulling up to the table of a quilting bee) and lovingly woven important pieces of their fabric into your life.

What if they wouldn't have taken the time to pull up alongside you? What if they wouldn't have offered a piece of their own life fabric? Would your life quilt be less beautiful? Would there be a significant piece missing?

It goes both ways. You, too, contribute many different pieces of fabric into the patchwork quilts of others' lives and stories.

You don't have to provide fabric for the *whole* quilt, just a piece of it. And you won't know how your piece will fit into God's ultimate design for the other person's life, but don't let that keep you from offering it.

Offer the pieces of your story freely, because they're really pieces of God's story.

SHARING YOUR PAIN

Some like to share only the pieces of their lives that demonstrate their strength and show that they have it all together. It's safe to share those pieces of fabric. It requires no risk. It doesn't tarnish their reputation.

At times, it can be good to share from your success stories. But the truth is, it's only a part of the fabric of your life and story. And it may not be the piece that others need.

Others may need to hear about your failures…and how God has been redeeming them. They may need to hear about your pain… and how God has been comforting and healing you. They may need to hear about your times of confusion…and how God has stayed close to you in the midst of your wavering belief.

These are the stories that often have the greatest power in others' lives because they reveal the depths of your frailty and how God is still working in you. They make you vulnerable, which allows others to feel safer in being vulnerable about their own frailties.

We all sense our need for God most desperately at our points of pain and weakness. But some may never open up themselves to His care until you open up yourself to them.

Sharing your own pain or weakness isn't usually an easy way to do ministry. But it can allow you to quickly and deeply build life-giving relationships with others who'll see you as someone authentic and credible to come alongside their own lives.

You don't have to look far to see how God has turned the tragedies of people's life stories into ministry tools.

God turned Chuck Colson's Watergate-related prison sentence into the international ministry known as Prison Fellowship.

He turned Joni Eareckson Tada's tragic diving accident—which left her a quadriplegic—into Joni and Friends, an extraordinary ministry to the disabled.

And God has greatly impacted many lives through the story of professional baseball pitcher Dave Dravecky, who lost his pitching arm to cancer. He has since used his painful story to honor God and to help others who are facing cancer, loss, or pain.

All three have chosen to offer the less-than-beautiful fabric of their life's tragedy to be divinely sewn into the lives of others. If God can use their tragedies on a national scale, couldn't He also use yours on a more local scale—in the life of one person at a time, in your own sphere of influence?

He not only *can*, but according to Scripture, He *wants* to.

> *"Praise be to the…God of all comfort, who comforts us*
> *in all our troubles, so that we can comfort those in any*
> *trouble with the comfort we ourselves have received*
> *from God. For just as the sufferings of Christ flow over*

into our lives, so also through Christ our comfort over-
   flows" (2 Corinthians 1:3-5).

If God has comforted you in your pain, you can use it to comfort others.

Just like Dawn did with Diana.

Everything about your life—whether painful or joyful—is employable by God for His Kingdom service.

It's all a part of your story. And your story is one of the greatest tools you can use to minister to others when you offer it to them out of the natural ease of your relationship with them.

Are you using this tool? Are you telling your story?

PART TWO

THE PROBLEM

*God's Plan A is to minister through
"ordinary," "uniquely designed," "along the
way," "up close," "life on life" ministers.
But there's a problem that
challenges the fulfillment of His plan.*

Are you part of the problem?

SPECTATORS

When I was nine years old, my parents took my brother, sister, and me to watch a parade on the main street of my small hometown. My sister and I were old enough to jump on our bicycles and ride ahead of the rest of the family so we could grab a choice spot along the parade route.

There wasn't a whole lot to the parade. Makeshift floats, men and women in thrown-together clown outfits, Boy and Girl Scout troops, civic clubs, politicians in freshly waxed cars, the high-school marching band, local fire engines, and police cars all paraded past us.

It wasn't until a group of my own peers passed by on their decorated bicycles that I got excited.

They were just riding their bikes—not really doing much—but I was thrilled that someone *like me* had a spot in the parade. These kids weren't just sitting on the curbside watching the parade with the rest of us. They were *in* the parade.

"Mom, those are *my* friends in the parade!" I shouted.

She immediately replied, "Do you want to join them?"

"I couldn't do that!" I insisted, assuming the kids in the parade belonged to some special group in order to take part in it. My mother knew otherwise. She knew it was a small-budget, open-to-anyone parade.

My heart pounded at the thought of actually getting to be *in* the parade myself, but I continued a half-hearted protest: "Mom, my bike isn't decorated like their bikes. My bike is just plain."

"You don't need to have it decorated," my mom persisted as she picked my bike off the ground. "Go ahead, it's your chance! Get out there with the rest of your friends! I'll find you at the end of the parade route."

"Really? I can *really* do that?" I asked, looking for one final bit of reassurance.

Then I made the mistake of glancing over at my father, just to be sure. My father is *not* a risk-taking, parade kind of guy, so he gave me little reassurance. He didn't have to say anything for me to tell he was concerned. I could plainly see it on his face.

But my mom—who's very much a risk-taking, parade kind of lady—won out. She grabbed me and walked me into the street.

"It's okay! Hurry! You're going to miss out if you don't get in there," she said.

I quickly caught up with the rest of my friends and joined the parade.

For the next thirty minutes or so, I savored the almost too-good-to-be-true reality that I was *in* the parade! I kept glancing in disbelief at all the spectators to my left and right.

I had the time of my life.

Despite my mom's coaxing, however, my sister wouldn't join in. She was too timid. Too afraid.

My family met me at the end of the parade route, and my parents threw my bike in the trunk of the car. As we drove home, I proudly recounted every moment of the experience to my parents.

In my young mind, I think I recognized that this wasn't just a different experience for me. Somehow, *I* was different.

SITTING ON THE SIDELINES

This childhood parade experience has become for me a metaphor for the way most Christians approach life and ministry. Most are sitting on the sidelines, watching the parade go by. They're content to watch others get involved while they sit in their comfortable seats at a safe distance away from the action.

I've come to believe that this is one of the greatest challenges to God's Plan A for reaching the world: spectators.

Here's why. According to a survey published by the Barna Research Group, eighty two percent of those who consider themselves Christians are not involved in any kind of active Kingdom service. That means eighty two percent of Christians have not answered God's call on their lives to become a Kingdom laborer.

Apparently, the harvest (ministry opportunity) is *still* plentiful, and the laborers (ministry participants) are *still* too few (Matthew 9:37).

This statistic reminds me of the eighty-twenty principle that pastors have talked about for years. The eighty-twenty principle says that, in most churches (and in the Body of Christ as a whole), twenty percent of the people do eighty percent of the ministry work.

God's Plan A for reaching the world is to mobilize *every Christian* (as an active laborer) into *every place* of human need. But how can He fulfill His plan if fewer than twenty percent of His people are involved in it? How can He fulfill His plan when more than eighty percent are spectators?

I think God wills to extend His grace, love, and power to so many more people in the world. But when He looks around to find a willing laborer through whom He can express His will, He finds none. There are just not enough active laborers for all the human needs of the world.

The problem isn't so much that there aren't enough Christians. The problem is that there aren't enough Christians who are willing to put their faith into action. Instead, they're content to be spectators—sitting on the sidelines.

A QUADRIPLEGIC BODY

I wonder how God must feel when he sees so many human needs and so few laborers who are willing to meet them. I wonder if it saddens Him. Frustrates Him. Angers Him.

I think I got a glimpse of how He must feel through another life experience that took place when I was in my twenties. It happened when I was a regular singer and an occasional interview host for *Day of Discovery*, an inspirational television program produced by RBC Ministries in Grand Rapids, Michigan.

On one program, I did an "informal," five-camera interview around the piano with Joni Eareckson Tada, founder and CEO of Joni and Friends, a ministry to the disabled.

Joni's story is widely known. She suffered a childhood diving accident that left her quadriplegic (paralyzed in her arms and legs) and bound to a wheelchair. Over the years, she'd allowed God to use her physical infirmity as a means of ministering to others with disabilities. By the time of my interview with her, her ministry was thriving.

And so was she. I found her to be radiant with the presence of God.

The director staged the interview around a grand piano. He put me in front of the keyboard and had Joni's assistant wheel her up to the side of the piano (facing me) with her arm resting naturally on the corner.

Soon, the cameras were rolling. I began the interview. I asked Joni about her new book and what God had been doing through Joni and Friends. We both forgot about the cameras for a moment and talked about meaningful heart issues.

At the end of the interview, I played the hymn "All The Way My Savior Leads Me," and we sang it together. But seconds before the song and interview ended, something happened.

As we were singing the last line—"I know whatever befalls me, Jesus does all things well"—I heard a loud "clunk."

At first, I thought someone must have dropped something off camera.

Out of the corner of my eye, I quickly tried to see what had caused the noise. What I saw nearly brought me to tears. In the worshipful moment of the song, Joni had tried to raise her arm in praise to the One she loves—as if to testify that no matter what happens in life, Jesus does *indeed* do all things well.

But her paralyzed arm—surrounded by a metal brace—wouldn't cooperate. Her neck and shoulder strength were enough to lift her arm slightly off the corner of the piano, but her arm couldn't continue to hold its own weight. It quickly fell back to the piano, and the metal brace smacked the wood.

What had been an otherwise powerful interview ended in an awkward moment.

Day of Discovery used the interview in its entirety. But I was deeply affected by what I'd seen. I thought about it nearly the whole next day.

What must it feel like for your head to tell your body to do something…and it won't? It must be more frustrating than I could imagine.

And then it hit me. Is that the way Jesus feels about *His* Body?

Scripture tells us Jesus is The Head and we are The Body. The Head continually communicates with The Body. The Head tells The Body to say this or do that, but what happens when The Body isn't willing to respond?

Far too often, The Body of Christ hasn't done what The Head wants it to. It hasn't cooperated.

There are many times when Jesus has wanted to speak words of love or encouragement to a hurting or searching person, but *His Mouth* won't cooperate.

I think He's often wanted to be close to people across a room, across the street, or even across the world, but *His Feet* won't cooperate—they won't go where He tells them to.

We know Jesus once held children in His arms and blessed them. And today, I think He still wants to pick up and hold children, but *His Arms* won't cooperate.

GRIEVOUS CONSEQUENCES

What happens when so little of The Body actively obeys Jesus?

Think about it for a moment. How does it affect the world? What are the consequences? I think there are at least several.

For starters, those in the active twenty percent of The Body are prone to burn out—despite the fact that fulfilling their ministry calling can be an incredible source of joy and purpose. They see so much need around them that they often try to do too much by themselves. They try to overcompensate.

On the flip side, the inactive eighty percent miss out on the joy and sense of purpose that come from getting involved in active, daily Kingdom service. They don't know the exhilaration and blessing that comes from giving themselves for the eternal good of others—even if it requires sacrifice and commitment.

The most disturbing consequence, however, is that a lot of Kingdom work doesn't get done. So many people need an involved Christian around them to notice their needs and reach them with the love of Christ. But often, there's none around them. There's no one who sees their need and stops to do something about it.

Around the world right now, there are orphanages filled with unwanted children. Streets filled with homeless and hungry people. Offices filled with unhappy and unfulfilled employees. Homes filled with single parents who are trying to raise their children without spouses. Schools filled with students who don't feel like they measure up to their peers. Bars filled with people who are trying to numb themselves to their loneliness and pain.

And, at the same time, there are churches filled with people who are content to do nothing about the needs around them. All of this must grieve the heart of God.

Having a fully functioning Body is critical to God's Plan A for reaching the world.

THE PRESSING QUESTION

I've often asked myself *why* so many are inactive in Kingdom service. I'm sure there are many reasons.

Some are distracted by worldly things that have little eternal value. Others put off ministry service for another day—a day that never comes—believing they're too busy at the time to do anything that requires a sacrifice of time or energy. And then there are those who are just too self absorbed to be concerned about the needs of hurting and hopeless people. All of these are matters of lordship.

But I think there's another prevalent reason why so many Christians haven't become active Kingdom laborers: ignorance.

They don't fully realize how important they are to God's Plan A for reaching the world. Perhaps they believe that ministry participation is only for a certain group of people. Perhaps they've been given the impression that ministry is not an open-to-everyone activity, even though Scripture clearly tells us that God has invited every one of His children to participate.

Some are paralyzed by fear and feelings of inadequacy. They think they don't have the stuff to do anything significant or special in God's Kingdom. Perhaps they haven't noticed the incredible lineage of people in the Bible and throughout history who initially thought the same thoughts—but moved past their fear and got involved.

Remember Moses—the one who thought he couldn't lead the Israelites out of Egyptian slavery because he couldn't communicate very well? Remember Gideon—the one God used to lead His army into battle, even though he thought he was too weak and had the wrong family lineage to do anything like that?

The Bible is full of people who didn't seem like very good candidates for a significant ministry assignment. But they were God's first-round picks.

Don't miss your opportunity to fulfill your ministry calling and potential because of complacency and fear. The master thief, Satan, wants to convince you to stay away from the action. He doesn't want you to get involved, because he knows your potential to impact the world for all of eternity.

And Satan doesn't want you to find the immeasurable fulfillment that comes from doing what you were made to do. He doesn't want you to see and experience things that can never be known or seen from the sidelines.

THE PARADE IS PASSING BY

It's time to stop watching the parade from the sidelines. It's time to grab your bike and join in.

The parade is passing by only *once*. What are you waiting for? There aren't more parades coming. This is it! You can't go back and reclaim a missed opportunity.

It's not the same to just *talk about the parade*. It's not the same to just watch, listen, read, and vicariously live through the ministry lives of others.

Being a spectator is not God's calling on your life! His Plan A for reaching the world includes your involvement.

Got your bike? It's time to get in there and ride.

PART THREE

THE POWER

*God's Plan A is to express
His love and power to the world
through His Kingdom Laborers.
He's the power source
and laborers are His connectors.*

12

40,000 VOLTS

Frank Clewer had no idea what was happening as he walked into a business building in Warrnambool, a small town in the state of Victoria on the southern coast of Australia.

Frank was wearing a wool sweater and a synthetic nylon jacket. As he walked, the two were rubbing together—creating friction and storing up an electrical charge.

He didn't feel a thing. He was totally oblivious to the electrical current that was building up in his clothing.

Others who were working at the business heard a popping sound, as if firecrackers were going off somewhere inside the building. But they couldn't figure out where the sound was coming from. Frank heard the sounds as well, but even he didn't know it was coming from his own clothing.

After taking care of his business, Frank left the building. But those who were still inside began to notice the smell of smoke—as if there were an electrical fire somewhere in the building. Then they noticed spots on the carpet where it was melted and smoldering.

Suddenly, one spot burst into flames. Startled employees called the fire department.

Firefighters arrived within minutes, and they immediately evacuated everyone inside and cut the electricity—thinking there might have been a power surge.

A few minutes later, as Frank was getting into his car, he also began to notice the smell of smoke—it was coming from the floor of his car. He looked down and was startled to find the plastic floor mat melted and smoldering where he'd placed his foot. He jumped out of the car and ran to get help from the firefighters who were walking outside the building.

It wasn't long before someone put the two together. They realized Frank was the source of both fires—in his car *and* in the building.

Firefighters quickly put a static-electricity field meter on his clothing to see how much electricity he was carrying. To their amazement, he had unknowingly generated nearly 40,000 volts of static electricity!

A fire official later told a news agency that Frank was dangerously close to spontaneous combustion!

INCOMPARABLY GREAT POWER

As hard as it is to believe, this incident was reported as a true story by news outlets all over the world on September 17, 2005. When I first heard it, I was utterly amazed. How could a guy walk around for that long carrying that much power...and not be aware of it? I couldn't fathom it.

But then I realized that it happens all the time—but in a different way than it happened to Frank Clewer.

It happens to Christians like you and me. We walk around with God's amazing presence and transformational power at work within us, and we're often not even aware of it.

> "Now to him who is able to do immeasurably more
> than all we ask or imagine, **according to his power**
> **that is at work within us**..."
> (Ephesians 3:20, emphasis added).
>
> "I pray also that the eyes of your heart may be enlight-
> ened in order that you may know...**his incomparably**

*great power for us who believe. That power is like the
working of his mighty strength, which he exerted in
Christ when he raised him from the dead and seated
him at his right hand in the heavenly realms..."*
(Ephesians 1:18-20, emphasis added).

The same power that raised Christ from the dead is at work
within us! That's more amazing than Frank's 40,000 volts! And it
explains why even those laborers who feel the most ordinary can
have an extraordinary influence on the lives of others—because
God desires to work *in* them and *through* them.

You're not the *source* of the power. You're the *carrier.* The *conductor.* The *connector.*

Imagine yourself as a carrier of 40,000 volts of God's hope...40,000
volts of God's love...40,000 volts of God's wisdom...40,000 volts
of God's life-changing truth...and 40,000 volts of His transformational power...to the world around you!

Can you imagine it? God wants to work His power in and
through *you.*

THE POWER SOURCE

The book of Acts tells about a time when the Jewish religious
leaders were "greatly disturbed" because Peter and John were
preaching about the death and resurrection of Jesus with great
anointing and power. Many believed their message and joined
their new movement.

The Jewish leaders had Peter and John arrested, and the next day,
the leaders questioned them: *"By what power or what name did
you do this?"* (Acts 4:7b, emphasis added).

"Filled with the Holy Spirit," Peter boldly responded to them,
declaring that their authority was in the name of Jesus.

But the reaction of the Jewish leaders to Peter and John is what's
truly amazing to me; it's an affirmation of the potential power of a
Kingdom laborer.

*"When they saw the courage of Peter and John and re-alized that they were **unschooled, ordinary men,** they were astonished and they took note that **these men had been with Jesus**"* (Acts 4:13, emphasis added).

The Jewish leaders were *astonished* because Peter and John had not been trained in the top rabbinical schools of the day. No one important knew who they were. They weren't part of the religious elite. And yet, they clearly spoke with authority and anointing.

Where did it come from?

Jesus.

Jesus had given them authority to minister in His name, and that made them bold.

He'd sent them His Holy Spirit when He returned to heaven, and that gave them power.

And they spent lots of time with Jesus, and that gave them an understanding of how to connect God's power to the world around them. They imitated what they saw in Him. And so can you.

If you're a follower of Christ, you've been given authority to minister in His name and the power to minister through His Holy Spirit. But you have to place your complete trust in Him and His strength.

It's common for us to misplace our trust in other things, and in so doing, we lose our power to serve.

We trust in the power of money.

We trust in the power of education.

We trust in the power of organizational effort.

We trust in the power of strong leadership.

We trust in the power of this world's wisdom.

And we often even trust in our own power to get things done.

But God has called us to trust in *His* awesome power—and nothing else!

"If anyone speaks, he should do it as one speaking the very words of God. If anyone serves, he should do it

with the strength God provides, so that in all things
God may be praised through Jesus Christ" (1 Peter
4:11).

"Our gospel came to you not simply with words, but
also with power, with the Holy Spirit and with deep
convictions" (1 Thessalonians 1:5).

"For Christ . . . [sent me] to preach the gospel—not
with words of human wisdom, lest the cross of Christ be
emptied of its power" (1 Corinthians 1:17).

Did you catch that last phrase? Whenever you misplace your trust—placing it in yourself or something other than God—you pay a price. You "empty the cross of Christ of its power" in your life.

Your potential is limited when you trust in yourself or other finite things. But your potential is nearly unlimited when you trust in God to work in and through you.

Is it possible that somewhere along the way, you lost your confidence that God still empowers ordinary people?

LITTLE IS MUCH

It's amazing what can happen when we allow God to work through our little acts of service and our seemingly insignificant words of encouragement. Little becomes much because He's involved in it.

I witnessed this firsthand when I was just a six-year-old little boy.

My father was the pastor of a small country church in rural Pennsylvania. It was a classic one-room, whitewashed church with a steeple—the kind you see in old photographs and paintings. It had a beautiful, sheep-grazing pasture on one side and a small, stately cemetary with large trees on the other. It even had an outhouse in the back.

It was heated by a single wood-burning stove that sat in the middle of the room, about a fourth of the way back. My mom sat our family toward the front of the room—close to the furnace—on cold winter days so we could stay warm.

I was an overactive kid—not one to sit still for long on a hard wooden pew. So, when we sat in the front of the room, *everyone* noticed. They couldn't miss it!

I didn't like the Sunday church hour much. It wasn't at all kid friendly in those days, and it was even worse for an antsy kid like me. Sitting still for even a minute seemed like an hour.

I'm not exaggerating: I was a distractive spectacle nearly every Sunday.

One Sunday after church, an elderly lady from the congregation approached my mom. She had gray hair and a black, "old lady" purse with a single clasp on the top.

"Does your son like peanut butter?" she asked.

She was talking about me, of course, and I knew it. I listened intently as my mother replied, "Yes, he likes it a lot."

"Good," she said. "I have an idea for next Sunday. See me before the church service begins."

The next Sunday, she approached my mother in the coatroom behind the sanctuary before the service started. We were running late, so the conversation was quick. She opened the clasp of her purse and pulled out a peanut-butter sandwich wrapped in foil.

"This is for Dwight," she instructed. "It's Jiffy peanut butter on Wonder bread. I've cut it into four pieces so you can give him one piece every fifteen minutes to keep him occupied through the service."

Have you ever eaten peanut butter on Wonder bread? It's work to chew and swallow it! It tastes good, but it also takes more than a little effort to get it cleared from the roof of your mouth. It didn't fill the whole hour, but it came pretty close.

I loved it! Church had never tasted so good!

She did the same thing for me nearly every Sunday while my dad pastored that church—occasionally deviating from sandwiches to peanut-butter cookies and candy.

Eventually, I started calling her the "Peanut Butter Lady."

Her legacy in my life is that she endeared me to the church by doing what she could with what she had. As little as her acts of service may seem, they impacted my life in ways that could only be realized in hindsight.

Before the Peanut Butter Lady stepped up, I started dreading each Sunday morning on Saturday night. But I started looking forward to church once she started bringing me treats. I couldn't wait to get there and see what she had waiting for me in her black, "old lady" purse.

And something else happened to me during those years. I actually started sitting still enough to notice what was going on in the services. I started singing some of the hymns (in between bites, of course!), I listened to some of the testimonies, I silently prayed during some of the prayer times, and I even started listening to some of the things my dad was saying.

I also first recall feeling the presence of God in that little church. And I first remember feeling drawn to music there. I started feeling like the church was a place where I belonged.

As I grew older, I looked forward to church gatherings with a spirit of anticipation. I became heavily involved in a youth group, where I grew closer to God. And my love for the church grew so strong that I eventually became a pastor.

When I get to heaven, I plan to find the Peanut Butter Lady and thank her. God used the little she gave to change the heart of a little boy who couldn't sit still. She found a way to get me to stop moving around so much, and God took it from there. He arrested my attention and eventually my heart.

Years later, when she passed away, my parents told me her real name—Klenna Slater. But I think when I get to heaven and ask where her mansion is, I'll simply ask where the Peanut Butter Lady lives.

One little old lady with a heart of love, a black purse, a jar of peanut butter, and a loaf of Wonder bread—that's what God first used to endear me to the church. And He took it even farther, endearing me to Himself and His Kingdom as well.

WHEN GOD IS IN IT

Klenna's actions remind me of a hymn I first learned in that little country church: "Little is Much, When God is in It." Even though it uses older language (it was written in 1924), its message is profound. Here's one verse and the refrain:

Verse Two
Does the place you're called to labor
Seem too small and little known?
It is great if God is in it,
And He'll not forget His own.

Refrain
Little is much when God is in it!
Labor not for wealth or fame.
There's a crown and you can win it,
If you go in Jesus' Name.

As I travel and speak, I find that there are Klenna Slaters all over the place who are doing little things for others in faithful (and often sacrificial) ways. What saddens me, though, is that they usually don't feel like such little acts of service can have much of an impact on others' lives.

When I take them on a journey through Scripture to show them that God values what they do, and He really wants to infuse their actions and words with His 40,000 volts of divine power, I sense a stir in them.

After one service, I had a college basketball coach named Mike tell me that he nearly jumped up on his seat and shouted, "hallelujah!" when I said that God wants to empower His ministry.

"I've always felt that my 'mission field' is on a basketball court with twelve kids at a time," Mike the Basketball Coach explained to me.

"But my role in God's Kingdom has always felt little to me—especially when I compare it with what pastors and missionaries do. I've known God wants to do a mighty work through them, but I never realized He wants to do a mighty work through me, too—through my job as a basketball coach. But why not? I have a mission field, too.

"I can't wait to get back out on the court and see what God does!"

Mike the Basketball Coach had realized that God's Plan A is to empower him and every laborer with 40,000 volts of love, wisdom, hope, and power.

That's why your little acts of service and words of encouragement can amount to much...because God is in them.

13

CONNECTORS

While speaking at a summer camp a number of years ago, I had a chance to spend some time with my friend David, who I hadn't seen in a long time. We were excited for the chance to catch up on each other's lives.

As David and I were talking one afternoon in an open area of the campground, I noticed he wasn't looking at me as I shared some really important things. He seemed to be distracted by something going on behind me.

I continued to tell my story, doing everything I could to regain his attention.

I added volume. I added intensity. But he still wouldn't look at me.

Suddenly, I saw panic in David's face. He jumped up from where we were sitting and dashed past me.

When I turned to see where he was going, I realized why he hadn't been listening very well.

Beyond me, he'd been watching a little boy who was playing too close to some electrical wires. David sprinted toward the boy when he saw him grab a live wire that had been improperly connected to a concession trailer.

By the time David got there, electricity was flowing through the boy's body.

Fortunately, David had the presence of mind to do something I wouldn't have known to do. He didn't grab hold of the boy and try to pull him free from the power line. Instead, he threw all his body weight against the boy's body and knocked him to the ground—free from the power line.

David saved the boy's life—and avoided being seriously injured himself—because he knew he shouldn't grab him. Why? Because the power coming from the source would have traveled straight through the boy's body into David. David could've been electrocuted because the boy would have served as a conductor between him and the power source.

The boy would have acted as a connector.

In a similar way, Kingdom laborers are also conductors through which God does His work in the lives of others. We're connectors. It's why our lives have so much Kingdom potential.

We aren't dependent on our own strength, our own love, our own wisdom, or our own power to do the work God has called us to. We can be conductors of *His* strength, love, wisdom, and power to those who are all around us.

God has always looked for people who are willing to be His connectors to the world.

THE GREATEST GIFT

Here's the deal, though: You can't be a connector unless you touch the heart of God (the Power Source). And the only way to touch God's heart is to spend time with Him. When you spend time in His presence—getting to know Him in deeper, more intimate ways—your life overflows with more of His love and power.

It happens naturally.

You can't pursue greater intimacy with Jesus without being transformed. You can't spend time in His presence without being filled with more of Him.

That's why I believe with all my heart that *the greatest gift you'll ever give the world is your intimacy with God.*

The more you spend time with Him, the more He'll show up

where you show up on the everyday scenes of life—in your home, your workplace, your church, your school. . . and all the other places you go.

You have wonderful talents and spiritual gifts that God has given you to share with others. But there's something people need more than you and your gifts.

They need God Himself. They need His presence, power, and love.

As much as you may have to give others, God will always have more to give:

> God's thoughts and ways are much higher than yours (Isaiah 55:8-9).

> His infinite love is much greater than your limited capacity to love (1 John 4:9-10).

> His foolishness is wiser than your wisdom (1 Corinthians 1:25).

> His weakness is greater than your power (1 Corinthians 1:25).

> You can reflect His light, but He *is* the light that pierces the darkness (John 1:4-5, 9).

> Your words can bring hope, but He *is* the hope of the world (1 Timothy 1:1, Colossians 1:27).

That's why the greatest gift you'll ever give the world is your intimacy with God. Because He has far more to give people than you do. And the more you've spent time in His presence, the more He'll move through you in your daily actions and words.

And it's also why He's called you to live your life "up close" to others—in the places where they live and work and play—because you have the capacity to usher in His presence wherever you go.

YOU CAN'T GIVE WHAT YOU DON'T HAVE

The catch, of course, is that you can't give what you don't have. You can't give your intimacy with God to others if you aren't experiencing it in the first place.

In Acts 3, Peter and John were going to the temple for their regular time of prayer. At the same time, a crippled man was being carried to the temple gate where he sat every day to beg for money.

When he asked Peter and John for money, Peter replied: *"Silver or gold I do not have, but what I have I give you. In the name of Jesus Christ of Nazareth, walk"* (Acts 3:6).

One way of looking at this story is that it shows how God does His work through us as we live our daily lives. Peter and John were going about their normal routine when an opportunity for ministry came up. It wasn't a preplanned activity or a ministry event; they just responded to a divine appointment that God had set in their path—"as they went" about daily life.

But there's another powerful way of looking at this story. It clearly shows that *you can't give what you don't have.*

Peter and John couldn't give the beggar the money he sought because they had none. Likewise, you can't share God's presence with others if you haven't had much intimacy with Him yourself.

You just can't give what you don't have!

You can try to fake it. You can produce a counterfeit that lacks the power of God's intimate presence. You can even try to appear spiritual in the eyes of others.

But if you're not close to God, you can't bring Him close to others.

Even Jesus needed to spend intimate time up close to His Father in Heaven. Even He needed to touch the Power Source. Time and time again, He escaped to quiet places to be with His Father for extended periods of time. If God Incarnate needed that time with His Father, how much more do we need it?

A PRESENCE-DRIVEN LIFE

Rick Warren's book *The Purpose Driven Life* has helped many of us think more about God's purposes for our lives. It's a great message that could even be included in the subtitle of this book. But there's another part of the equation that works hand in hand with being purpose driven—we must also be presence driven.

Let me put it a different way: The world needs more than purpose-driven people; it needs presence–driven people. It needs people whose lives are led and empowered by their intimate time with God.

The world needs presence-driven people because the world needs God, and presence-driven people usher His presence into the lives of others.

Paul told the Roman church that "God has poured out his love into our hearts by the Holy Spirit, whom he has given us" (Romans 5:5).

That's what the world needs: His love. And if His love has been poured into our hearts, we have it to give to others.

A Kingdom laborer, then, is a person who is in a love relationship with God and brings His love and presence into everyday relational encounters. They're connectors.

IMMANUEL

God wants *us* to be up close to the lives of others because *He* wants to be up close to their lives. That's the message He was expressing when He sent His only Son to the earth as a human being.

What did God call His Son? Immanuel. A name that means "God with us." God is with us!

God was with us when Jesus came into the world. And when Jesus went back to be with His Father in heaven, He sent His Holy Spirit to reside with us.

God is still with us!

He desires to be a personal Immanuel in the life of every person, and He extends His direct-from-the-source, life-changing power to others through us. Through you!

When He looks to accomplish His will "on earth as it is in heaven," He looks for a willing laborer through whom He can get the job done. That's Plan A. When He wants to show His love to someone, He looks for a willing laborer to use as an up-close vessel of love. Plan A. When He wants to bring hope or purpose to someone's life, He searches for a willing laborer through whom He can say or do something. Plan A.

In a sense, Kingdom laborers are God's power lines. They spend time in a loving relationship with the awesome God of the universe who, in turn, expresses His love and power through them.

The world needs laborers like you...because the world needs Him. Are you connecting Him to others?

14

LETTING GO

Five-year-old Alaina climbed up on my lap as I sat at my living-room piano, preparing to lead a group of friends in a time of worship. Alaina is the daughter of a close friend and ministry colleague, and since I had no children at the time, we'd adopted each other as uncle and niece.

Alaina was the only child in a room full of adults that night, and she and I were both well aware there were no toys in our home for her to play with. She was bored.

"Give me your hand," I said to her as she squirmed on my lap. "Would *you* like to play a song?"

"I don't know how to play," she quickly replied.

"It's okay, I do. We can do it together."

She smiled and nodded.

I asked her to point with her index finger and then folded her other fingers under the palm of her hand. I then began to press the keys of the piano with her index finger to sound out a melody.

At first, Alaina's arms were rigid. I could hardly move her hand where I wanted it to go. I knew we could play a song together if she'd loosen up and let me move her hand. But she remained inflexible.

"Just relax," I said. "Relax your arm and let *me* move it."

In the next few minutes, she got the hang of it. She slowly relinquished control of her arm and recognized the tune we were playing.

She looked at me with surprise and delight, realizing we were *really* playing a song.

"Wow! I know that song!" she shouted, as she quickly glanced over at her parents to see if they'd been watching.

"I did it!" she said with great pride. "I played a song!"

I don't know if something was born in her at that moment, but she's now (as a young adult) a gifted musician. She plays the piano and guitar, and she's an anointed worship leader. (She's even given guitar tips to my daughter.)

As I sometimes tell this story to groups of young adults, I ask them a question: "Did Alaina *really* play that song?"

Most take a moment to ponder the question, but usually a few quickly blurt out, "No, *you* played it."

"Are you sure?" I press harder. "It was Alaina's finger that touched the keys."

They usually reply with something like, "Yes, but you didn't *need* her to play the song—you could've played it by yourself. But she couldn't have done it without you!"

"But isn't that the point?" I reply, "I wanted her to have the joy of doing something she couldn't do on her own."

After further discussion, most come to the conclusion that I played it *with* her and *through* her. I didn't need her in order to play it, but it was so much fun—for both of us—to do it together. We both enjoyed the experience more than if I played that little tune on my own.

TOGETHER

Alaina's story is a powerful picture of the work God *chooses* to do through us. The parallels are many. To begin with, I think He's asking each of us the same question I asked Alaina: "Do you want to play a song?" Or to paraphrase, "Do you want to do important work in my Kingdom?"

It's an invitation. An opportunity. He won't force it on us, but I think He looks forward to our joy—and maybe even surprise—when we discover how much He can do through us.

I also think it's a welcome response to Him when we say, "I don't know how."

It's hard to direct people who think they already know how to do it. "I don't know" is a response of humility and teachability. It's a response that launches new faith ventures. And it's a response that ultimately produces greater Kingdom work.

But even when we let God take our hand, we often start out rigid. We're not used to relaxing and giving up control.

We have to learn to let go.

Leaning into His leadership is a new experience for us. It requires a daily posture of listening for His voice, which is not a life discipline we usually learn in our formative years.

We often struggle against God's leadings, sometimes telling *Him* what to do. We try hard to figure it out and do it on our own. But over and over, we're brought back to the realization that our way doesn't work nearly as well.

Maybe we just haven't experienced the rich joy and pleasure of Spirit-directed living and laboring. Maybe we haven't heard how much more beautiful and powerful the music is when He plays it through us. Maybe we're just too proud to allow ourselves to sit on His lap and let Him do the work through us. Or maybe we're too afraid to let go of control.

Regardless of the reason, I think most people never find out how much God can do through them, because they just can't bring themselves to relax and let go.

The result? They downscale the impact of their lives.

But there are some who get to the place where they really do relax, realizing the ease and joy of His rhythm as they live out their daily lives. They let God do *His* thing. And before long, they begin to recognize that He's playing a tune. He's playing it *through* them.

The part we play may seem little—perhaps not much more than when I used Alaina's finger to play the keys. But that's how God chooses to work— *through* us. That's His Plan A. It requires nothing short of our willingness to let go and lean into His moment-by-moment leadership and empowerment in our lives.

Picture yourself sitting on His lap in front of a piano. Are your arms rigid, or are they relaxed? Are you fighting against His movement, or are you allowing Him to play a tune of His choosing? Are you experiencing the joy of hearing the song as it's played? Are you watching those around you enjoy the blessing of the music you're playing together?

That's a picture of your life.

Relax and let go.

PART FOUR

THE POTENTIAL

The potential impact of one Kingdom laborer is powerful. Imagine what could happen if more and more laborers around the world would fulfill their personal role in God's Plan A.

15

RIPPLES

Ed Kimball was a simple and ordinary man who loved God. He was also a true Kingdom laborer who put his faith in God into action. And God used him.

Although he lived in the Nineteenth Century, the effects of his life are felt by millions today. Maybe even by you.

Ed taught a youth Sunday school class at Mount Vernon Congregational Church in Boston. It was a pretty humble ministry assignment, really, but he did it faithfully for years—serving the boys in his class in practical ways.

One of his students was a seventeen year old named Dwight, a new transplant to Boston. He'd moved there to work in his uncle's shoe store.

Dwight had little interest in spiritual things, but his uncle required that he attend church.

So he did. Dwight got up on Sunday mornings and went to Mount Vernon Congregational Church, where he met Ed. He didn't care much for the church service—he thought it was boring—but he enjoyed Ed's Sunday school class. And he especially enjoyed spending time with him.

The two became close friends.

After months of friendship, Ed visited Dwight at his shoe store with a clear mission in mind. He asked Dwight to commit his life to Christ. Dwight was ready for Ed's request, and he eagerly knelt wn and prayed right there in the middle of the store!

From that point on, Dwight began sharing Christ with others.

THE LEGACY OF ED KIMBALL

You've probably never heard of Ed Kimball before now, but I'm guessing you *have* heard of the "Dwight" in this story: Dwight L. Moody. This is how he became a Christian in 1855.

You may also know that Moody went on to become a well-known evangelist, and he started Moody Bible Institute in downtown Chicago.

But my focus in this story isn't so much on Dwight Moody as it is on Ed Kimball. You see, Dwight Moody was just the beginning of Ed's legacy. He was the first ripple of Ed's influence that eventually spread in every direction.

In time, Moody moved from Boston to Chicago. During the course of his life and ministry, he prayed with a young man named J. Wilbur Chapman, helping him be certain of his salvation.

Chapman went on to become an itinerant evangelist and connected with another young man—a former professional baseball player named Billy Sunday. Sunday helped Chapman organize his evangelistic meetings. Chapman discipled Sunday and, before long, Sunday was preaching on his own.

Sunday preached at an evangelistic meeting in Charlotte in 1924, which birthed a men's prayer group that lasted for years afterward.

Sunday's impact on the group was profound, and the group prayed earnestly for God to send revival to Charlotte. In 1934, the prayer group invited another evangelist, Mordecai Ham, to hold a revival meeting there.

By now, the group had invested ten years of prayer into this evangelistic meeting—and God answered their prayers. Many came forward to receive Christ. One was a young man named Billy.

Billy would go from there to be one of the most anointed evangelists in American history.

His counsel has been sought after by the last six U.S. presiden[t] and his crusades have been instrumental in bringing hundreds o[f] thousands of people to belief in Christ.

The story I have just recounted is Billy Graham's spiritual lineage.

But it's more than that. It's the spiritual legacy of Ed Kimball, an ordinary (but faithful) Sunday-school teacher who served God in humble ways and trusted Him to do the rest.

It's about the ripple effect of Ed Kimball's life. It's about his legacy.

REVERBERATIONS

Each of us has a ripple effect on the world around us. Each of our actions is like a small drop of water in a big lake, causing ripples that spread out in every direction. As small as these drops may seem, the reverberations are felt by people we don't even know for years after we die. That's partly why the potential of your life and Kingdom labor are so great.

These reverberations multiply the power of even our small acts of service because they spread out their influence over time through the lives of others. You needn't look any further than Ed Kimball's life for a clear example.

Even the most shy and inhibited of us have the capacity to impact the lives of countless thousands of people.

A number of years ago, I came across the book *101 Ways to Improve the Self Concept in the Classroom*. (It's now out of print, and I haven't been able to find a copy since.) There was one sentence in the book that I wrote down, and it's stuck with me over the years. It said, "The most inhibited person will influence at least 10,000 people in the course of [his or her] lifetime."

I've since seen several studies that come to similar conclusions. The bottom line? We all have more influence than we'll ever see. Even if the drop of water that represents our life seems small and inconsequential, it leaves a spreading ripple.

...very one of our lives has a ripple effect.

AMPLIFIERS

The ripple effect is evident throughout Scripture, but the most powerful example is in how Jesus chose to spread the influence of His Good News through His disciples. He taught them His Plan A for reaching the world over the course of three years and then sent them out to spread the Good News all over the world.

I was reminded of the disciple's influence a number of months ago, when I spent some time with Abraham, my Indian friend. Abraham trains pastors throughout India and starts and supports churches in Bihar, a state that's known for its hostility to Christianity. I spent time with him when he was traveling in the U.S. to raise money to start a new set of churches in Bihar.

While I was with Abraham, I asked him how he became a Christian. I was surprised at his answer. Rather than talking about his own personal conversion experience, Abraham gave me a bit of a history lesson.

"I am a Christian today because one of Jesus' disciples brought the Gospel to India nearly two thousand years ago," he said.

I'd never heard anything like that before. To be honest, I was a little skeptical.

"Which one?" I asked him.

"I am a Christian because of the Apostle Thomas," he replied. "He first brought the Gospel to parts of India, and now I am carrying on his work as I help spread it farther into India—into places where people still have not heard about Jesus."

Talk about a ripple effect!

Abraham has a sense of his own spiritual heritage that goes all the way back to Thomas—and ultimately to Jesus Himself. He even feels a connection to the ministry mission of Thomas, believing that he's carrying on the work that Thomas started.

The reverberations of God's love started long before you and me. And, like my friend, Abraham, we get to be amplifiers of them in our generation to places where they might not otherwise be

FROM GENERATION TO GENERATION

While I was writing this book, I had an encounter that under
scores how God uses our ripple effect. I was speaking for a Spiritual Emphasis Week at a Christian university in the Midwest, and
a student approached me after one of the services.

"Hi, I wanted to introduce myself to you," he said. "I think I'm
your great-great-great grandson in the faith."

He then walked me through the spiritual generations that connect us.

Years ago, I'd led a teenager Mick Veach to Christ and discipled
him. I spent a lot of time with Mick for several years—pouring into
him—and he became one of my closest friends. I taught him to do
the same with others, and his life had a powerful impact on many
of his peers.

He eventually pastored a youth group, where he led a kid to
Christ and mentored him. That kid went on to do the same for
another kid, who did the same for another kid. And that kid led
this student to Christ and discipled him.

I walked away from my great-great-great grandson in the faith
very thankful for the work God had done in the twenty-plus years
since I'd spent time with Mick. But I was also moved by the realization that I'll never know many of my spiritual grandchildren this
side of heaven.

And that leads me to a word of encouragement for you: God
wants to use the ripple effect of your life to impact countless others
for many spiritual generations. Your ministry potential is greater
than you can probably imagine!

Through you, He wants to impact the lives of people you don't
even know!

That is, if you'll let Him.

You may be among the faithful who've sacrificially poured into
others' lives for years—and you've wondered whether or not you've

made much of a difference. Let me remind you that you may
see (in this life) many of the reverberations of your life from
person to another and one generation to the next—any more
an Ed Kimball did.

Think about it. Kimball never saw the role he would play in training thousands of students to minister to others through Dwight Moody's Bible institute. And he never saw the role he would play in the life of Billy Graham and the countless others who Graham's life would touch—even American presidents. Kimball's faithfulness in the life of one teenage shoe salesman has had reverberations from person to person and from generation to generation.

God wants to do a reverberating work through you as well. That's part of His Plan A. Will you offer your life to Him as a Kingdom laborer and follow His leading to impact the lives of others around you? If you do, your impact could be felt throughout all of eternity.

16

IMAGINE

The pastor stood at the front of the sanctuary and anointed Kara to go back to the mission field God had called her to. He dipped his index and middle fingers into a small glass bowl filled with oil and touched her forehead.

"I anoint you with oil for the ministry service God has called you to...in the name of The Father, The Son, and The Holy Spirit," he said.

He then added a few encouraging words as he sent her forth.

In some ways, it was nothing unusual. It was a formal ministry commissioning service like the ones you've probably seen in your church.

But in other ways, it was *very different* from a typical commissioning service.

You see, Kara is not an overseas missionary who's returning to a field like Kenya or Thailand. She's a mother of five whose primary place of ministry service is in a suburban neighborhood about twenty minutes away from the church.

She's a "stay at home" mom. And her primary ministry service for her current season of life takes place in "motherhood" kinds of places—in her home, down the street, at the swimming pool, on playgrounds and practice fields, in her kids' schools, and at the grocery store and doctor's office.

Kara was not the only one being anointed that Sunday. All

und the sanctuary, other Kingdom laborers were consecrating emselves to God and gathering in front of pastors and elders to eceive the same kind of commissioning.

By the time all five services were over, thousands of laborers had been anointed!

The pastors and church leaders had clearly communicated something important that morning. They'd validated every laborer's personal ministry, and they'd sent them out to "be the church" wherever they went.

But that's not all they communicated. In the same symbolic act, they showed how powerful a force the Body of Christ could be if every Christian would fulfill God's Plan A by becoming a Kingdom laborer.

As I watched laborers being anointed all over the sanctuary, my imagination took over.

"What could happen if most churches around the world equipped and commissioned their 'attenders' to be active Kingdom laborers?" I asked myself.

"What if the eighty percent of uninvolved and 'unemployed' laborers in the Body of Christ would stand up and report for duty?"

"What if there were services like this all over the world and the 'commissioning line' was so long that it took weeks for all the pastors and elders to anoint and send out all the laborers?"

God had sparked something in me, and my imagination was running wild!

UNTAPPED POTENTIAL

The Body of Christ is full of untapped potential. It's like a sleeping giant! And it's time for us to wake up and fulfill the redemptive possibilities of God's Plan A!

You've probably heard the famous quote about "the sleeping giant" that's attributed to Japanese admiral, Isoroku Yamamoto. He supposedly said it after his fleet attacked Pearl Hearbor in World War II. The line has been immortalized in movies like *Tora! Tora! Tora!* and *Pearl Harbor*: "I fear all we have done is to awaken a sleeping giant and fill him with a terrible resolve."

If Yamamoto said this line or even thought this thought, he was right.

The U.S. had the power to influence the outcome of the war long before Japan's attack, but it remained uninvolved—content to be a spectator. (Sound familiar?) The war seemed so far away, so removed from the daily lives of most Americans. But when the Japanese surprised the U.S. at Pearl Harbor, it awakened the "Sleeping Giant" and brought it into the war—with great resolve.

So, what will it take to wake up the Sleeping Giant that is the church? What will it take to fill it with such great resolve?

The New Testament ideal of the church was not so much about buildings or programs as it was about God, His people, and the collective influence they would have on each other and the world.

The future of God's Kingdom does not hinge on how big or great our buildings and programs are (as useful as they may be). *The future of God's Kingdom is in human resources.*

It's in you and I (and all Christians) accepting our God-given calling to become His Kingdom laborers and usher His presence into the lives of others in the everyday places where we find ourselves.

Because the church is made up of people, it has no boundaries. And because the power behind this movement comes from the almighty God who reigns over the universe, it has more power than we realize.

The church truly is a Sleeping Giant! And God is calling for us to wake up.

I believe He's fueling a grassroots movement of laborers whose influence will be felt throughout the world.

YOUR ROLE IN THIS MOVEMENT

You have a role to play in this laborership movement. And you don't need to wait to get started. Here are some things you can do as soon as you put this book down in a few moments:

surrender your whole life to God, and offer yourself as a living sacrifice for obedient service in His Kingdom.

2. Live the life of a Kingdom laborer, making yourself available to be an "in the moment," "along the way," "up close," "camouflaged," "life on life" minister in your sphere of influence.

3. Pray that God would raise up more laborers for His harvest field.

    *"Then [Jesus] said to his disciples, 'The harvest is plentiful, but the laborers are few; **pray** therefore the Lord of the harvest to send out laborers into his harvest'"* (Matthew 9:37-38, RSV, emphasis added).

4. Come alongside other potential laborers, helping them see the role God wants them to play in His Kingdom work, and equipping them to do it. (See the list of resources on page 152 that can help you equip and encourage other laborers.)

5. Pray that God will show you other ways you can be a catalyst for a larger "Plan A," laborership movement around the world.

Don't wait. Take some immediate steps that will push you further away from the sidelines and into the middle of the parade—in step with what God wants to do in and through your life!

A FINAL PRAYER

God, may you raise up the readers of this book to be active and obedient laborers as they participate in your Kingdom-building Plan A. May you draw them closer to You, fill them with your 40,000 volts of power and love, and lead them into places of greater Kingdom influence.

And may you awaken the Sleeping Giant—including the vast army of Christians who are currently "missing in action"—and send it into every corner of the world.

We can imagine it. We're beginning to see it happen. May you powerfully carry forth your Plan A in our generation. Amen!

PLAN A

A SUMMARY

THE PLAN

LABORERS ARE GOD'S PLAN A FOR REACHING A LOST WORLD. AND GOD HASN'T GIVEN A PLAN B.

WHO:

God does his extraordinary kingdom work through ordinary people who Jesus called "laborers."

- Laborers are Christians who put their faith into action through ministry service.
- *Every* Christian is called to be a laborer and to play a significant role in building God's Kingdom. There are no exceptions.
- Ordinary people are God's first-round draft picks for ministry service.
- Laborers are ministers—not just the "professional" kind like pastors and missionaries, but the common, ordinary kind like students, "stay at home" moms, teachers, nurses, artists, businessmen, construction workers, and the like.
- Laborers are willing to be used by God in their everyday places of influence.
- "Christian celebrities" aren't the answer to the great harvest need. Ordinary laborers are.

God is not calling just a few select people to make a difference in the world. He's mobilizing an army of His laborers who will go into every corner of the world.

- The kingdom of God needs all kinds of laborers who do all kinds of work.

WHAT:

Laborers participate in God's redemptive Plan for the world by engaging in ministry service that's as distinct and unique as they are.

- Each laborer's service is as unique as his or her fingerprints.
- Ministry does not have to be expressed in a form that we've seen hundreds or thousands of times. It can be creative and entrepreneurial.
- God has made every one of His laborers for a ministry purpose. And He's uniquely designed them with that purpose in mind.
- You'll experience an incredible joy when you discover and fulfill God's ministry purpose.
- Nearly every aspect of your life can be creatively employed for ministry service—even your hobbies and recreational interests.
- As a part of your ministry design, God has outfitted you with a "camouflage" ministry uniform that allows you to naturally connect with others *in their world,* ministering to them out of the overflow of who you are—in the places where their pain and needs most naturally emerge.
- Camouflage comes in many different forms.

WHEN:

Laborers minister to others in the everyday moments of life— whenever they encounter a ministry opportunity or sense that God is prompting them to act.

- Ministry doesn't just happen at preplanned times. It often happens when we're going about our daily lives.

- When Jesus walked the earth, He ministered to people *as went*, and now He wants to minister through His Kingdom laborers *as they go*.
- He wants you to embrace a lifestyle of Spirit-directed living and laboring.
- God *wants* to speak to you and guide you *in the moment*—not just in your morning quiet times with Him, but throughout your everyday life.
- When it comes to hearing and obeying God's voice, don't let the fear of getting it wrong keep you from getting it right.
- You can't hear God's voice if you're not listening...if you're too focused on your own "important" agenda...if you're too busy getting other things done.
- If you're rushing through life "on task," you may be missing important Kingdom-advancing moments along the way.
- You may not understand why He's asked you to do something at the time you're doing it. You may not know for a long while. In fact, you may never know this side of heaven. But *He* knows.

WHERE:

The most powerful places of ministry are those that bring laborers up close to the lives of others—where they live, work, struggle, gather, and play.

- God never meant for ministry to primarily happen inside "the four walls of the church." Jesus told His followers to "go and tell," not just ask people to "come and see."
- When people are in desperate need, they don't need distant celebrities. They need *on-the-scene* laborers.
- People need laborers *up close* because they need God *up close* to them.
- You impress people from a distance, but you impact them up close.
- Meal tables are among the most natural up-close places where you can build relationships with people and minister to them.

145

If you like to eat, you have *great* ministry potential!

How:

The ministry of a kingdom laborer is most effective when it's done in highly relational settings—one life at a time.

- While large-event ministry can be very powerful in people's lives, nothing can replace ministry that happens one laborer to another—over time in relational settings.
- Spending more time with fewer people can equal a greater Kingdom impact.
- It's difficult to see the value of *life-on-life* ministry when most of our culture sees more value in using mass-production methods. But, over time, mass-production methods aren't as effective as relational methods for reaching the world with God's love and truth.
- Over time, spiritual multiplication is a ministry strategy that reaches more people, and it reaches them in a deeper, more impactful way.
- Spiritual multiplication is not about your multiplying yourself. It's about multiplying other followers of Jesus. Your goal is to help others set and keep their gaze on Him.
- As a part of His relational ministry strategy, God gives each one of His laborers a personal story to share with others.
- *Your* story is powerful because it's an expression of *His* story.
- People can argue with logic and information, but they can't argue with your story.
- Your story helps you establish common ground with others.
- Some need to hear the stories of your failures and pain—not just the stories that show your strengths and successes.
- God has comforted you so that you can comfort others.

THE PROBLEM

GOD'S PLAN A IS TO MINISTER *THROUGH* KINGDOM LA-
BORERS. BUT THERE'S A PROBLEM THAT CHALLENGES THE
FULFILLMENT OF HIS PLAN: SPECTATORS.

- The vast majority of Christians (approximately eighty percent, by some estimates) have not responded to God's call for them to become active laborers and engage in ministry service.
- The Body of Christ is quadriplegic in that its various parts don't obey the Head.
- A fully-functioning Body is critical to God's Plan A.
- There are grievous consequences when so many Christians don't participate in Kingdom service:

  The active twenty percent of laborers are prone to get burned out because they often try to compensate for the inactivity of the majority of Christians.

  The inactive eighty percent of Christians miss out on the joy that comes from living a life of ministry that flows out of God's design on their lives.

  A lot of Kingdom work doesn't get done.

THE POWER

GOD'S PLAN A IS TO EXPRESS HIS LOVE AND POWER
TO A NEEDY WORLD THROUGH HIS KINGDOM LABORERS.
GOD IS THE POWER SOURCE AND LABORERS ARE HIS
CONNECTORS.

- Laborers have been given the authority to minister in Jesus' name. They've been empowered by His Holy Spirit. And they can learn how to express that power by spending time with Jesus.

- Laborers are God's connectors. But you can only be a connector if you're up close to the Power Source. If you're not close to God, you can't bring Him close to others.
- That's why the greatest gift you'll ever give the world is your intimacy with God.
- The more time you spend with God, the more He'll show up where you show up on the everyday scenes of life.
- As wonderful as you are, there's something that others need more than you. They need God.
- Before laborers are purpose driven, they must be presence driven.
- Laborers often drain their ministry of its power by depending on the wrong things—money, education, organizational effort, strong leadership, the world's wisdom, or their own limited abilities.
- Your resources are limited. God's resources are unlimited.
- God wants to use you as a connector to reach the world around you.
- God can only use you if you let go of control. When you hold on to control, you downsize the impact of your life.

THE POTENTIAL

THE IMPACT OF ONE LABORER'S LIFE IS POWERFUL. IMAGINE WHAT COULD HAPPEN IF MORE AND MORE CHRISTIANS FULFILLED THEIR ROLE IN GOD'S PLAN A BY BECOMING KINGDOM LABORERS.

- We all have more eternal impact than we'll ever see because our influence on one person's life is passed on to another, who passes it on to another, and so on.
- Even the most inhibited of us has the potential to impact the lives of tens of thousands of people.
- The reverberations of Jesus' love started long ago and have traveled through generations. We now have the opportunity to

amplify His love to future generations.

- Each laborer must answer the question: What am I doing v
  my God-given opportunities for Kingdom influence?
- The Body of Christ is a "sleeping giant." God desires to awaker
  it and unleash its untapped potential throughout the world.

ABOUT THE AUTHORS

DWIGHT ROBERTSON

Dwight Robertson is founder and President of Kingdom Building Ministries, Aurora, Colorado. He's also a popular speaker for various kinds of events, including university chapels, conventions, seminars, retreats, and pastor's conferences. He's the author of several other print resources—including *The Spiritual Life Notebook*—and he frequently writes for *The Laborer's Journal*, the ministry magazine of Kingdom Building Ministries. Dwight lives in Aurora with his wife, Dawn, and their children, Dara and Dreyson. To schedule Dwight to speak at your event, call Kingdom Building Ministries at 1-800-873-8957.

MARK VERMILION

Mark Vermilion is Vice President of Communication for Kingdom Building Ministries and Executive Editor of its quarterly magazine, *The Laborer's Journal*. He's authored or co-authored numerous magazine articles and resources and he's also a gifted teacher and speaker. Mark lives in Aurora, Colorado, with his wife, Katrina, and their five children: Lauren, Brandon, Madeline, Nathan, and Kaylen. To schedule Mark to speak at your event, call Kingdom Building Ministries at 1-800-873-8957.

ABOUT THE MINISTRY

KINGDOM BUILDING MINISTRIES

Kingdom Building Ministries is a nondenominational, evangelical, itinerant-speaking ministry that challenges people to fully devote their lives to God and equips them to live lives of active ministry. Its dynamic speakers are in demand for various kinds of ministry events all over the world, including conferences, festivals, retreats, camps, church services, and training workshops. Kingdom Building Ministries also offers laborer-training programs, including high-impact summer sessions for young adults and regional weekend conferences for adults. It also offers books, message CDs and DVDs, and other resources as well. To find out more, log on to Kingdom Building Ministries' website at *www.kbm.org* or call 1-800-873-8957.

PLAN A CONNECTION

The *Plan A Connection* is an online resource for those who want to grow closer to God and live lives of greater Kingdom influence. Check it out! You'll find powerful spiritual-growth articles and resources—as well as free computer wallpaper screens that feature some of the most powerful quotes from the *Plan A* book. You'll also find a place to tell stories of ordinary Kingdom laborers (like James the Roofer) who are impacting others in the everyday places and circumstances of their lives. And you can find out locations of *Plan A Conferences* around the nation. You can get connected by logging on to the Kingdom Building Ministries website at *www.kbm.org* and clicking on the "Plan A Connection" link.

PLAN A STUDY SERIES

If you'd like to lead others through a deeper study of the content presented in this book, then grab a copy of the *Plan A Study Series*, available January 1, 2007. The *Plan A Study Series* is a high-impact, eight-session multimedia resource, ideal for use in one-on-one discipleship settings or in group studies of all sizes. It includes a Leader's Manual, a Study Workbook, and a CD/DVD of Dwight Robertson teaching the *Plan A* content in a live setting. Additional Study Workbooks are also available for each person in your group. To order your copy of the *Plan A Study Series* and/or additional Student Workbooks, visit *www.kbm.org* and click on the "Plan A" link—or call us at 1-800-873-8957.

PLAN A CONFERENCE

Kingdom Building Ministries partners with local churches and groups to hold Plan A weekend conferences, featuring Dwight Robertson. Conferences are available for 2007 and beyond. If you'd like to learn more about hosting a *Plan A Conference* at your church or helping bring one to your area, call us at 1-800-873-8957.

THE LABORER'S JOURNAL

The Laborer's Journal is a digest magazine produced quarterly by Kingdom Building Ministries. It contains powerful devotional content that's designed to strengthen your intimacy with God and help you live out your faith through a life of ministry. Its articles will challenge you, encourage you, and equip you to live more fully and actively as a Kingdom laborer. To receive a free copy of *The Laborer's Journal* or to order a subscription, visit our website or call us at the number listed at the bottom of this page.

WWW.KBM.ORG

Visit Kingdom Building Ministries' website to find out more about our organization and to access some great resources. The website features a library of free spiritual-growth articles, information on when and where Kingdom Building Ministries' itinerant communicators are speaking, archives for *The Laborer's Journal*, and information about life-changing laborer-training programs for youth, young adults, and adults.

SPIRITUAL LIFE NOTEBOOK

Dwight Robertson has developed a practical tool called *The Spiritual Life Notebook* to help you grow daily in your walk with God. The *Spiritual Life Notebook* has sections for journaling; writing down sermon or Bible-study notes; and tracking your prayer requests, financial giving, Scripture memorization, and encouragement to others. It will help you engage more consistently and effectively in spiritual disciplines and Kingdom service.

**For more information or to place an order,
call us at 1-800-873-8957
or visit our *website* at *www.kbm.org*.**

For my wife,
who always makes the blank page bearable.

Acknowledgements

I wish to thank my agent and good friend, Leona Trainer, for her integrity and unfailing encouragement. Thanks as well to my very talented editor, Lynne Missen, whose expertise and humour always make the process of finding my way through a story enlightening and enjoyable. Finally, I want to thank Kelly Barro and the health care workers like her who helped me explore the physical and emotional journey of rehabilitation. They are the true heroes of this book.

I know just how it feels
To think of the right thing to say too late.

— ROBERT FROST
"The Death of the Hired Man"

PART ONE

Chapter 1

"C'mon, Reef! Let 'er fly!"

"Yeah, man! Toss 'er!"

Reef felt the weight in his hand. Hefted it. Saw in his mind's eye the smooth arc it would make when he launched it out over the busy highway below them. Saw, as well, the ripple of expressions on the faces of the drivers, who would react first with startled surprise, then fear, then anger. He knew that tangle of emotions well, the sudden transformation from shock to stormy outrage that left you weak and hollow inside, like those Hallowe'en pumpkins that little kids still carved. He and the others had stolen pumpkins last October and thrown them off the Everett Street overpass. He remembered the orange explosions they'd made as they hit the highway, the slash of meaty pulp crushed and dragged along by sliding, squealing tires. He grinned. Leaned back. Wound up for the throw.

Jink grabbed his shoulder a split second before his arm shot forward. "Cool it, Reef!"

"Yeah," hissed Bigger. "Cops!"

3

A white Metro Police car pulled out of Carver Avenue and cruised down Birmingham on a course that would take it under the Park Street overpass on which they stood. They waited motionless, watching the white car move toward them, then flash its turn signal and pull over to the curb. They could see the patrolman behind the wheel take a microphone from the dash, hold it to his mouth and begin talking, all the while looking up at the three teenagers standing by the metal railing that kept vehicles and pedestrians from falling into the traffic below.

Reef swore. Pocketing the rock in his leather jacket, he muttered, "Be another one 'long in a minute. Let's get outta here."

He and the others cut across to the other side of the overpass where the cop couldn't see them, then loped northward up Park Street. From below, the cop wouldn't know which direction they'd gone, or even if they'd left the overpass at all, but they kept jogging anyway till they'd made it to Patterson, cutting through the empty lot between Fishman's Mini-Mart and yet another used CD store. This one didn't even have a sign up yet. Not that it mattered—it wouldn't last any longer than the one before it.

By the time they got to The Pit, they'd slowed to a walk, sharing swallows from the bottle they'd snagged earlier off a bum on Wickham. Bigger had been worried they'd catch some kind of disease, but Reef and Jink had laughed at him, called him an old woman, shamed him into taking the first gulp. The rum had burned their throats, but it took the edge off their rancor and put—as Reef's grandmother used to say—"a bit of a glitter" on what otherwise had been a lousy day.

For a moment, Reef could almost hear her voice in his head. Coming from a woman who'd never swallowed a drop of alcohol in her life, those words had always been funny. He tried now to think of the last time he'd seen Nan alive, but the image of her lying in the cheapest casket Proule's Funeral Home offered eclipsed his other memories of her. She'd been wearing the black dress she had bought two years earlier at Zellers, the only dress he'd ever seen her buy new. Even at 70 percent off on the Final Clearance rack, it had been an extravagance, but she'd needed something to wear to her husband's funeral. He remembered how Nan had wept quietly all through the service. Reef had just been glad to see the son of a bitch laid out.

He drained the bottle, then drove it into the alley between The Pit and Wade's Laundry. Miraculously, it bounced twice before shattering, the combination of sounds boomeranging between the brick buildings. No one came out to investigate. Lou Wade had learned the hard way that it was bad for business to worry about what went on in the abandoned building next door— that fires had a habit of starting next to his laundry's ventilation stack after police showed up at The Pit.

Owners of the few other remaining businesses on the street knew too. Knew that the decaying eyesore once known as the Patterson Hotel was off limits to prying eyes and wagging tongues. No one called the police any more. And the few times they came by on their own, they just flashed their light and doo-wopped the siren a couple times to scare kids off. Not that it worked, but it allowed everyone to pretend it did.

They sidestepped a mangled grocery cart, a rusted hubcap, the remains of a child's stroller, and climbed the crumbling stone steps to what had once been the main entrance of the hotel. Gone were the ornately carved double doors and leaded glass windows that had adorned the original threshold. In their place were battered, graffiti-covered sheets of plywood nailed over the entryway, and similar sheets covered most of the basement and first-floor windows. To discourage people even further, someone had spray-painted "DANGER! KEEP OUT!" in fluorescent orange letters across the plywood that blocked the doorway, but some joker had altered it so it now read "DANGER! KEEP PARTYING!" It was clear from the broken bottles littering the steps that the hotel's newest tenants were following this instruction to the letter. It was also clear that city maintenance workers had given up the notion of ever keeping the building's steps and walkway clear of debris, resigning themselves instead to the task of keeping it from overflowing into the street.

His head now fuzzy from the rum, Reef stumbled as he climbed the steps, banging his knee on the worn stone and cursing. Bigger began to laugh, but Jink shot him a look that shut him up, and he coughed twice instead. At the top of the steps, Reef tugged at the bottom left corner of the "KEEP PARTYING!" plywood, easing it far enough away from the door frame to allow Bigger and Jink to slip inside. They, in turn, pushed against it from the inside, enabling Reef to enter easily. There was a time, Reef remembered, when they used to climb the rickety fire escape and crawl through one of the second-floor windows at the back. Now it didn't matter who saw them. The Pit was theirs.

Bigger belched, the sound a long, hollow gargle that seemed to come from his toes. "Gotta take a leak," he said.

"So do I," offered Jink.

Reef's back teeth were floating too, and all three turned toward the rear of the building. Although the plywood on the windows darkened the first floor, they made their way easily through the gloom. They knew The Pit so well they could find their way through it blindfolded—and they had one afternoon when they'd all been bored.

Lately, the hotel had really begun to show its age. Huge chunks of plaster, weakened from rain that seeped through the roof and blew through paneless upper windows, had begun to let go. The latest, the size of a small driveway, had fallen on the second floor the week before last. Zeus Williams had been lying under it when it came down, but he'd been so stoned he hadn't realized what had happened till he'd regained consciousness in the hospital. The paramedics who'd pulled him out said it would have killed a normal person, but Zeus—who'd never wasted time worrying about being normal—just laughed. The city, of course, reacted true to form: within hours, a building inspector had tacked up four additional "THIS SITE CONDEMNED" signs, one on each side of the building. They didn't last long, though. In fact, Bigger stuck one on the end of Zeus's emergency room bed that same day. The nurses weren't amused, but Reef and Jink laughed like hyenas until Security came and escorted all three of them out.

The Pit was built on a hill that sloped down toward the harbor, so the rear of the building's first floor hung a story above an alleyway even narrower than the one that ran alongside the building. In the days of the hotel's operation, this alley—barely wide enough to accommodate a dumpster—had served only to park delivery vehicles and to dispose of garbage. The only first-floor rooms with windows facing the rear had probably been used as offices—no paying customer would have appreciated that view. One of these first-floor windows lacked its customary plywood curtain, and it was toward this window that Reef, Jink and Bigger headed.

Standing in front of it, they unzipped their jeans and relieved themselves, sending three yellow arcs into the alley.

"Yes!" Bigger yelled. Months ago, some clown had painted a crude target on the asphalt below, and Bigger invariably scored a bullseye. Today was no exception.

Reef and Jink grinned. Bigger sure had the height advantage when it came to trajectory. They'd long ago accepted the fact that their huge friend was stronger and more agile than they were. Than anyone they knew, in fact, including Bigger's own brother, Kirk. Three years older, and recently laid off from the shipyards, Kirk Ellis was a massive guy who could bench-press 250 pounds without breaking a sweat. But even he was dwarfed by Bigger, and people had referred to the younger Ellis brother as "the bigger one" for so long that few of them used his real name, Bobby. *Bigger* suited him better, anyway.

When they'd finished and zipped up, Reef patted his jacket for his smokes and lighter and his fingers found the rock he hadn't thrown. Annoyance at having been interrupted by the police flickered through him: he hated seeing a good rock go to waste. He pulled a pack of Rothmans from his other pocket and tapped out a cigarette, then offered one to each of his friends. All three lit up, then made their way to the staircase behind the lobby, Reef in the lead.

No one else was in The Pit, which wasn't unusual.

The warm June day wasn't forcing anyone inside, and it was far too early for a crack party. Later, though, the place would be jumping.

Their footsteps echoed hollowly as they climbed the stairs. Bypassing the lower floors, they stepped out of the fifth-floor landing and crossed to the west-facing rooms at the front of the building. The afternoon sun pierced the interior shadows, flooding what had once been the Presidential Suite with yellow light. This was Reef's favorite place. Two stories above the surrounding flat rooftops, the Presidential Suite on sunny days made him feel like he was standing on a huge stage washed by spotlights, the city stretching before him like an expectant audience.

Avoiding pigeon droppings, he sat down on the foot-wide window ledge and leaned back against the rotted casing. The breeze blowing through the glassless opening felt good on his rum-warmed face. If he wanted to, he could close his eyes and pretend he was standing with Nan on Citadel Hill, the sun on their faces as they watched tourists from as far away as California enter the fortress. But he didn't. He'd been nine the last time he was there. Before Nan's cancer had got so bad Social Services had taken him away from her, put him in a foster home. The first of many.

Reef frowned. Bending down, he picked up a fist-sized fragment of windowpane and held it up to his face, looking for evidence of that frightened nine year old in his reflection. Instead, the pitted glass mirrored the face of a defiant young man whose dark eyes had stared down more than a few social workers, even a principal or two. The glass also reflected someone who was used to getting appreciative glances from the females he encountered. Curly black hair accentuated tanned skin and contrasted dramatically with white, even teeth. His straight nose and square, beard-stubbled jaw made him look older than his seventeen years, and his tall, tightly muscled frame only heightened that impression. For the briefest moment, he wondered whether Nan would recognize him now, and then he opened his fingers. The fragment shattered as it hit the floor.

"Scar meetin' us here?" asked Bigger.

Reef turned to him, shook his head. "Her ol' man's back."

Jink pinched one nostril and blew fiercely through the other, sending a green, scab-like projectile into the street below. "Probably got her runnin' all over the city," he said, before reversing nostrils and blowing again. Twice. Nothing.

"Better 'n standin' around waitin' for a hand upside her head," Bigger offered.

Reef nodded. He used to think it was Scar's red hair that set her father off, like waving a flag in front of a bull—neither of her parents had hair that color, nor did anyone else in their family. It was her father who had named her Scarlet. Reef had seen a picture of Scar taken when she was only a few days old, and even then her hair had been the color that usually earns kids nicknames like Carrot-Top or Red. Of course, no one called Scar those names. Not more than once, anyway.

Bigger sat on the ledge beside Reef, yawned, scratched his armpit. "Jeez, I'm hungry."

Jink chuckled. "You were *born* hungry."

"Ain't as bad as bein' born *ugly*," Bigger replied. "Least I get *full* from time t' time. You're *always* gonna be ugly."

Jink grinned, three missing teeth like darkened doorways in his mouth. Along with his broken nose, the holes in his smile were souvenirs of several confrontations that had earned him a reputation as a formidable fighter. Not that these features made him any less attractive than he would have been without them. His too-wide face and sloping forehead made him look menacing even in mid-grin, an impression further emphasized by a tattooed snake that curled around his thick neck and bared its fangs below his right ear. Reef couldn't remember the last time Jink had lost a brawl. Couldn't, in fact, even imagine it happening. Although not as massive as Bigger or as razor-quick as Reef, Jink had pit-bull tenacity and a wild-eyed demeanor that, combined with the chip on his shoulder a mile wide, made people turn and cross the street if they saw him coming. Even his teachers were afraid of him.

Except Mrs. Gregory, who'd taught Jink and Reef eighth-grade English three years ago. Reef had just changed foster families again, which had meant another change of schools, which in turn had made him the new kid in Mrs. Gregory's class. But it hadn't taken Reef long to realize that Stan Eisner, the crazy kid with the wild eyes, was on a collision course with anyone foolish enough to get in his way. The old woman stared him down time after time, never flinching, even the day Stan completely lost it and threw his chair across the room. It had been a lazy last period and the teacher had split the class in half, offering as a reward no homework to the team that could spell the most words correctly. Stan spelled about as well as he did math, which he failed regularly. In fact, Reef learned that Stan had failed almost everything once, and the only reason he'd made it to grade eight was the school board's rule about no one repeating a junior grade more than once. Stan was, as Reef had overheard a teacher comment, "on the two-year plan." It wouldn't have mattered if he'd stayed home during the even years of his education—he was guaranteed a pass "for social reasons."

Reef had realized on his first day something that everyone else at that school had known for years: Stan hated school, but he hated teachers even more. He especially hated when they singled him out, forced him to demonstrate his ineptness to everyone in the room, and teachers soon learned it was better for everyone involved not to call on Stan Eisner. Mrs. Gregory, however, was the exception. All of five feet tall, maybe ninety-four pounds soaking wet, and prone to putting a blue rinse in her graying hair, Mrs. Gregory was intimidated by no one. So when the next person in line to spell *jinx* was Stan Eisner, she refused to back down as he glared at her, muttering about "friggin' teachers" and school being a "buncha bull." She waited. Waited for Stan to risk being wrong and take a chance on being right for a change. While the rest of the students in the room held their breath.

Finally, his face black with muted rage, Stan attempted the spelling, spitting the letters one at a time through clenched teeth: "*J . . . i . . . n . . . k . . . s.*"

The tension in the classroom was mattress-thick, and someone at the back, longing for release, gulped. The sound, like a too-ripe pear being squeezed in a fist, was too loud for the room.

"The word isn't a plural form," Mrs. Gregory explained. "You don't say 'one *jink*, two *jinks*.'"

Suddenly someone giggled, then someone else, then laughter erupted all around them.

Humiliated, Stan rose to his feet. "I can goddamn well say *jink* if I *want* to!" he roared. "*Jink! Jink! JINK!*" For effect, he kicked his desk, sending it clacking into the one in front of it.

"Sit down, Stanley."

"I *ain't* sittin'!" he bellowed.

"I said sit *down!*"

In response, Stan Eisner picked up his chair and

threw it against the wall behind him, narrowly missing Eddie Blake, who sat in the last seat of the adjacent row. The whole class jerked around, staring in awe as the chair, one leg bent at a crazy angle, crashed to the floor.

Sitting two rows over, Reef grinned. This was infinitely better than the hoedown he'd given Michelle Hatt during phys ed, her face crimson as she'd yanked her gym shorts back up over her bare ass. "*Jink*," he crooned. Then he repeated it. Louder. "*Jink!*"

Students around him grinned, and a few were even brave enough to take up the chant: "*Jink, jink, jink, jink . . .*"

"That'll be *enough*!" Mrs. Gregory's voice. An ice pick in their throats. Then, "Stanley, the chair."

Stan stared at her a long moment, then hissed, "Bite me, bitch!" and sauntered past her out the door.

Of course he'd been suspended for the remainder of the school year, but since that was his second time in grade eight, he'd gone on to nine the following September anyway. In the process, he'd acquired a nickname he'd worn proudly ever since.

"What's goin' on down there?" Bigger asked. He pointed to a green truck that had pulled up in front of The Pit, the lettering on its side impossible to read from where they sat. Two men got out and stood looking up at the crumbling facade, talking and making notes on clipboards. Then they turned their attention to the buildings on either side of The Pit. One man pulled something out of his pocket and moved over to the alley between the hotel and Wade's Laundry, and the something turned out to be a retractable tape that he used to measure the width of the alley, more information that ended up on the clipboard. The other man returned to the truck and started it, then drove it into the alley and out of view.

"More buildin' inspectors?" Jink asked.

Reef shrugged, his rum buzz gone. "Maybe. I dunno. Let's check it out."

They made their way back down the stairs, pausing twice to peer into the alley. There was no sign of the men.

"Narcs?" Bigger suggested.

Reef shook his head. "Don't think so. They were payin' more attention to the buildin' than what's inside." Reef had had run-ins with undercover narcotics officers before. These two didn't seem the type. Their busyness looked real.

They reached the first floor and made their way to the entrance, where Jink eased his shoulder against the plywood, allowing Reef to peer through the upside-down V between the plywood and the door frame. Surveying the street for the two men, he saw no one, then pushed through the opening into sunlight.

"Aww, *Christ!*" he moaned.

Almost simultaneously, the two called, "Cops?"

Reef slumped back against the crumbling wall. "I wish."

Bigger and Jink eased out onto the step beside Reef, turned in the direction he was staring.

This time their voices were exactly simultaneous. *"Fuck!"*

Chapter 2

"You can take this garbage and shove it up your—"

The final epithet was lost in the crash and clang of dishware and dinner tray meeting hard tile floor. Mashed potatoes, peas and meatloaf slid across the broad expanse of white, followed closely by a pot of tea and a dish of custard. The girl who had just placed the tray on the bed table turned an astonished face toward the nurse in the doorway.

Mary Clayton sighed wearily. "I should've warned you about Mr. Harris, Leeza. He doesn't think much of the—"

"Pig slop!" the elderly man snorted, banging the rail on the side of his bed. "Nothin' but *pig slop* in this place! Where's my Maggie? Maggie! Look what they're tryin' to feed me!"

Leeza Hemming braved a smile as she turned back to the patient. "It's okay, Mr. Harris. You don't have to eat this if—"

"Maggie knows what I like!" he snapped. "*Maggie* knows." He looked past her toward the doorway and called, his voice cracked and thin, "Maggie! Where *are* you, girl?"

Nurse Clayton clucked softly and moved toward the bed. "Now, Mr. Harris, you know Maggie isn't here. Remember?"

The old man turned to her, his lower lip quivering. "She's not here?"

The nurse's tone was low, professionally sincere. "No, Mr. Harris. Maggie's not here."

He looked toward the door again and started to cry, his thin shoulders quaking as he sobbed.

Ignoring the mess at her feet, Leeza placed her hand on the man's arm, gently squeezing it and speaking in soft tones. "It's okay, Mr. Harris. No need to get yourself all upset now. Everything'll be fine."

The old man looked up at the girl as if seeing her for the first time. "Maggie?" he asked.

She shook her head. "No, I'm not Maggie. But I'm sure she'd want you to eat something, wouldn't she? How about some soup? Does that sound like something you'd like?"

"You're not Maggie?" The man's voice seemed to come from somewhere far inside him.

"No. I'm Leeza. But I bet the cook's been saving a bowl of soup for someone special like you. Would you like me to check?"

His eyes still leaking tears, he reached for her hand and gripped it like a lifeline. "Will you bring it to me?"

"Of course I will. You just lie back and rest and I'll take care of everything." She turned to pick up the fallen items, but Nurse Clayton waved her away. "I'll look after this. It's my fault for not warning you in the first place. You go see about that soup."

Thirty minutes later, the nurse poked her head in the door again to see the teenager sitting by Mr. Harris's bed, chatting softly as she spooned the last of some chicken broth into the elderly man's mouth. He watched her with bright, interested eyes as she got up to leave. "You'll come see me again?" he asked.

"Sure. I'll be here again tomorrow after school." She leaned over and patted his hand. "You won't forget me now, will you?"

He shook his head.

"He already has," said the nurse a moment later in the hall. "Forgotten you, I mean." She took the bowl and spoon and set them on the meal trolley with the other dishes, then accompanied the teenager down the corridor past the nurses' station.

"Oh, I know," Leeza said. "He still thinks I'm Maggie."

"His wife," said the nurse. "She was a resident here too. Passed away last year, poor soul."

"Sad," said Leeza. "But, in a way, he's lucky." Seeing the surprise on the nurse's face, she continued, "I mean that he doesn't remember she's gone. This way, she'll always be alive for him."

The nurse nodded. "For someone so young, you

know a lot about older people. You must have grand-parents."

Leeza shook her head. "They died before I was born."

The nurse seemed about to say something else, but they'd arrived at the elevators. Leeza pressed the *down* button. "It was nice meeting you," she said.

"So you're back again tomorrow?" asked the nurse. "The director said something about you and a course requirement."

"Not exactly. I had to do some volunteering for a high school credit I was taking, but that's all finished."

"What was the course?"

"Career and Life Management. It's compulsory, and my teacher included twenty hours of volunteer service as one of the completion requirements. But I finished those last semester."

The nurse looked puzzled. "Then why—?" Her unasked question hung in the air.

Leeza hesitated, wished she'd been able to leave before the questions began. Then, "I just really enjoyed doing it. When I finished at the Children's Hospital, they put me in touch with the director here at Silver Meadows, and she said she could use me."

"Can we ever. We've really been short-staffed since the government cut back our funding. But why'd you choose this place?"

Leeza looked back in the direction of Mr. Harris's room, a sudden throb of sadness catching her unaware. She took a hard breath, used it to force back the feeling, then turned to the nurse. "I can't stand the thought of someone being . . ." She paused, groping for a word. "Helpless. Trapped in a room. I spent time with some kids like that at the Children's, and it really felt good when I could take their minds off being there."

Mary nodded. "That's the reason I became a nurse in the first place." She smiled, but there was no humor in it. "Unfortunately, it often gets so busy here that we end up doing far less of that than our patients need. That's why volunteers like you are so important." The elevator arrived with a *bing* and the doors glided open. "Thinking about a career in medicine, Leeza?"

The girl shook her head. "Not really. Volunteering is one thing," she said as she stepped inside, "but a career is something else. I really don't know what I want to do just yet."

"Well, in the meantime, you're certainly welcome here."

"Thanks."

"No, thank *you*," Leeza heard as the doors slid closed.

Out in the parking lot, she scanned the cars for her parents' green Subaru, momentarily forgetting where she had parked it. She was thinking about the things she had said to Nurse Clayton. Or really, the things she *hadn't* said. Things like why she had chosen to do her volunteer service in hospitals and senior citizens' homes rather than in community centers and daycare facilities like the rest of her classmates. She'd had a hard enough time trying to explain it to her mother and stepfather, who felt that being around "all that pain and suffering," as they'd put it, was the last thing Leeza needed. "You don't have to prove anything," they'd said.

Well, maybe they were wrong. Maybe there was plenty she had to prove. Like there was a reason she was still living and breathing when her older sister, Ellen, had stopped doing both six months ago. Ellen, who had been Student Council president, top scorer on the senior girls' basketball team and the lead in two of the school's drama productions. And managed to maintain an honors average at the same time. That is, before the cancer brought everything to an end, faster than Leeza could have imagined possible.

Besides, it wasn't as though Leeza had much else occupying her time anyway. Her sister had been one of those people everyone loved to be around, and it was only when Ellen got sick that Leeza discovered the people she spent time with were more Ellen's friends than hers. There were some, like Robin and Jen, who still called once in a while and even dropped by from time to time, but without Ellen there to make the moments seamless, getting together had seemed to become—for her friends, anyway—more obligation than pleasure.

The air had cooled somewhat since she'd arrived,

but the late-afternoon sun still felt warm on her neck as she crossed the parking lot and unlocked the Subaru. Although she'd been driving for more than a year, she was still grateful for the freedom she felt each time she slid behind the steering wheel. It was driving that had helped her cope with losing her sister, being able to point the vehicle in whatever direction she wanted and just go. Even now, when thoughts of Ellen began to seep into every moment, welling up like water in a footprint after a rain, she'd ask her parents for the keys to the car. It wasn't just the mechanics of driving that helped turn her mind away from the horror of that hospital room, it was never knowing exactly what lay ahead. Even driving through familiar neighborhoods gave her opportunities for surprise: the kid who rode his bike into the street without looking, the driver who didn't yield the right of way or turned without signaling. During those final days, when her family had waited—even prayed—for the inevitable, it was those moments of not knowing that had somehow made bearable the tragedy that was Ellen. Even going home wasn't something Leeza was certain she'd do; it always seemed to be a conscious choice she made at the end of every drive.

Like the choice she'd made to volunteer at the Children's Hospital. And now here, at Silver Meadows. She needed the feeling those places gave her—that her being there made a difference. Unlike the times she'd sat with Ellen, who in those last few days hadn't even seemed to know there was someone holding her hand, someone sponging her forehead, someone choking back sobs in the stillness of the room.

For a moment, memories of her sister washed over her—Ellen laughing on the phone, Ellen singing in the shower, Ellen lying in the burnished mahogany casket at Proule's Funeral Home—and Leeza had to grip the steering wheel to keep from shaking, from sobbing. Her long fingernails bit into the flesh of her palms, and the pain somehow made sitting there, alive and breathing, less wrong.

When the final wave shuddered through her, she slid the key into the ignition and started the car. Glancing at the clock on the dash, she saw she still had time for a drive before heading home.

Chapter 3

"They can't *do* this!" Bigger snarled.

"Goddamn right!" agreed Jink. "The Pit belongs to us!"

Reef said nothing, just kept looking at the sign painted on the green truck: "SCOTIA DEMOLITION: We Turn Eyesores Into Assets."

The two men were nowhere in sight, probably around back of the building with their measuring tapes and clipboards. Reef moved down the steps and toward the truck as if wading through deep water, his steps slow and deliberate.

"Reef?" Jink called. "Whatcha doin', man?"

Reef didn't answer. He reached the truck and stood staring at the words on the side, the letters formed from a continuous stylized fuse. The fuse stretched back to a picture of a detonator being pressed by a hand, giving the absurd impression that Scotia Demolition had blown up the rest of the body along with whatever eyesore had required their attention.

Jink and Bigger came down the steps to stand beside Reef. "Ya think they can really do this?" Bigger asked.

"No way!" Jink said. "No jerks with measurin' tapes are gonna tear down The Pit. Not while *I'm* here."

Reef turned to them. "It ain't *them* that's doin' it."

"Yeah, they're just the math guys," said Bigger.

"Engineers," corrected Jink.

"Right," Bigger agreed. "They prob'ly got minimum-wagers to set the explosives."

"That ain't what I meant," Reef snapped. "They're only the guys *paid* to take it down. It's the ones who *own* The Pit that're doin' it."

"I din't think nobody owned it."

Reef scowled. "*Somebody* owns it, asshole. *Everything's* owned by *somebody*. Even if it's just the city!"

Bigger picked up a shard of glass glinting on the sidewalk, a fragment of a bottle broken a long time ago. "Well," he vowed, "I don't care who owns it. It ain't comin' down." He glanced toward the street for cars or pedestrians. Seeing none, he strolled over to the truck and held the shard against the back fender, then dragged its jagged edge along the full length of the vehicle. When he had finished, it looked as though there were now two stylized fuses, the second a thin white line spelling an expletive between the words *Eyesores* and *Assets*.

Jink hooted, then pulled a switchblade out of his back pocket. Bending down, he flicked open the blade and inserted it with almost surgical precision into one of the Michelin all-season radials. As the air hissed out, he sauntered around the truck, repeating the surgery on each of the tires while the vehicle settled geriatrically to its rims.

Reef grinned, remembering the rock inside his jacket. He reached into his pocket and felt the cool smoothness beneath his fingers, all the while admiring the expanse of windshield before him. He pulled the rock out and eased his arm back, winding up for—

"Hey! What're you doing?" All three whirled to see the two men with clipboards running toward them down the alley. One took out a cellphone and punched numbers as he ran. Three numbers.

"Let's get outta here," Reef ordered.

"We can take 'em," said Bigger.

"They called 911," Reef hissed. "Cops'll be here in a minute." He jammed the rock back into his pocket. "C'mon." He turned and ran. Jink and Bigger followed.

"Sonsabitches!" they heard behind them. "Look what they did to my truck!"

Jink hooted again, his laughter high and wild as the three raced out of the alley and down the street. Reef looked back to see the man with the cellphone in pursuit. "You lousy punks!" he shouted. "Wait'll I get my hands on you!"

He was more agile than his forty-some years had led Reef and the others to expect. More than a block from The Pit, the man was still behind them and showing no sign of flagging. It reminded Reef of the times his grandfather would drunkenly roar his name, calling

him a "good-fer-nothin' sonuvabitch bastard" as the
boy he once was cowered outside whatever rathole
they were living in, listening through sobs to his
grandmother's gentle voice inside. Settling his grandfather, soothing him, making everything all right
again. Until the next time.

"Let's split up!" Reef shouted as they pounded down
Patterson. He knew they could outrun the truck
owner, but there was no sense in prolonging the
inevitable. "He'll give up when he can't chase all of us."

Bigger grunted and veered to the right, darting into
an alley between Bob's House of Billiards and a greasy
spoon that sold fish and chips wrapped in newspapers.

"Later," Jink called, and turned down North Street.

Reef looked back and saw the man pause, uncer-
tain. He laughed and, feeling the rock bounce in his
pocket, suddenly knew where he was heading.

Leeza showed her volunteer parking permit to the
attendant at the gate, waited as he raised the barrier,
then eased the Subaru out into traffic. She liked rush
hour driving, liked constantly having to watch the
cars around her weave in and out of openings that
appeared and dissolved like eddies in a stream. She
didn't even mind the jerks that cut her off without so
much as a nod or a wave, so intent on saving those two
seconds or three yards that apparently were worth the

risk of collision. Already she'd seen two cars pulled over to the side, their red-faced drivers exchanging insurance details over crumpled fenders.

Traffic seemed even heavier this afternoon, thanks to a work crew on Elgin Avenue that had diverted drivers to an alternate route on Bentley. Vehicles slowed to a crawl and, without meaning to, Leeza found herself playing the driver game Ellen had invented years ago when they were bored on long drives. She looked at the driver in the Camry on her right, a man in his mid-thirties whose face was set in determined lines. He glanced at his watch, grimaced, drummed his fingers on the steering wheel, glanced at his watch again. "Robert," murmured Leeza. "Divorced. Promised he'd take his kids to their soccer game." In her rearview mirror, she saw a woman with blond hair piled high on her head driving a battered Buick Century. "Raylene. Mary Kay representative. Still hoping for the pink Cadillac."

A horn blew somewhere up ahead, followed by a squeal of tires as a blue Durango beat a yellow light. The Camry turned right and a minivan took its place, the air around it throbbing with bass. A boy about her age played air drums and bobbed his head to the beat of an urban rap. *Too easy*, she could hear Ellen say. Leeza shook her head, rose to the challenge. "Kyle. Just got his license. First time out alone without his mom." She grinned. "Tough to be cool in a minivan, Kyle." She imagined Ellen laughing, her teeth perfectly white. Before the medications darkened them, turned them the sallow color of legal notepads.

Leeza gripped the steering wheel, tried to swallow around a sudden fist in her throat. She stared straight ahead, refusing to look at the other drivers jockeying for space around her.

Reef took another look over his shoulder. Nothing. He hadn't seen the guy with the cellphone since he'd cut through the vacant lot behind Fishman's. About time. The man had stuck with him long after Reef had figured he'd give up and go home. Pain in the ass. Reef hated it when things interfered with his plans. He waited another moment just to be sure, then turned left on Belcher.

Leeza listened to the steady *tink-tink-tink* of the turn signal as she waited for the light to change, grateful to see traffic flowing steadily on Carver. She'd decided to shortcut her way home, no longer interested in the extended-play version of the drive. Without realizing it, she glanced at her watch again, grimaced, leaned back against the headrest. The traffic light glowed immutably red. She fought to keep from drumming her fingers on the steering wheel.

• • •

Reef stood on the overpass above Birmingham, his hand in his jacket pocket squeezing and releasing the rock. The thing he liked about Park Street was its lack of traffic, especially during rush hour. Most of the traffic was on the multi-lane outbound highway that ran perpendicular to it. The people who used Park Street and this overpass were mainly those who lived in the few houses scattered along its length and people heading toward the green belt at its south end. And rush hour wasn't a time many people headed toward the park, which suited Reef just fine. He didn't need an audience for what he was about to do.

The stone fit in the hollow of Reef's palm like a piece of a puzzle, an extension of his own hand. Reef had loved rocks for as long as he could remember. Not that there were many around the places he'd lived. The tenements he'd called home over the years had been surrounded by concrete and asphalt, oceans of hardness. It was his grandmother who had somehow made the hardness bearable, and it was she who had placed the first stone in his hand.

He'd been almost five and they'd been on the way to Truro in the old Dodge Dart his grandfather drove. Reef had grown carsick, and his grandfather had had to pull over on the 102 so he could puke. Car after car whizzed by as he retched on the side of the road, his grandfather cursing him, warning him he'd better not throw up in the car if he knew what was good for him.

During the tirade, Nan slipped down into the ditch,

where she moved aimlessly about in the long grass like someone lost. When she returned she had in her palm a small, round stone as smooth as glass. "It's a sick-stone," she explained when his grandfather had gotten back in the car. She placed it in Reef's hand and closed his fingers over it. "When you feel like you're gonna throw up, just squeeze it hard. It'll take the sick feelin' away." It worked. Each time the waves of nausea rolled up over him, he gripped that stone like a lifeline, trying not to watch his grandfather's thick fists pound the horn at whoever was stupid enough to cut him off. And each time he squeezed that rock, he felt stronger, like he was somehow in charge.

Like he felt right now.

There had been other sick-stones after that. And stones whose purpose was to prop open doors, to hold up windows to let the breeze blow through, to level a chrome table whose leg had bent when his grandfather had rammed it against the kitchen wall. And then there had been stones that had no purpose except to be stones. In the months following that afternoon on the 102, he'd started bringing home rocks he found on the playground, adding to the collection Nan helped him hide in his closet. When his grandfather wasn't home, the two of them would take the rocks out and arrange them on the kitchen table, sorting them according to color and texture and size. There were always rocks that didn't seem to fit into the groups Reef would devise, and these they loved the best. "These are special stones," Nan would tell him. "Just because they don't fit with the others don't make 'em less important." It was then he'd realize she was talking about more than just stones, and he'd wait for her to get that faraway look in her eyes when she'd begin to speak about the girl who had been his mother. The girl whose deafness had made her different, had set her apart, had trapped her in a world of silence and shame.

Reef shrugged, pulled out the rock he'd carried with him all afternoon. Turning it over in his hands, he thought of the night two years ago when Bigger had coined his name. They'd been passing around a joint, and Reef—who, at the time, was still Chad Kennedy—had taken the final shred of it from Jink for one more drag. Already high, he'd sucked too strongly on it, pulling the burning remnant inside his mouth. Jink and Bigger had rolled on the ground guffawing as he'd choked and spat and cursed, his tongue already swelling from the burn.

"Man, you're one hell of a toker," Jink had sputtered through his laughter.

"Yeah, man," echoed Bigger, "you're the Grim Reefer. Hey, Reef!"

Reef had liked the name, but not for the reasons Jink and Bigger thought. Years earlier, Reef's fourth-grade teacher had shown his class a science film on coral, and while nearly everyone else had dozed or whispered in the dark, Reef had sat mesmerized by the images of the living rock that formed protective barriers around tropical islands. He liked what a reef could do, liked thinking of himself as living rock, liked pretending that it was possible to protect those you loved.

In the end, he hadn't been able to save the one person who'd meant everything to him. Had had to watch the cancer burn her up, her body like an ember that crumbled into ash.

Horns below him on Birmingham brought him back to the overpass, and he looked down at the traffic through tear-filled eyes. He gripped the rock, seeking its strength, and chose a target.

The traffic was moving more steadily now, picking up speed as it neared the Park Street overpass. Leeza glanced up and saw two figures there, one on the end with his hand to his ear, the other in the middle with one arm up, waving at her. Amused, she raised her hand to wave back.

Then something hit her windshield and the world exploded.

Chapter 4

"And you saw everything, Mr. Ryan?"

"Yes, sir. After they trashed my truck, I chased all three of 'em until they split up. Then I followed *that* one."

Reef slouched in a chair by his lawyer, Hank Elliott, not even looking at the Crown attorney or the man on the witness stand. He longed for a drink or a joint or a line of coke, anything to make this interminable questioning more bearable. He imagined disembodied mouths moving wordlessly in space and thought briefly about his mother, craved the silence her deafness must have provided. He looked again at his watch, scowled, slouched farther in his chair.

Scott Phillips, the Crown attorney, addressed the judge. "Let the record show that the witness indicated the accused, Chad Kennedy." He turned back to the witness. "Go on, please."

"He thought he lost me, but the 911 dispatcher had told me to hold back, not to let him know I was followin' him. I was keepin' track of him so she could relay his location to the police."

"And when he got to the overpass?"

"He just stood there for a minute or two, watchin' the traffic pass under him."

Reef glanced up to see the man staring at him, shaking his head in disgust. *Screw you*, Reef thought.

Ryan's eyes held his as he continued. "I had no idea what he was gonna do, or I would've tried to stop him."

"And what exactly did he do, Mr. Ryan?"

Ryan turned to the Crown attorney, disbelief underscoring his words. "He took a rock out of his pocket and threw it into the oncoming traffic."

A strangled sob rose from the back, but Reef didn't need to turn to guess who'd made it. Probably the woman who'd stared at him when he'd entered the courtroom. He'd seen newspaper photos of her and the man sitting beside her right after the accident. The parents of the girl in the car. *Screw you, too*, Reef thought. He yawned, louder than he'd intended, and he could feel the judge's eyes on him. *Screw you most of all, bitch.* He longed again for a drink or a hit. Or both.

"What happened then?" Phillips asked.

Ryan looked again at Reef, who recognized the I'd-like-to-kick-your-ass glare. *Bring it on, dipshit*, Reef telegraphed back, and was satisfied when the witness looked away. "The rock," Ryan responded, "hit the windshield of a green Subaru. The driver lost control—"

"Objection." Hank Elliott was on his feet. "Mr. Ryan doesn't know what happened inside that car."

"Sustained," Judge Thomas ruled. Frowning at the Crown attorney, she instructed, "Please tell your witness not to speculate, Mr. Phillips."

Ryan colored and turned to the judge. "If a rock the size of a fist suddenly hit *your* windshield hard enough to cave the glass in, *you* wouldn't be thinkin' straight either."

Elliott was on his feet again. "Your Honor—" he began.

The judge nodded. "Just tell us what you *saw*, Mr. Ryan."

Reef made no attempt to hide the smirk that played around the edges of his mouth, and he enjoyed watching its effect on the witness. Ryan glowered at him, ran a nervous hand through his hair, then began again. "The Subaru swerved right as it passed under the overpass and hit a van in the lane beside her. Rammed into the driver's door."

The Crown attorney moved over to three easels positioned near the witness stand and removed a large sheet of white cardboard from the first to reveal a poster-sized photograph. "Is that the van the Subaru hit?" he asked.

"Yes, sir." Ryan nodded.

There were several audible reactions to the photograph, and even Reef was surprised by what it showed: a late-model Dodge minivan, its left front fender caved in and twisted so it nearly touched the battered driver's door. Who knew steel could crumple so easily?

"And then what happened?"

"I guess you'd call it a chain reaction. The van veered to the right and hit the curb, then suddenly pulled back again. The driver must've panicked and overcorrected—"

"Objection."

"Sustained. Mr. Ryan—"

"Sorry, Your Honor. The van suddenly swung left and hit the Subaru."

"And then?"

Ryan pulled his eyes away from the photograph and looked out across the courtroom, and Reef could tell he was looking at the girl's parents, searching for some way to describe the scene that had unfolded below the Park Street overpass. For a moment, Reef saw the nightmare in his own head, then he pushed the images aside. Nobody had died. And only the girl had got hurt. Everybody else had walked away with cuts and bruises. Reef had seen worse.

Ryan was still looking out across the courtroom as he continued. "By this time, they were on the other side of the overpass. The Subaru ricocheted into the left lane and was struck by an inbound truck."

"Is this the truck?" Phillips removed the white cardboard covering the second easel, exposing beneath it a picture of something that looked like a delivery truck, except the front end was pancaked into a tangled mass of hood and grille.

"Yeah," Ryan replied softly.

Judge Thomas leaned toward the witness. "You'll have to speak louder, Mr. Ryan. Is that the truck that struck the Subaru?"

"Yes." Ryan took a deep breath before continuing. "It spun the car around so it was facing the oncoming traffic. At least three more vehicles piled up before the traffic finally got stopped."

"And this," asked the attorney, "is the Subaru that Chad Kennedy hit with the rock?" He pulled the white cardboard off the third easel.

Reef heard the girl's mother dissolve into sobs, followed by the soothing tones of a man's low voice. Angry muttering rose from several places in the courtroom but died when the judge scowled darkly.

"Yes, sir," said Ryan, visibly shaken by what he saw. "That's the Subaru."

Reef stared at the third photograph, saw the shattered front end, saw the trunk rammed up into the back seat, saw how rescue workers had had to cut the door off to get the girl out. And he saw something else.

He felt Ryan's eyes on him, and this time it was Reef who turned away. He looked at his watch again. How long was this shit going to last?

Phillips nodded at the witness. "Thank you, Mr. Ryan. No further questions, Your Honor."

The judge nodded to the defense. "Your witness, Mr. Elliott."

Hank Elliott got up and stood for a moment looking at the photographs displayed near the witness. He frowned. "All this must have taken place in a very short time, Mr. Ryan. A matter of seconds. Are you sure about everything you saw?"

Ryan was clearly annoyed by the question. "You ever work with explosives?"

The lawyer frowned again. "The way this works, Mr. Ryan, is that I ask *you* the questions. Now if you'll—"

"My work is demolition. I stay alive by payin' attention to details."

Elliott seemed about to say something, then thought better of it. "I have no further questions for this witness, Your Honor."

Bigger and Jink were waiting with Scar on the back steps of the courthouse when Reef and his lawyer came out of the building. After sitting in that air-conditioned courtroom all morning, Reef felt the late-June heat hit him like a hammer. Even the breeze off the harbor hadn't diminished its intensity. It was shaping up to be a hell of a summer.

"Kennedy!"

Reef turned to see a reporter coming out the door carrying a video camera. "How about giving us a statement?" the reporter called.

Reef was about to offer his favorite comment when Elliott shook his head. "You know better than that, Peterson."

The reporter sneered. "He can't hide behind the

Youth Criminal Justice Act forever. How old are you, Kennedy?"

"And how old were *you* plannin' on gettin'?" growled Bigger, moving up the steps toward the reporter.

The lawyer stepped between Bigger and the reporter, whose bravado had disappeared in the face of Bigger's menacing bulk. He scowled at the group and shook his head, then took his equipment back inside.

Reef gave a low whistle of admiration as he high-fived Bigger. "How old were *you* plannin' on gettin'?" he echoed. "That was *premium*, man."

Bigger grinned as Jink slapped him on the back. "I wish I'd decked the little prick," he said.

Elliott stared at them, his face a mask of incredulity. "That would've been a *big* help," he said. There was no mistaking the scorn in his voice.

Jink looked at Reef and nodded his head toward the lawyer. "What crawled up *his* ass?"

Elliott wheeled toward Jink, his eyes blazing. "What crawled up my ass, as you so elegantly put it, is your attitude that all this is just a joke. An inconvenience."

"Take it easy, man," Bigger said. "Reef's only seventeen. What can they do to him anyway?"

Elliott looked at the huge teenager and shook his head. "They can do plenty. Haven't you seen all those reporters? What does it take for you to realize this case is very high-profile? You're just lucky that witness didn't get a good look at you, and that Reef didn't name you and your friend as accomplices in the truck vandalism. Otherwise, you'd both be sitting through your own hearings."

"We been in courtrooms before," Jink bragged.

"I'm sure," Elliott remarked. "And I see it's done all of you a world of good."

"Jesus, Reef," Jink said. "Great to have *this* guy on your side."

Elliott exploded. "Haven't any of you been listening to what was said in there?"

Reef, Jink and Bigger looked at him in stony silence. Only Scar nodded. "It doesn't look good?" she asked.

"It *never* looked good, which is why I advised Reef to plead guilty." A pager in Elliott's pocket hummed, and the lawyer pulled it out, looked at the display and scowled. He clicked it off and returned it to his pocket. "The purpose of this hearing is to provide the judge with the relevant facts prior to sentencing. With eyewitness testimony like the kind we just heard, there was no defense. The best strategy was to admit the crime up front and hope for a lenient sentence."

Bigger frowned. "You tell all your clients to plead guilty?"

Elliott sighed. "This case was over the minute the details hit the papers. Why do you think this hearing was held so quickly?" He didn't wait for a reply.

"Pressure from the public. People have zero tolerance for youth crime."

"Some shit-hot lawyer *you* turned out to be," Jink said.

Elliott shook his head wearily. "I guess you get what you pay for," he said, his Legal Aid status reflected in his sarcasm. He reached into another pocket and pulled out a cellphone. "Look, I have a couple calls to make, Reef. I'll see you back inside when this recess is over. Don't keep the judge waiting." He turned and headed back up the steps and into the courthouse.

No one said anything for a moment. Bigger looked down at his shoes, size fourteen Nikes he'd lifted from a store display at the Halifax Shopping Center. Jink had his hands shoved deep in his pockets like he was checking for loose change. Reef stood motionless, staring at the courthouse as though seeing it for the first time, a tourist in downtown metro. Only Scar seemed capable of movement. She drifted over to Reef, stood in front of him as if waiting.

"Forget him," Reef said. "This'll all be over in a day or two." He pulled a pack of Rothmans out of his shirt pocket and tapped out a cigarette, then offered the smokes to the others. Both Jink and Bigger took one. Scar did not. She watched as they lit up, the three glowing ends of their cigarettes like punctuation in the air.

"You saw those pictures?" she said.

Twin contrails of smoke streamed from Reef's nostrils as he looked at the sky. "Hard not to when you're sittin' front row center."

"Jeez, man," said Bigger. "That Subaru was shredded."

Jink snorted. "Sounds like some kinda cereal. Subaru Shreddies."

Bigger cackled and punched Jink's shoulder. Grinning, Reef turned to see Scar's wooden face.

"She's still in a coma, Reef," she said softly. "The newspapers—"

"Fuck the newspapers!" he hissed, then regretted it. The look on Scar's face told him she'd noticed more than the mangled metal and shattered glass. She'd seen what was all over the inside. Not red, though, like you'd expect. Everything was covered in black, pools and streaks of it like motor oil thrown from a bad piston. From farther back in the courtroom, it probably looked like shadows. But Scar had known what it was. Who knew a person had so much of it to lose?

Scar's fingers brushed Reef's arm. "They don't know when she'll come out of it."

He looked at Jink and Bigger, who were trying to one-up each other with more grisly breakfast foods. Obvious choices like Captain Crash and Ram Flakes were giving way to more gruesome names like Shredded Meat.

"She's our age, Reef."

"Which is a *good* thing," he said, refusing to look at her. He watched Jink and Bigger escalate their cereal competition. "We heal fast."

"But what if—?"

He wheeled on her. "*Jesus*, Scar, whaddya want me to do? Visit her? Hold her hand? What's done is done, for fuck's sake. Ain't nothin' I can do about it now. Even if I wanted to. Which I don't."

He turned away, but not before he saw the look in her eyes. Something between frustration and outright anger, that save-the-world shit he'd never understood about her. Strangers meeting her for the first time—hell, even people who got to know her a bit—would miss that about Scar, her need to protect the underdog, to make everything right. They'd see a cool, hard-edged teenager whose slim frame emphasized her bluntness, telegraphed her refusal to take crap off anyone. He'd certainly seen *that* side of her the first time they'd met.

Two years ago, Reef and Jink and Bigger had been sitting in the school bleachers making fun of the kids trying out for the junior girls' soccer team—a bunch of Barbie dolls trying to impress Ken, a.k.a. Glen Whidden, Reef's phys ed teacher the previous year. He'd had more than one run-in with the athletic asshole that year over what he called Reef's "undisciplined and unsportsmanlike behavior," and Reef still enjoyed any opportunity to make Whidden's life miserable. Like watching his tryouts. He and Bigger had been laughing and jeering every time someone missed a kick or fumbled a block, and Jink had been prancing back and forth along the sideline, imitating the girls' awkward movements, his socks balled up and stuffed under his T-shirt like adolescent breasts. Twice Whidden had called over to them to take a hike, and both times they'd ignored him.

But it had been hard to ignore the redhead who'd appeared from nowhere and told them to shut the fuck up.

At the sound of her voice, Reef had turned expecting to see an annoyed parent or a disgruntled preseason fan. She was neither. He'd seen her around the school a few times, usually alone. Kept to herself. He'd heard she was into some heavy shit, that her dad had done some time for dealing drugs and now she was muling for him. Oddly, though, she was in the accelerated program, so they shared no classes. He looked her up and down, appreciating the curves in all the right places, grinning at the nerve of the bitch. "Hoo, baby, ain't you a fireball," he breathed.

"Goes with the hair," said Jink.

He and Bigger began to laugh again, but Reef silenced them with a wave of his hand. He smiled broadly, but his eyes were ice. "You don't wanna mess with me, Red," he warned.

She smiled back. "The last guy who called me that found his nuts up his ass."

Reef casually got to his feet, swung down off the bleachers and stood in front of her, his chest scant inches from her face. Staring down at her, he waited for her to flinch. She didn't.

It hadn't taken long for them to become friends.

And then lovers, although that was off more than it was on. There were things about her that made him crazy. Like that day on the soccer field, standing up for Whidden. Couldn't she see what a jerk he was? Like they all were?

Apparently not.

Much later, she would tell him it was Whidden who had encouraged her to try the accelerated program. Besides teaching phys ed and coaching soccer, he administered the Canadian Mathematics Competition at the school each year, and she had entered. Not from any desire to win, or even because she liked math that much, although she was good at it. She'd nearly flunked one of her math courses, but that was because she'd missed so much time, not because she couldn't do it. She'd told Reef there was something in her head that made problems unfold, helped her see inside them. He couldn't understand any of it—for him, math was a puzzle with a hundred goddamn missing pieces—but he understood what drew her to Whidden's math group. It was the opportunity to stay after school twice each week for the month prior to the competition. Scar was a loner who would never try out for a team, but extracurricular activity had its advantages. After-school practice meant two afternoons each week she wouldn't have to make a drop for her father.

And she'd surprised everyone when she'd placed first in the school and third in the province. Certainly Glen

Whidden, who suddenly took a big interest in Scar. He told her it'd be a crime for her not to challenge the math mark that had kept her out of the accelerated program. In fact, he'd helped her do it. Reef knew the asshole just wanted to play the big hero and maybe cop a feel for his trouble, but Scar couldn't see it. There were so many things Scar couldn't see that were Windex-clear for Reef.

Like this shit about the accident.

"So what d'you think's gonna happen?" she asked him now.

Bigger looked over at them. "Aww, she'll be outta the hospital in no time," he offered. "You wait 'n' see."

Scar frowned. "No. About the sentence. What d'you think the judge will decide?"

Reef's face twisted. "What's the worst she can do? Send me to Riverview? I been to that corrections center before. Put me on probation? I ain't finished my last one yet. Move me to another foster home? Like *that* ain't gonna happen anyways. I already heard the Barkers talkin' about it. They're just waitin' till after the hearin' to move me out."

Jink took a final drag on his cigarette, then flicked the butt into the street. It danced in the wake of a passing car, throwing off a brief shower of sparks. "No need to worry, Reef. Remember the time they got Zeus for bashin' that guy with the baseball bat? Slap on the wrist."

"I ain't worried," Reef replied. "Just sick 'n' tired 'a sittin' in that courtroom. Not like the movies, huh?"

Bigger snorted. "You got that right, man. How's that judge keep from noddin' off?"

Scar frowned, opened her mouth as if to say something, but at that moment the door swung open and a court clerk beckoned Reef back inside. The recess was over.

Chapter 5

She was in the forest again, cool green reaching up on either side of her as she lay facing the white expanse of sky above. She was alone, as she had been so many times before when she'd found herself here. Off to her right, a bird called incessantly, its high-pitched chirp continually punctuating the emerald stillness. She'd heard that bird before. She turned toward it, or tried to turn, but pain sledgehammered through her body and she cried out, her exclamation a muted gasp. The bird chirped more rapidly until its call became a shrill, insistent whine that made her teeth vibrate. She cried out again, her voice breaking in a series of sobs.

"There, there, Leeza," came a voice beside her. A woman in white leaned over her and suddenly the chirping ceased. Everything was still, except the sledgehammer that continued to pummel her. "I turned off the monitor, dear. We won't need it now that you're awake."

"Where . . . ?" It was all she could manage. There wasn't room for both language and that sledgehammer inside her.

"You're in the hospital, dear. Acute Care Unit. I'm Joyce. I've been here nearly every day since they brought you in."

"When . . . ?" Like the five *W*s of a news story: *Where*, *When* . . .

"Almost three weeks now. You've been unconscious most of that time."

Leeza's voice was little more than a croak. "Why . . . ?" The third *W*.

The nurse looked at her watch and made a notation on a chart. "I'll let the doctor tell you all you want to know. She'll be along in a bit." She inserted a needle into a vial and drew a colorless liquid into the syringe, checked the amount, then injected it into a clear plastic tube that hung over Leeza's bed. "This will help. You get some rest now."

She could not rest. Would not possibly be able to r—

"Leeza." A pause. "Leeza, can you hear me?"

She forced open her eyes to find a tall, heavyset woman standing by her bed. Graying hair pulled back in an unforgiving bun, narrow black glasses perched on the end of her nose, stethoscope jammed into the pocket of her white hospital coat like some serpentine creature caught trying to escape. On her lapel was a tag that said "Julia Mahoney, M.D.," but she easily could have been a female bouncer in one of the downtown bars.

"I'm Dr. Mahoney," she said, and the musical quality of her voice erased Leeza's severe first impression. In those few words were the softened edges of an Irish accent, and as she spoke she placed a hand gently on Leeza's arm. "You've been my patient since you were admitted to the ACU. We've spoken before, but you weren't completely conscious. It's good to see you fully awake. I won't ask you how you're feeling. I think I know." She smiled, and Leeza could see in her eyes that she *did* know. "Your parents are waiting outside. I thought it would be a good idea to have them here when I spoke to you. Is it all right if I ask them to come in?"

The sledgehammer was still there, but it seemed less immediate, as if striking her softly from a distance. "Unh," Leeza said. She'd meant to say *yes*, but her mouth seemed full of cotton and wouldn't form the word.

"Good." The doctor nodded to someone behind her, and a door opened. Two people came in.

"Leezie, honey." It was her mother's voice, but surely it wasn't her mother who had spoken. Diane Morrison was much younger than the person who stood at the end of her hospital bed. Lines now carved a face that in the past had elicited many admiring comments. *Your mother could have been a model*, Leeza's friends often said. Would they say that now? Her hair, once thick and richly auburn, looked thin and lifeless, pulled carelessly back in a metal clip. Her slim figure, so envied by friends and neighbors, now looked frail, almost gaunt, and her slender fingers, long accustomed to intricate work with pens and graphics software, looked like white bones that fidgeted aimlessly with the strap of her purse. "We've missed you so much. Welcome back." Her voice caught and she brushed at sudden tears with the back of her hand.

Standing behind her, Jack Morrison put his hands on his wife's shoulders. He was a tall, athletic-looking man who kept in shape with regular visits to the gym, but he, too, seemed different—older somehow than the last time she'd seen him. Could that really have been three weeks ago? Clearing his throat, he said, "Great to see you awake at last, Leeza."

Don't cry, Mom, Leeza intended to say, but her mouth wouldn't manufacture the words properly and they came out "Donnn rrryyyy." She frowned, moved her tongue around inside her mouth, but the words refused to form.

"It's the medication we've given you for the pain, Leeza," said Dr. Mahoney. "You'll get used to it after a bit."

"How long will she have to be on it?" Jack asked. "The morphine." Even in her drug-fuzzy condition, Leeza heard the catch in his voice, knew what he was thinking. Jack didn't even take Advil for headaches. The thought of his stepdaughter getting regular shots of a narcotic would be difficult for him to accept.

"In light of her injuries, it's likely she'll be on it for

some time," the doctor said. Turning to Leeza, she continued, "Do you remember what happened that brought you here?"

Leeza thought for a moment, but the only memories that surfaced were of other hospital rooms, these ones with beds that held her sister. She tried to shake her head, but pain zithered up her neck and she could only grimace.

"Is it necessary that she remember?" her mother asked. "What if it's too painful . . . ?" Her voice trailed off.

The doctor ignored her. "You've been in a coma, Leeza, and it's important to determine if you have any significant memory loss. Think back. Do you remember the last thing you were doing?"

Leeza tried to concentrate and, for a while, her mind was as blank as the white ceiling above her. Then a memory of another hospital room floated out of her subconscious, a room that didn't have Ellen in it. Instead, there were dishes on the floor. And an old man.

She tried to tell them. "Ollll mannnn," she murmured.

"Van?" asked Jack. "Did you say van, honey?"

Her mother clutched her stepfather's arm. "She must be remembering the accident," she whispered.

Accident? The memory of the old man and the dishes vanished as Leeza's mind groped, grasped at the word. *Accident?* What had happened? Had she gone off the road? Hit someone? Had someone been hurt because of her? Without knowing it, she began to moan.

"Leeza, it's important that you don't upset yourself," said Dr. Mahoney. "I'm going to give you something to calm you down."

She reached for the IV, but Leeza was barely aware of the doctor's movements. Unconsciously, she clawed at the sheet beneath her right hand, caught and twisted it between her fingers. *Accident?*

And then it came to her, out of nowhere, like the object that had struck her windshield. "C-c-crash," she sobbed, her head filled with sudden sounds and images of metal colliding with metal. Not like in the movies, though, where the scene would play out in slow-motion frame after frame after frame. These were quick and final, like hitting the wall with your fist. *Whump! Whump!* Twice? Three times? She'd lost count as the cars had careened into her, could only watch them coming and hold on. And scream.

Leeza sobbed again. "Cra-a-ash," she moaned, the word slurred this time by tears.

"So. What do you think?"

Leeza's eyes fluttered open long enough to see her stepfather standing by her bed, then closed again. Her eyelids were folds of lead. She would need her fingers to keep them open, but they were attached to hands heavy as houses. Useless.

"I'd like to say the worst is over, but that wouldn't be entirely true." The doctor. Syllables like water tumbling over itself.

"But she's out of the coma now." Her mother's voice, high and thin. Like a guitar string wound pitch-tight. "That has to be good news."

"Yes, Mrs. Morrison. It *is* good news. But the coma hasn't been our greatest concern. That was her body's means of preparing itself for the healing process."

"So she *is* healing. Getting better." Jack again.

"All the tests indicate her brain activity is normal."

"Thank God."

Leeza forced her eyelids apart again, momentarily saw her mother dab at her eyes with a tissue, Jack's hand on her arm. Leeza wanted to tell them she was awake, but her eyes wouldn't let her. The dark came down again.

". . . know this has been very difficult for you," the doctor was saying softly, "especially following the loss of your other daughter."

Leeza tried to open her eyes again. Could not. Had she slept?

"You don't know. No one can. It's like a bad movie that won't end." Leeza heard her mother blow her nose. It was a sound of hospital waiting rooms. And funeral homes.

Then something crept into her mother's voice.

Something hard. Whiplike. "And then to sit in court and watch that lawyer try to make excuses for what that boy did." Her tone made the word *boy* sound as ugly as *pustule* or *gangrene*. "How can he sleep at night?"

"I'm sure he's just doing his job." It was the doctor who offered this.

"I mean the son of a bitch who did all this. How can he look himself in the mirror?"

Someone did this? Leeza thought. *To me?* An image swam out of her memory. Someone waving. At her. *Someone did this?* The image shimmered, fragmented, dissolved.

"That's not for me to say," Dr. Mahoney replied. "I'm more concerned about how all this has affected your daughter."

A curtain drifted over Leeza. She fought it, struggled to pull it back. Tears leaked out of the corners of her eyes, slid in increments down the sides of her face. One hung suspended from her jaw and she willed it to fall to the sheets but it wouldn't.

"Is there something you haven't told us?" Even with her eyes closed, Leeza could sense her stepfather's distrust. Of hospitals and doctors. And drugs.

She heard the doctor draw a long breath, then let it out slowly. "It's not what I haven't told *you*. You've known every detail of Leeza's condition from the moment she was brought in here. It's what Leeza doesn't know that bothers me."

The curtain again. Drawn lazily over her mind. *No*, thought Leeza. *Not now*. But the curtain wouldn't listen. *What is it? What don't I—*

Chapter 6

". . . you even *looked* at the news stories they been writin' about this? Have you even *thought* about that girl and what's been happenin' to her?" Karl Barker slid the newspaper across the table toward Reef. "You're just lucky there were no other serious injuries. Or that someone wasn't *killed*, for God's sake. You could be in a whole lot worse mess than you are right now, young man."

Reef felt the heat work its way up the back of his neck. Once his foster father got launched into one of his *young man* speeches, there was no stopping him until he'd had his say. And that could be quite some time. Depending on whether he got whipped up to full bore, it could go on for fifteen, maybe twenty minutes. Sometimes longer. Reef thought casually about flipping the kitchen table over on its side and walking out, but it wasn't worth it. It was the price you paid for living with a foster family like the Barkers. You were just two ears on a body, ears that had to listen to every complaint and criticism and rant they threw your way. Speeches that began with such gems as *While*

you're livin' under my roof and ended with observations
like *You don't know how lucky you got it.* Yeah. He felt
pretty goddamn lucky, all right. Living under what
amounted to house arrest with the Barkers until
Social Services could find another place for him. Sitting here watching Karl's lips move, spit forming in
the corners of his mouth, and sometimes getting
caught in the spray of words he aimed at Reef, at the
ceiling, at the floor. Karl had missed his calling. He
should have been a preacher instead of a postman. Or
a politician.

Avoiding the damp fallout of Karl's barrage, Reef
glanced down at the newspaper and saw a picture of a
man and a woman being interviewed by reporters
outside the courthouse where he'd sat the last three
days. He read the caption below the photograph: "Jack
and Diane Morrison respond to questions following
the pre-sentence hearing of the young offender guilty
of causing the accident that seriously injured their
daughter, Elizabeth." The young offender. How often
had he heard *that* phrase in the last few weeks? He'd
laughed at the way Jink said it, like it had capital letters, like it was the title of one of those old movies they
played on the Superstation. *The Young Offender*, star-
ring Reef Kennedy.

Of course, Jink and Bigger hadn't guessed where his
laughter had come from, hadn't known he'd pulled it
up from some hollow place inside him, forced it out
between lips frozen in a grimace that he'd somehow

transformed into a grin. Over the years, he'd pulled other things out of that place inside him: the sneer he wore in principals' offices, the mocking tone he used in police stations, the stony silence he'd shown his grandfather each time the drinking began.

It was that same stony silence he called on now as his eyes again found the name beneath the photograph: *Elizabeth*. There'd been no pictures of her in the paper. No family photos or yearbook headshots. "At the request of the family," he'd read, and momentarily wondered how ugly your kid had to be for a parent to ask reporters not to print her picture. *Elizabeth*. His eyes kept returning to her name. And he imagined once more the feel of the rock in his hands, imagined its sudden release, the journey it made from his fingertips to the windshield of the car the girl had been driving: *causing the accident that seriously injured their daughter.* Imagined for a moment his fingers gripping rather than letting go, pulling back, returning the rock to its place in his pocket. Imagined that faceless girl at home with her parents instead of hooked up to monitors in a hospital downtown. Just like Nan.

He swallowed hard, reached deep inside for the safety of that silence, skimmed the article below the photo: ". . . spokesperson for the family reported that the seventeen-year-old accident victim has finally regained consciousness." Reef released the air in his lungs, softly. At least there was that.

". . . and I can't for the life 'a me understand how none 'a this seems to bother you . . ."

Yeah, well, thought Reef, *that's because your Ph.D. in Postal Delivery don't include Reef's handy Life Lessons for Dummies.* Like Life Lesson Number One: *What don't kill you makes you stronger.* That's what his grandfather used to say. When he wasn't drunk and cursing his bastard grandson for every breath he drew.

". . . like none 'a this matters, like you're just along for the ride . . ."

Reef watched Karl's lips move some more, thought again about the disembodied mouths he'd imagined in the courtroom. When you came down to it, that really was all people were. Mouths. Endlessly talking mouths. People didn't even need ears any more. His mother had actually been an improvement to the basic design. Too bad she never knew.

Reef's eyes returned to the article: ". . . the prosecution and defense presented closing statements . . . groups lobbying for stiffer sentences to deter youth crime . . . high-profile case is expected to put pressure on Judge Hilary Thomas to present her ruling soon . . . under the Youth Criminal Justice Act, the teenager who threw the rock cannot be identified . . ."

Right. Like the hundred or more people who filed in and out of that courtroom each day didn't know that the person sitting beside Hank Elliott was a ward of the court named Chad Kennedy. Not getting your name and picture in the paper didn't exactly mean no one knew who you were. It was like being invisible in plain sight.

People knew, all right. Like the kids during those last few days at school who'd suddenly grown silent when he'd walked by, their eyes following him down the hall. Lately, he'd even begun to sense a coolness among some of his own buddies. Like Zeus Williams, who had nearly beaten that guy to death last year with a bat. Last week, Reef had walked over to see what was left of The Pit and Zeus had been standing by the barricade watching cranes loading the rubble onto a fleet of trucks. Zeus had said hey, and they'd shot the shit for a while about The Pit being gone, but there'd been something in the air between them. Like a word that hadn't been spoken. Invisible in plain sight. Zeus had left after a few minutes, and Reef hadn't seen him since. *Well, fuck him.*

". . . you don't know how lucky you got it . . ."

And fuck you, too, Karl.

The phone on the kitchen wall rang, mercifully interrupting Karl's postmortem on the sad state of youth as he saw it. Karl reached for it. "Hello," he said. Then, "Yeah, he's here." Handing Reef the phone, he muttered, "It's your lawyer."

"They're called external fixators," Dr. Mahoney said.

Leeza had slept nearly two hours. Her tongue felt

thick and her mouth was dust-dry, but she was awake and alert. Now that the curtain had lifted, though, she longed for its return. Her eyes widened in horror as she gazed down at the ruin that was her body.

Holding up the bedsheet, the doctor moved on to her other injuries, pointing to the cast that encased Leeza's left arm and carefully describing the dislocated shoulder and the two breaks that occurred above and below the elbow. But all Leeza could see was the metal hardware that seemed to grow out of her pelvis and left leg.

"I know," the doctor said softly. "It can be frightening the first time you see them."

Her mother stood on the other side of the bed, holding her right hand. She focused on Leeza's eyes, silently communicating her support. Somehow, though, Leeza sensed that her mother was not looking *at* her as much as *away* from what lay under the sheet. Clearly, her mother had already seen her injuries, could not bring herself to look at them again.

More tears slipped down Leeza's face as she stared at several metal bars that crisscrossed the left side of her lower body. Thick as ballpoint pens, the bars were connected to metal rods about three inches long that protruded directly from her flesh. "They go right . . ." Leeza choked, tried bravely not to sob. She took a shaky breath, let it out slowly. "Right into my skin."

"Yes, they do. They were surgically implanted to keep the bones in your leg and pelvis aligned so they heal properly. They'll be taken out after they've done their job."

Leeza continued to stare at them, her lower lip quivering. She barely heard the doctor as she continued with the explanation of her injuries.

"Along with the fractures, two of your ribs were broken, and you had a severe concussion that caused the swelling in your brain and resulted in the coma." She paused a moment, as if to let the reality of Leeza's injuries sink in. Then, "Your ribs, arm and shoulder are healing nicely, and we've been exercising your legs each day to keep them strengthened. We bring in a portable machine called a CPM that provides continuous passive movement so your muscles don't atrophy. You'll see it later."

Her head raised on pillows, Leeza continued to stare at the roadmap of incisions beneath the fixators and the fading, blue-yellow bruises that ran up both legs and across her pelvis. The muffled throb of her body that had set her teeth on edge all morning was forgotten as her eyes traced and retraced the damage below her waist. Even the earlier humiliation of the catheter—"We have to change it four times a day," Joyce had explained as she'd inserted the plastic tube—was a dim memory.

"I know it looks bad, Leeza," the doctor admitted. "But you'll heal. You've already begun doing that. The important thing is to get you walking again."

At last, Leeza's mother spoke. "They're transferring you to the rehab center tomorrow, honey. The sooner you start therapy, the sooner we're going to get you home."

Leeza's eyes did not leave the wreckage of her lower body. "I need . . ." She choked, and her mother squeezed her hand lightly.

"Yes, dear? What is it you want?"

But the dam broke and Leeza was sobbing, unable to continue.

Dr. Mahoney lowered the sheet and reached around behind her, pulling something out of a drawer in the sidetable. "This is what you want, isn't it, Leeza?" She held out a mirror.

Leeza looked up and nodded. Releasing her mother's hand, she took the mirror and held it in front of her face. And gasped. The person who used to look back at her—the pretty, blue-eyed girl with the oval face and long, blond hair—was gone. In her place was a stranger. For a long moment Leeza stared at the fading bruises on her hollow cheeks and lined forehead, the sunken eyes that looked like holes burned in a white sheet, her bluntly cropped hair.

"There were two lacerations on your scalp that we had to suture," Mahoney explained. "Fortunately, there were no serious cuts on your face. You were lucky. It could have been much worse."

Leeza lowered the mirror to her chest, looked at the

ceiling through streaming eyes. Tried to feel how lucky she was.

"I knew things were moving quickly, but the judge surprised even me." Hank Elliott seemed younger on the phone. Maybe it was not seeing that pasty, Legal Aid face of his when he spoke. Wearing his I-can't-believe-I'm-doing-this expression that made Reef want to puke. Or punch him out. He looked out the window at the Barkers' back yard, the grass long since choked out by weeds and cinch bugs. He said nothing.

"So," Elliott continued, "can you make it to the courthouse by three o'clock?"

Reef looked across the table at Karl. "Oh, I got someone here who's just dyin' to take me."

Karl glanced at him sharply. Scowled. "Smartass," he said.

Reef flipped him the finger.

"Phone call for you, Mrs. Morrison," the nurse said from the doorway. "You can take it at the nurses' station."

Leeza gripped her mother's hand, then thought of all the times her sister had lain in beds like this one, being strong for everyone. Now here *she* was, clinging to her mother like Velcro. She forced herself to let go.

"Thanks, Joyce," Diane said. She turned to Leeza. "Must be Jack." She pointed to her purse. "You can't use cellphones in the hospital. I'll be right back, honey." She patted her daughter's hand and hurried out of the room.

"Joyce," said Dr. Mahoney, "I've adjusted the dosage of Leeza's pain medication. You'll see it on the chart."

"Yes, Doctor," the nurse replied. She came around by the bed, checking instruments and recording notes on a chart.

"And she'll be moving to rehab tomorrow."

"Good for you, Leeza," said the nurse. "I'll be sorry to see you go, though. We didn't have much chance to get to know each other."

"I'll check on you later this evening," Mahoney told Leeza. "See you then," she said, then left.

Leeza said nothing, gripped the handle of the mirror in her white-knuckled fist.

"So," the nurse said as she flipped through the chart, "I've been meaning to ask you about your name. I've heard Lisa lots of times, but we don't get many Leezas here."

Leeza swallowed audibly. Forced back tears. She didn't think she could speak and was grateful the nurse pretended not to notice, busying herself with the chart.

"Is it a given name or short for something?" the nurse asked brightly.

Leeza swallowed again. "Short for Elizabeth."

The nurse turned to her. "Is that right? I have a sister named Elizabeth. Everybody calls her Liz."

Leeza said nothing for a long moment, and the nurse continued checking instruments and recording information. She hummed a bit as she worked, seemingly unaware of the continued silence.

Finally, Leeza was able to force out the words. "It's the name my sister called me."

"Really?" the nurse asked without looking up. "Did she hear it somewhere?"

Another pause, this one shorter than the last. "When I was born, she couldn't say my name. Called me Leezabit. Then just Leeza."

"That's sweet," the nurse said. "I had quite a few names for my little sister when we were growing up, but, fortunately for her," she grinned, "none of them stuck."

Despite the pain that ground its teeth along her left side, and even despite the horror she'd seen under the sheet and in the mirror, Leeza smiled. A wan, fleeting thing, but still a smile. Apparently encouraged by this reaction, the nurse was well into a humorous account of how she'd sabotaged her sister's first date when Leeza's mother returned.

"I have to go out for a while, Leeza," she said, her face ashen. "Jack's on his way now to pick me up."

"Where?" Leeza asked.

"The courthouse," she replied, her voice hard as ice chips. "That was the Crown attorney on the phone. The judge is sentencing the boy who put you here. I want to see his face when she throws the book at him."

Chapter 7

The courtroom was packed. As soon as they'd arrived, Karl Barker had hurried directly into the courthouse, his postman pants making sandpaper sounds as he'd threaded his way inside. Unlike Karl, Reef hadn't been worried about getting a seat. The one advantage of being the guilty party. He turned now to look at the crowd and saw there was standing room only, most of which was occupied by numerous reporters at the back. The one Bigger had threatened on the steps gave him a hard smile, but Reef ignored him. Sitting on the left a few rows in front of Karl were the man and woman in the newspaper photo. The woman was looking directly at him, as if trying to fry him with laser vision. He looked away, continued scanning the crowd.

Scar and Bigger waved from seats very near the back, but Jink wasn't there. And wouldn't be. Reef had told them so when they'd spoken outside.

"Why *isn't* he here?" Scar had demanded.

"Jink's got his own troubles right now. He don't need more 'a mine."

"What happened?"

"Cops picked him up last night for disturbin' the peace. Fightin' at Rowdy's."

"There's always fights at Rowdy's," Bigger had added. "Usually better 'n the floor shows at that dump."

"This time," Reef said, "the cops got there before it broke up, 'n' they nailed Jink for drinkin' under age. They shut the place down."

"Jesus," Scar muttered. "How could Jink be so stupid?"

"I know," agreed Reef. "Rowdy may lose his liquor license. He told Jink he better hope it don't happen." Reef knew that losing the income from the run-down joint called "Rowdy's" would be no hardship for its owner—Jink had said many times that Rowdy didn't make a helluva lot off the few boozehounds that frequented the place anyway. It was the bar itself that Rowdy needed; it was a front for more than a dozen shady operations that attracted more police attention than almost any other place in the city. Everyone knew the cops had been trying for years to find ways to shut it down, even citing the place for Health Code violations—but a rumor that Rowdy had a friend in the Health Department seemed to have proven true when the violations were suddenly rescinded. Now Jink had handed them a gift that, combined with all the other infractions, could very well be the one to close Rowdy's for good.

Bigger had whistled softly under his breath. "I wouldn't want Rowdy and his goons lookin' for *me*."

If the situation hadn't been so grim, Reef would've chuckled. "That's why I told Jink to stay put," he'd told them. "The cops don't need to see him connected with this shit. Don't need another reason to put the screws to him."

So Jink would miss the big show. Somewhere there were hearts bleeding purple piss.

"All rise."

Reef turned to see Judge Thomas enter the courtroom, her black robe making her tiny frame seem even smaller. For a bizarre moment she looked a bit like Nan, but then he looked again and the illusion was gone. She was just a short woman with a long coat—and the power to put him away for a few months. But so what? *What don't kill you makes you stronger*. And then there was Life Lesson Number Two: *Shit happens*. Looking at Judge Thomas, Reef was reminded that it's a whole lot better being the shitter than the shittee. Something else his grandfather used to say.

Reef ignored the court clerk's opening crap about the presiding judge and the court proceedings. He'd heard all of it so many times he could recite it chapter and verse. He glanced at Hank Elliott, who must have heard hundreds of court-now-in-session intros, but the lawyer appeared to be listening intently as though it were his very first time. The guy was a trained chimp.

"You may be seated."

About time, thought Reef, as everyone settled into their seats. *Let's get this show on the road.*

The judge perched a pair of dark-rimmed glasses on the end of her nose and opened a thick file. She paged through it silently, as if entering each piece of paper in some photographic memory bank. Reef got the feeling, though, that she knew every detail of the file already, that this was a performance just for his benefit. *Well, fuck you, Judge. It takes more than a dwarf in a black bathrobe to scare me.*

Judge Thomas closed the file and leaned back in her chair. At that angle, her eyes barely topped the judge's bench, and Reef grinned as he imagined her feet dangling above the floor.

His grin did not go unnoticed. The judge frowned. "Counsel, would you and your client please stand?"

Elliott stood so quickly that Reef wondered if there were a spring-loaded ejection device in the lawyer's seat. Reef ambled to his feet.

"Chad Arthur Kennedy, under Section 430 of the Criminal Code, you are guilty of two counts of mischief resulting in the vandalism of a privately owned truck and an accident that damaged six vehicles and injured three people, one of them seriously."

A murmur rippled across the courtroom, and Reef could hear a few people mutter their disgust as if all this were a big surprise. Assholes. Hadn't he pleaded guilty almost three weeks ago? What a show.

The judge waited for silence, which fell almost immediately. "Do you have anything you wish to say?"

Reef had *plenty* to say, but Elliott, who'd chosen not

to have him testify for that very reason, had made him promise he would keep quiet, even made him practice the five words a few times: "No, Your Honor, I don't."

"Well then," she continued, "I am prepared at this time to sentence you."

Another ripple, this one lasting longer than the first. Thomas glared at the spectators and silence returned to the courtroom. "This case has attracted the attention of the general public as well as many members of the media. All of us here have seen many editorials in the paper and on television regarding the need to get tough on youth crime, to make examples of the perpetrators of these heinous acts that will deter others from performing similarly in the future . . ."

Reef watched as her lips moved, but he no longer heard what she was saying. Words, words, words. Meaningless, like the "KEEP OUT" signs on The Pit. His whole life had been a "KEEP OUT" sign. He'd listened to it described in detail over the last few days as though listening to people talk about someone else, someone not even in the room.

Elliott had called three people to speak in his defense. The first was Royce Gould, a social worker, who gave a detailed account of the poverty of Reef's early childhood, the emotional abuse he'd endured from an alcoholic grandparent, the short-lived experiences in numerous foster homes since he was nine. Next was Karl Barker, who offered—in Karl's eyes, anyway—valuable insight into life spent with troubled teens. The last person was a surprise: Elvira Gregory, his eighth-grade English teacher, who commented on Reef's vast potential as a student—potential that, upon cross-examination, the Crown attorney had shown to be unfulfilled.

". . . but the courts are not institutions to be manipulated by public opinion. If the public is dissatisfied with a law, it is the duty of each citizen to become actively involved in the repeal or amendment of that law. The forum for discussions such as these is Parliament or the provincial legislature, not the courtroom."

Reef had no idea what she was talking about, but he could sense movement behind him. The reporters at the back.

The judge paused again, was rewarded with silence, then continued. "Despite the fact that the public is demanding stiffer punishments, I firmly believe that punishment is not the way to dissuade individuals like yourself from committing crimes such as this one. Numerous studies have shown that incarceration of young people only leads to further instances of criminal behavior. A case in point is your own prior stay at the Riverview Correctional Institute." A moment passed and, when she spoke again, she addressed the spectators. "More important than fear of punishment is the need for compassion, the need for better choices, the need for young people who commit crimes to recognize that they are and will continue to be members of a society, and that the actions of everyone in that society impact in some way on every other member."

More movement at the back. Reef could hear pens scratching furiously on notepads. Where was this going?

"The Youth Criminal Justice Act recognizes that there is no quick fix to youth crime. It supports constructive, long-term solutions intended to foster values of respect and accountability. At the heart of the Act is the principle that criminal behaviour will result in meaningful consequences."

The judge took off her glasses and folded them carefully, placing them on the file in front of her before continuing. She turned again to Reef. "Mr. Kennedy," she said, "you have pleaded guilty to criminal acts and, in doing so, have saved the court considerable time and expense. However, you have not shown remorse for your actions." She shook her head sadly. "In fact, from what I've seen in this courtroom, you have demonstrated no concern whatsoever for what you have done." She paused. "I believe that you need to experience the results of such actions firsthand so you will understand their ramifications and, hopefully, learn to make better choices in the future. I am assigning you to the North Hills Group Home, where you will live for the next twelve months under the supervision of Mr. Frank Colville. When school begins again in the fall, you will attend classes at Bonavista High School, where you will work to your potential."

She picked up her glasses and brandished them at Reef. "And you *will* work, young man. Teachers face enough problems in their classrooms without having to deal with people who are sentenced to school. Ms. Rita Hamilton, principal of Bonavista, has agreed to report directly to me every two weeks on your performance, and I'll be expecting to hear positive news. If I don't, you'll find yourself standing in front of me again."

There was now a buzz in the courtroom, and the judge bristled. "If I have to clear this courtroom to be heard, I'll do it!" she snapped.

The room fell silent again.

"During the school year, you'll attend classes and take part in at least two extracurricular activities. Judging from the distance you threw that rock, I'd suggest you try track-and-field events like shot put and javelin." There was sudden laughter from the back of the room, and the judge shot a stern look at the people who had produced it. Returning her attention to Reef, she resumed, "Beginning this summer and continuing through the school year, you will volunteer your help at one of the city's rehabilitation centers on two week-day afternoons or evenings and every other Saturday. You'll learn intimately what suffering is all about, young man. Many of the people in those facilities suffer from crippling illnesses. Others are victims of trauma caused by a variety of accidents, including motor vehicle mishaps resulting from careless actions such as your own." She leaned forward. "When Mr. Colville feels you are ready, you will conduct a series of presentations to high school classes and youth groups telling about your experiences and the insight you've gained as a result of them. And believe me, young man, you *will* gain insight. You *will* feel remorse. I'm going to make certain of that."

Reef blinked at her. Extracurricular activities? Volunteering at rehabs? *Youth groups?* Was the woman crazy?

"I can see from your reaction, Mr. Kennedy, that you're not thrilled with my ruling." She glanced around the room. "Many others will no doubt share that reaction, but for very different reasons. There's nothing I can do about that. However, what I *can* do is try my best to ensure that you become a productive citizen. I'll be watching you, Chad, and it's my hope that, when you complete your sentence, you will have a new appreciation for the people with whom you share this planet."

"She's outta her goddamn mind!" Reef muttered as the courtroom emptied.

"Shut up," Elliott hissed. He'd told Reef to remain seated, and the two were now alone except for the handful of people the court security officer was still ushering out. That, however, wouldn't last long. They still had to run the gauntlet of reporters on the steps outside. "You don't know how lucky you are."

That line again. "Fuck off," Reef snarled as he got to his feet.

Elliott glanced around as he stood up, saw no one within earshot, and spoke through clenched teeth. "Now you listen to me, asshole. I have clients who *give* a shit, so the last thing I need is to waste more time with the likes of you. But I want you to understand one thing. Judge Thomas could have crucified you. Instead, she gave you a second chance. Don't screw it up."

"Chance to do what? Improve my public speaking? Give me a break!" Reef turned away savagely, kicked a nearby chair so it flipped over backwards and crashed to the floor.

Elliott's voice was low, but that didn't mask the venom in his response. "You don't get it, do you? You've just been given a break. You get to walk out of here and make a difference in your life. That is, if you have the guts to do it."

Reef whirled to face him. "What do *you* know about guts? I could kick your ass from here to Sunday." It was out of Reef's mouth before he realized where that line had come from. His grandfather.

The lawyer shook his head. "That's the problem with you, Reef," he said as he reached down and pulled the chair upright. "Courage and kicking ass aren't the same thing. Maybe that's something you'll learn in the next twelve months. If not," he sighed, "I expect I'll see you here again." He opened his briefcase, slid his files inside, and took a deep breath. "Now comes the hard part."

"Mr. Elliott! What's your response to the judge's ruling?" The throng of people around Reef and his lawyer was overwhelming and questions came quickly.

"Of course we're pleased," replied Elliott as he and Reef made their way down the courthouse steps. As instructed, Reef said nothing. He kept his hands inside his jacket pockets so the reporters wouldn't see his fists. Clenching, loosening, clenching again. He scanned the area for Scar and Bigger and spied them waiting across the street. Scar waved to him.

"Surprised?" called the reporter whom Bigger had confronted.

"We think the judge was fair," Elliott replied.

An angry sob rose from another knot of people on the steps below them and a woman's voice shouted, "Fair? It was anything *but* fair!"

Reef's glance slid across several faces and he saw, surrounded by television cameras, the man and woman he'd seen in the newspaper and in the courtroom every day. The man had one arm around the woman's waist, supporting her as she spoke through tears.

"That ruling was a slap in the face!" she sobbed. "My daughter is lying in a hospital bed with injuries to more than half her body, and that animal," she pointed at Reef, "was sentenced to be a *volunteer*! For Christ's sake, can *anyone* call that *fair*?"

A number of spectators watching from the sidewalk shook their heads and muttered, and Reef could hear grumbled comments like "Lousy punk!" and "God-damn psychopath!" One individual who obviously had come prepared held up a sign that said "I'M OFFENDED BY YOUNG OFFENDERS!" Reef pulled one hand out of his jacket to flash them all the finger, but Elliott gripped him by the shoulder and hurried him down the steps past the cameras, the crowd, the hysterical woman.

Chapter 8

The elevator eased to a stop and Matt McKillup announced, "Sixth floor, Hotel Rehab. Any guests for the sixth floor?" The ambulance attendant grinned broadly at Leeza as the doors slid open, but she didn't respond.

Carly Reynolds, the nurse who had met them at the ground-floor entrance, moved back to allow Leeza's stepfather to press the button on the elevator panel to keep the doors apart. Her mother stepped out first, making room for Matt and Carly to wheel the stretcher out into the hallway. It was obvious they were taking care to ease it gently over the gap between the elevator and the tile floor. Despite her recent morphine injection, Leeza was in considerable pain, and she appreciated their efforts to keep her from feeling any more discomfort than necessary.

Keeping his finger on the *open* button, Jack said, "Sorry, but I've got to get back to work." He appeared to be speaking to Leeza, but it was her mother who turned to face him.

"Right now?" Diane asked.

He nodded. "I've missed a lot of time. Things are piling up. You understand."

Gritting her teeth, Leeza found it hard to concentrate on what he was saying. But she didn't really need to hear the words. She could read the look on her stepfather's face, see him groping for whatever excuse would permit him to leave. Nor did she blame him. Now.

He reached out of the elevator and gently squeezed Leeza's free hand. "I'll see you soon, honey." Then, to his wife, "I'll take a taxi so you can keep the car." He released the button and the doors slid shut.

Leeza watched her mother stare at the elevator for a moment, trying to rearrange the expression on her face into something other than disapproval. Leeza wanted to tell her it was okay.

Of course, it hadn't been okay at first. She'd learned that Jack had been to the hospital only a handful of times while she was in the coma, and he hadn't stayed long after she'd regained consciousness. In the short time he was there, she'd noticed how he avoided her eyes when he spoke to her, his gaze fixed on some point above her head. Not that Leeza commented on this. She was only concerned about one thing now: the next morphine injection that made the pain less immediate, more bearable.

She'd watched her stepfather that morning as they'd wheeled her stretcher down the hospital corridor toward the elevators and the waiting ambulance in preparation for the ride to the Halifax Rehabilitation

Center. Watched him glance furtively through open doorways at patients in rooms along the hall. If someone's eyes happened to meet his, he looked away quickly, his face drawn, his lips a straight line. It was then that she realized how hard this had been for him. First Ellen. And now her.

No, she didn't blame her stepfather. How could she? The night before, she had tried to look at the pile of cards and notes she'd received, but the pain had made the task unbearable and she'd given up after reading only a few. She'd noted, however, that nearly all of them had arrived within a day or two of her accident, and only Jen and Robin had called her mother in the last two weeks to ask about Leeza and pass along good thoughts. Neither had asked when they could visit.

No, she couldn't blame her stepfather for not wanting to be there. No one else did, either. Herself less than anyone.

"Well, then," her mother said, and Leeza could hear her trying her best to mask the annoyance in her voice as she turned to the others. "Lead on."

Rolling the stretcher down the hall, the ambulance attendant resumed the steady patter he'd begun the moment he'd arrived at the ACU. He'd talked about growing up in Conception Bay, Newfoundland; about the basketball team he played on in his spare time; about the best choices for pets, the rising cost of gasoline, how buying in bulk never seemed to save him any money. Leeza hadn't been able to focus on his words and was thankful that her mother had responded with equally meaningless small talk. But now her mother was quiet.

As if sensing the sudden awkwardness, Matt McKillup began cracking jokes nonstop in his thick Newfoundland accent. By the time they'd reached Leeza's room, the nurse was laughing out loud, and even her mother had begun to smile. Leeza, however, stared straight ahead. The rehab's sixth floor was where she'd be living for at least the next three months, and she fought to keep a lemon-sized lump of homesickness from rising in her throat. How different this place was from their cozy two-story on Connaught Avenue. There, everything was color and light. An interior decorator, her mother had transformed their home from its original traditional blandness into a stylish combination of comfort and elegance that drew admiring comments from everyone who saw it. Now, as the attendant steered the stretcher through a doorway near the end of the hall, Leeza's heart sank. She closed her eyes to the beige walls and listened to the sounds around her: voices low in conversation, a television host describing fantastic prizes to be won, a toilet flushing, footsteps at the other end of the hall, a guttural moaning that suggested someone in terrible pain. That last sound reminded her of the agony awaiting her when the nurse and ambulance attendant would move her from the stretcher to the bed. She clenched her teeth and opened her eyes.

"Ride's over," Matt announced. He eased the stretcher to a stop beside one of the room's two beds. Although both were empty, a hairbrush, several chocolate bar wrappers and other personal items on the table next to the bed by the window were evidence of another occupant. Leeza saw a name written in marker on a card at the head of the bed: Brett Turner. She was sharing a room with a guy?

The nurse must have noticed her startled expression. "It's not what you think. Brett's a woman. You'll like her. She's only a couple years older than you are."

"I brought her in . . ." Matt looked to Carly for confirmation. "What's it been? Six weeks ago? Seven?" The nurse nodded as the ambulance attendant moved around to the other side of the bed. "A real character, that one," he said. He and Carly grasped opposite edges of the stretcher sheet and gently eased Leeza onto the bed, then slowly drew the sheet out from under her. Despite their efforts to move her smoothly, Leeza gasped as white-hot needles jabbed at her left side, and she tried to focus on Matt's steady stream of words. "You'll have to be on your toes, Leeza, sharin' a room with the likes 'a her."

"I heard that." Although the result was another stab of pain, Leeza couldn't help turning slightly to see a tiny redhead grinning at them from a wheelchair in the doorway. "Carly, do they still let goofy Newfies in this place?"

Matt grinned. "Speak 'a the devil."

"Devil?" the redhead chided. "This from a guy with a stretcher for a back seat?"

Matt shook his head at Carly. "By now I should know better than to tangle with that one, eh?"

Smiling, the nurse made introductions. "Leeza, meet Brett Turner. Brett, this is Leeza Hemming."

The wheelchair rolled into the room and around to the other bed. "Hi, Leeza. Guess we'll be bunk-buddies for a while."

Leeza's response—a muted "Hi"—was fainter than she'd intended. She cleared her throat to repeat it but her mother was already introducing herself: "I'm Diane Morrison. Leeza's mother."

"Nice to meet you, Mrs. Morrison. Despite what Matt the Rat here says about me, I'm pretty harmless."

"Pretty, yes. Harmless, no," Matt said. "I still have a bruise from that time you rolled over my foot."

The girl lifted herself out of the wheelchair and lay back on her bed. "That'll teach you to get in front of a wheelchair race."

Carly turned to a clearly startled Diane. "We don't allow races, Mrs. Morrison. But Brett, here, never met a rule she didn't break."

Brett threw an arm over her eyes in a gesture of eternal suffering. "That's right. Pick on the gimp."

Carly chuckled, and Leeza could tell her mother was impressed by the easy relationship between patient and nurse. Leeza was more cynical. After all, what wasn't there to like about a person who brought you pain medication on a regular basis? She'd be Carly's best friend as long as the morphine was on time.

"Well, Leeza," said Matt, lifting the brake on the stretcher, "looks like you're all settled so I'll be leavin' you with the rehab race queen. If she gives you a hard time, just call me." He nodded at the other three people in the room. "Later, ladies," he said, then he guided the stretcher into the hallway and was gone.

Leeza lay back on her pillow and tried not to think how much time would elapse before her next needle, tried instead to focus on her mother bustling about the room. "Where's the best place for this?" her mother asked the nurse, pointing to the blue suitcase at her side.

Carly turned to the two narrow metal doors in the corner. "Both these lockers are yours, Leeza. You might want to put your shirts, sweaters, things like that in the top locker and your footwear in the bottom one. But it's up to you. Whatever you find easiest." She glanced at Diane. "Maybe you could just leave that there and let Leeza deal with it when she's feeling up to it."

Leeza's mouth opened. She managed to close it before speaking the words her lips had nearly formed. How in hell was she supposed to unpack a suitcase when she couldn't even imagine lifting her head off her pillow? There wasn't enough morphine in the world to make *that* happen. Her suitcase could sit there until someone fell over it. It wasn't as if she needed what was in it anyway. It'd be a hell of a long time before she could wear something besides the hospital gowns that had been her only clothing since the accident.

The nurse spoke again. "I have some papers that need to be signed. Perhaps we could go take care of those now and leave Leeza to get settled."

Diane nodded. Leaning over the bed, she kissed her daughter lightly on the cheek. "I'll be back in a bit. Okay, honey?"

"Mmm." Leeza stared at the ceiling.

"She'll be fine," Leeza heard the nurse say as she led Diane out of the room.

A long moment passed. *She'll be fine.* Right, thought Leeza. Dislocated shoulder, broken arm and ribs, fractured leg and pelvis, metal sticking out of her like she was one of those half-human, half-machine characters in a sci-fi film. Or worse: something real. Like the turtle she'd once seen at summer camp flipped over on its back, unable to right itself, its legs waving uselessly in the air. Helpless. Like the feeble residents at Silver Meadows, diapered, washed and fed like babies. Completely dependent. Like Leeza was now. *She'll be fine.* She fought to keep a sob from tearing her chest apart, focused on the white tiles above her, tried to ignore the bass-drum throb that began in her legs and ended in her left shoulder.

Then, "The sprinkler on the left."

Leeza turned slightly toward the voice from the other bed, gasped as cruel fingers scrabbled up and down her neck. "Pardon me?" she asked, her voice little more than a whisper.

Brett lay on her back too, pointing at the ceiling. "Up there, the sprinkler on the left. That was my focal point. When the pain got too much for me, I'd concentrate on that one thing. Sometimes it worked."

Leeza scanned the ceiling and saw four chrome-plated sprinkler heads. She'd seen hundreds like them in the past—in school, in department stores, in the many hospital rooms where Ellen had lain. Inside each was a thin, mercury-filled glass tube designed to burst when heat from a fire expanded the red liquid. Leeza felt exactly like that tube—fragile, ready to burst. She swallowed hard to keep from crying. "Why that one?" she asked, and was immediately ashamed of how pathetic her voice sounded. Like a croak.

Brett didn't seem to notice. "The four of them make a rectangle and that one's in the top left corner. I've got a thing about top left corners. Like with envelopes? Most people focus on the name of the person they're going to. Or the stamp. Me, I look at the return address. Top left corner, right? I guess I'm more interested in where letters have been than where they're going."

Leeza tried to follow the logic in what she was hearing but gave up, listening instead to the musical quality of the girl's voice. She sounded like one of those radio personalities whose voices run up and down three octaves when delivering everything from ads to late-breaking news.

"So. Where're you from?"

It took Leeza a moment to realize it was a question that required an answer. "Here. I live in Halifax."

"I'm from the Annapolis Valley. Little town called Brookdale, about two hours' drive from here." She chatted about growing up there and how she still lived with her parents; about clerking at the Brookdale Home Hardware store; about Sam, her boyfriend, who worked shifts at the air force base in Greenwood, so he didn't get into the city often to visit but called at least once every day. Brett continued to talk, but Leeza's mind held on to only one fact: the size of Brett's community. "You could probably fit all the people in Brookdale inside this one building," she'd said.

Leeza tried to imagine that. Having everyone you loved in one building. Her house had been like that once. Before Ellen had died. She turned her attention to the ceiling again. Focused on the top left sprinkler. Became aware that the chatter had stopped. A long silence followed, a silence Leeza had neither strength nor inclination to end.

Finally, "Carly told me you were in a car accident."

Leeza didn't respond. It hadn't seemed like a question.

"Uh . . . Anybody die?"

Leeza said nothing for a while, listened to the moaning that filtered through the doorway from somewhere down the hall. Then, "Just me," she said.

Chapter 9

Greg Matheson's rusted Ford Escort hesitated, wheezed and belched blue smoke each time the social worker floored the gas pedal, threading the car in and out of traffic. Several of the Saturday morning drivers passing him made throat-cutting motions, and an attractive young woman on the passenger side of a Land Rover held up a "PUT IT OUT OF ITS MISERY!" sign hastily scrawled on the back of a McDonald's napkin. Greg just smiled and waved good-naturedly, but Reef's face reflected his humiliation, and he avoided eye contact with anyone.

The judge had assigned Reef a new social worker following the hearing, and when he'd first met Matheson he'd been pleasantly surprised. For one thing, Matheson was much younger than all the other social workers he'd had, and he wasn't wearing that Only-Five-More-Years-Till-Retirement look of weary desperation that Reef was so accustomed to seeing on the faces of government employees. They'd talked for a couple hours then about North Hills, what the judge expected of both of them, the whole christly package.

But, to his credit, he'd at least pretended to enjoy meeting Reef, even showed him pictures of his kids, telling him about this one's favorite toy and that one's favorite cartoon show. Not that Reef gave a shit. But it was a break from the Barkers, who'd been watching him like a hawk since the hearing, perhaps afraid they'd be murdered in their beds.

Now, though, as much as he disliked the idea of moving to the North Hills Group Home, he'd have gladly stopped anywhere to avoid being seen in Matheson's geriatric subcompact.

It was bad enough that Scar, Jink and Bigger had been there when Matheson had arrived to collect Reef and his things. Despite the early hour, the Barkers had been out—Saturday was the big open-air flea market in Sackville, and Karl liked to set up early before the crowds arrived. Reef always marveled that people actually bought the junk the Barkers lugged there each weekend. Karl got most of it from the people he delivered mail to—usually seniors with attics or garages filled with stuff they wanted to get rid of. Some of them even paid Karl to take it away, and then he and his wife would clean it up and put ridiculous prices on it so the bargain-hunters could beat them down and everybody walked away feeling good. It didn't matter that most of the things would just end up collecting dust in someone else's attic or garage. It was thinking you'd got a deal, put something over on someone. "Free enterprise at its finest," Karl had described it one

Saturday—the only Saturday—Reef had gone with him. Reef had shaken his head in disgust.

Much as he had when Matheson's Escort had rattled into the driveway to pick him up.

"Jeez, Reef," Bigger had said, "how far you plannin' on gettin' in that thing?"

"End 'a the goddamn driveway," Reef muttered.

"I feel your pain, man," said Jink, watching as the car wheezed to a stop.

Matheson climbed out. "All set?" Reef saw he'd had to lift up hard on the door handle because the bottom hinge was about to let go. As the car idled, an ominous knocking sound reverberated under the hood.

Reef tore his eyes away from the automotive ruin and nodded toward the tattered nylon gym bag sitting on the front step. "Would 'a been all set if you'd called two *minutes* ago. Where ya been the last hour?"

"Had a little trouble with the car."

"Imagine that," Scar murmured.

"Got a neighbor to boost me. I plan on leavin' it running till I get home."

The four teenagers just stared at him.

"Hey, so it's a little old." Matheson grinned. "You just wait till *you've* got a mortgage, Visa bills and kids who need braces. Then we'll see how choosy you are about cars."

Hunkered down now on the passenger side of the Escort, Reef hoped his life never got so pathetic that he wound up driving a shitbox like that and calling it a car. Not that he spent much time thinking about what his life was going to be like. Reef Kennedy lived in the moment. Life was now. Not ten years, ten months, ten *minutes* from now. He could be dead in ten minutes, and riding in this rustbucket only increased the likelihood of that event. Why waste time worrying about couldabeens and gonnabes?

Scar. Now, *she* was a person who thought about gonnabes. She and Reef had been together off and on since they'd met that day on the soccer field, and most of the time she was great to have around. But there'd always been a *What now?* between them that took the edge off whatever feeling he had for her, made him seek out other girls to remind himself—and Scar—that the less you carried with you, the less you had to lose. Reef's Life Lesson Number Three.

He thought now about the goodbyes they'd said above the knock of Matheson's motor. Scar had put her arms around Reef's neck, drawn his face toward hers. She'd kissed him, their tongues a warm tangle for a long moment before she pulled back. "So," she said.

Reef hated situations like these when people expected him to say or do something, like they had a picture of the moment in their heads and he wasn't doing his part to make it happen. He looked at her. Waited.

She turned away, stuck her hands in her jeans pockets, and he tried not to notice the wounded-deer expression on her face. "They tell you anything about what the school's like?" she asked finally.

"It's just a school." He hated that he felt awkward, like he'd been far away for a long time and had just got back. At least, that's how he imagined it would feel. He'd never been out of Nova Scotia. Hell, he'd only been out of Halifax four times, and never farther than Truro. Reef Kennedy: World Traveler.

"Anybody else from the group home go there?"

"Jeez," Bigger said. "What *is* this? Twenty questions?"

Scar's face turned the color of her hair, and she shrugged. "Can't a person be interested? It'll be weird not having him at school with us." Then she grinned. "With *me*, I mean. You two losers are never there anyway."

Bigger grinned back but Jink only stared at her. School was always a sore point with him. Nothing he joked about. Ever. "Yeah," said Jink, "like *you* never miss a day. Or five."

Reef recognized where this was headed, could see Scar suddenly on the defensive. Of the four of them, Scar was the only one who actually enjoyed school, could even make sense of the stuff the teachers made them do. In fact, Reef had overheard Mr. Morse, the principal, telling her in the hall one day how she could be on the honor roll if she really wanted to be. Which was his way of saying come to school every day. But that was her old man's fault, not Scar's.

Scar twisted her face up for a comeback but Reef

interrupted. "I ain't gonna be that far away," he said.

"Might as well be Dorchester," Jink said, referring to the New Brunswick penitentiary where his uncle was serving time for armed robbery. "What's that place called again?"

"North Hills Group Home. Out near Waverley." According to Matheson, a half-hour bus ride, including transfers.

"Any groupies there?" Bigger elbowed Reef in the gut.

Reef jabbed him back. "I wish." This he said for Scar's benefit, too, and it worked. He saw her clench her teeth, the muscles in her jaw tightening in annoyance. But she said nothing.

"Well, man," Jink said as he gripped Reef's hand, "we'll be by to see you after you get settled in."

Greg Matheson cleared his throat. "No can do, guys. At least not for a while. One of the rules."

"Screw the rules," Bigger snarled.

"Yeah, well, that's pretty much been the order of things so far, and where has it got you?" Despite Matheson's smaller size, he didn't seem intimidated by Bigger's bulk. "Unless Reef keeps his nose clean and follows the judge's ruling to the letter," he said, "his next stop very well *could* be Dorchester."

The car lurched now, backfired twice, and emitted a huge plume of blue smoke as Matheson stuck his arm out the window and turned left. "Signal light doesn't work," he said. "Gotta fix that."

"Yeah," Reef muttered. Matheson's arm out the

window was drawing even more attention. "I'd be real worried about that."

Matheson glanced at him and grinned, then pointed right. "Here we are," he said, pumping the brakes and pulling the car into a driveway that led up a short incline to a rambling, two-and-a-half story Victorian structure. Although clearly an older building, it was still impressive. "Used to be a single-family home before someone bought it and cut it up into apartments. After that it went to hell. Frank Colville got it for way less than market value and restored it himself before opening it as a group home. What do you think?"

Reef ignored the building and looked instead at the sign on the narrow front lawn. Above a painted backdrop of rolling hills, a star—which, he presumed, was the North Star, although it looked more like an exaggerated Star of Bethlehem you'd see on Christmas cards and nativity scenes—shone jagged yellow rays down on the silhouette of a figure carrying a heavy load. Reef sighed. If the corny symbolism was any indication of life at North Hills, it was going to be a long twelve months. He grunted noncommittally.

"If you don't mind," Matheson said, "I'm just going to drop you here. I'm low on gas and I want to get the car home before I have to shut it off."

"No problem." Actually, Reef was relieved. The sooner that piece of shit was out of his sight, the better. He reached into the back seat for his gym bag and got out.

"That's Frank, there," Matheson said. "You'll like him. He's a good guy." He leaned across the seat and smiled through the passenger's window at a tall man coming out the door. "Frank!" he called. "How're you doin'?"

"Hey, Greg," Colville replied. "Good to see you, man. Got time for a coffee?"

Matheson shook his head. "Thanks, some other time. Gotta get my car home before it quits on me. This is Chad Kennedy. Goes by Reef." He turned to the teenager. "You're gonna do fine here, Reef. I've already given Frank a copy of your file. I'll stop by in a couple days to see how you're settling in. If you need to talk to me before then, though, you have my number." The Escort sputtered and Matheson revved the engine to keep it from stalling. "Gotta go. You take care 'a yourself, okay?"

"I'll just do that." Reef's sarcasm was lost in the cacophony that was Matheson's departure. The social worker ground the Escort's gearshift into first and the car lurched down the circular driveway to the street, the motor hammering away like someone was trapped under the hood. Reef watched it trail blue clouds that lingered after the vehicle had gone, then turned and climbed several steps to a veranda that stretched the length of the house.

"Greg's still driving the clunker, I see."

Reef looked at the ham-sized hand extended to him, then at the smiling face above it.

"Hi. I'm Frank." The guy looked like an ad for L. L. Bean, his square, rugged face a roadmap of crinkled lines around steel-blue eyes. The plaid shirt and jeans he wore were snug on his large frame, but certainly not because he was overweight. Colville was well over six feet and two hundred pounds, and it was clear from the thickness of his shoulders and arms that what wasn't bone was solid muscle.

To many people meeting him for the first time, Colville would have been an imposing presence on that Victorian veranda, but Reef wasn't intimidated. Life Lesson Number Four: *The bigger they come, the harder they fall.* He looked at Colville's hand for a long moment, then hawked up a wad of phlegm and spat into the bushes at the foot of the step.

Colville's hand dropped to his side, but his smile never faltered. "Glad to have you here, Reef. I've been looking forward to meeting you. So have the others. Bring your bag inside and we'll get you settled before breakfast. We eat late on Saturday mornings."

He turned and led Reef into a large, oak-floored foyer that opened up to a living room on the left and what appeared to be an office on the right. Straight ahead was a hallway and a curved staircase that led to the second floor and beyond. Reef's eyes were drawn to the newel post at the foot of the stairs. Thicker than his thigh, the post was a solid piece of oak, the upper part of the wood ornately carved in the shape of a pineapple and burnished to a high gloss.

"Most people notice that right off," said Colville. "It's hand-carved. Found it in an antique shop in Lunenburg." He moved to the staircase and rested his hand on the pineapple. "My only extravagance, as you'll soon see. I spent more on this than anything else in the whole house. It isn't even Victorian," he said, shaking his head, "but I bought it anyway. It just seemed to belong here."

Reef said nothing, allowed the comment to hang in the air.

"The pineapple is a traditional symbol of hospitality," Colville added. "During colonial days, a host's ability to serve such a rare treat to his guests said a lot about his rank and resourcefulness."

Reef yawned loudly. "You're pretty big on symbols," he said dryly.

Colville grinned. "You're referring to the sign out front, right? Not my idea, really. One of my first residents painted it before he left. It was a gift."

"Some gift." This time there was no roaring motor to mask Reef's sarcasm.

Colville stared at him for a long moment. "Gifts come in many forms," he said. He sat down on the stairs, his long legs draped over several treads. "Your being sent here was a kind of gift, Reef. The judge could have put you some place far worse than North Hills."

Reef snorted. "You think I ain't been in worse places?" he asked.

"No, I'm sure you have. I've read your file. But you're here now. This is day one, okay?"

"What's that s'posed to mean? Some First-Day-Of-The-Rest-Of-Your-Life psychology crap?"

Reef expected a reaction from Colville, but not the one he got. The tall man put his head back and laughed, the deep bass sound almost too loud for the foyer. Even when he stopped, the sound seemed to linger, as if its echo were embedded in the rich wood. "You're a hard case, aren't you?" Colville said at last.

Reef stared at him. "I can take care of myself."

"Right. And that's important. But here you'll learn you have to look beyond yourself. There's a whole world out there that needs taking care of."

"My ass bleeds," Reef replied.

Colville grinned. "Guess I'm not the only one who's big on symbols, eh?"

"Fuck you."

Colville laughed again. Standing up, he said, "This is day one, so that won't cost you. After today, though, every curse out of your mouth will mean a job over and above your regular chores." He nodded his head toward the newel post. "You think this was that shiny when I first bought it? It's had a lot of polishing since North Hills became a group home." He waved his hand toward the rest of the house. "There're always lots of extra jobs that need doing in a place as old as this, Reef. You might want to bear that in mind the next time you feel a 'Fuck you' coming on."

Reef felt far more than that headed his way, but he was also smart enough to know what battles to pick, something his grandfather had taught him well. So he said nothing. Sometimes silence spoke louder than words anyway.

If Colville thought he'd won the first round, he didn't show it. He smiled again and nodded toward the room on the right. "Come into my office and we'll get the rest of the day one stuff taken care of."

"You mean I gotta sign this even if I don't want to?" Reef asked. The document he held in his hands bore an official-looking crest at the top, a miniature black-and-white version of the sign on the front lawn. Although much smaller than the original, it looked even more ridiculous. In Reef's mind, the figure with the heavy load was now a dwarf with a hunchback, and the North Star resembled those aluminum space-ships you saw in "B" movies on late-night TV, hovering ominously in the sky. Looking at that graphic, Reef thought, a person might wonder if North Hills was a home for alien abductees.

"It's a contract," Colville replied, leaning back in his chair. Although crammed with a desk the size of an aircraft carrier, three chairs, two filing cabinets and a bank of shelves filled with binders, the office did not appear disorganized. On the contrary, even the in/out baskets on the huge desk reflected a sense of order and purpose, papers in each arranged neatly rather than dropped carelessly into piles. "And no, you don't have to sign it if you don't want to. It's your choice. Just like it's your choice whether you stay here or not. If you want to stay, you sign it. If you don't, I call Judge Thomas and she arranges for you to spend the next year or so of your life elsewhere. Simple as that."

Yeah. Real simple, thought Reef. Blackmail all dressed up to look like free choice. He wanted to tell Colville to take a flying fuck at the moon, but he wasn't sure how far he could go even on day one.

"Read it," Colville said. "All it says is you understand and agree to abide by North Hills's regulations. They're printed on the back."

Reef turned the paper over, expecting to see dozens of rules all beginning with the words "Do not." Instead, he found five short statements:

> *Respect yourself.*
> *Respect others.*
> *Be accountable.*
> *Honor your commitments.*
> *Do the right thing.*

Reef blinked. "Pretty vague, ain't they?"

Colville shook his head. "They spell out everything I think is important. Like the first one. People who respect themselves don't need to swear to make themselves heard. Nor do they need to put drugs or alcohol into their bodies to keep from feeling the things they can't face. There's a whole lot tied up in those seven letters."

"Please don't get him going," came a voice behind Reef. "He's five seconds away from his Aretha Franklin impression."

Reef turned and saw a teenager with long, blond hair standing in the doorway. The teen's fine features and slim build suggested a female, but the voice was deeper than any girl's Reef had ever heard.

Colville made introductions. "Reef, this is Alex Praeger. Alex, meet Reef Kennedy."

Alex stepped forward and held out his hand. But not like a guy would to shake with another guy. His outstretched hand dangled limply from his wrist. "Charmed," he said.

Reef's face reddened. *Fuckin' fairy.* He glanced at Colville, who was watching him closely, then looked down at the paper in his hands and knew what Colville was waiting for. The second rule. More than anything he wanted to cram that contract up both their asses, but he was fairly certain one of them would enjoy it. He shrugged, took the fairy's hand and shook it quickly. "Hi," he grunted.

"We're almost finished here, Alex," Colville said. "In a minute I'll get you to give Reef the ten-cent tour. That is, if he's staying."

Reef shot Colville a look that would have withered

granite, but Colville only smiled. "So," he said, nodding toward the contract, one eyebrow elevated in an expression Reef could not read. "You signing or not?"

Reef gripped the contract in his hands and fought the urge to shred it. Maybe Dorchester wasn't such a bad alternative after all. But then he thought of the stories he'd heard about prison homos and gang rapes. Probably better dealing with one fag here than five there. Or fifty. He took the pen Colville held out to him and signed his name at the bottom, then passed both the pen and the paper back to him.

Colville put the contract in a folder and stood up, holding out his hand. "Welcome to North Hills, Reef."

Despite the urge to do otherwise, Reef shook it.

"And this is *your* room," Alex said. His long-sleeved silk shirt made a shirring sound as he opened the door with a flourish. "You're right across the hall from *me*."

Colville was right—if you were paying by the hour, it was a ten-cent tour. Alex had first shown Reef the grounds. Besides the postage-stamp lawn and sign out front, there was a back yard with some large trees, a deck with the biggest barbecue Reef had ever seen, an herb garden and an old greenhouse. Along with the living room, foyer and office, the first floor included a large kitchen, a dining room, a bathroom and a family room, the last of which his guide had gushed over. "Ooooh, the *family* room," he'd bubbled. "Just wait till you see what happens in *there!*" Resisting the urge to tell the fag to fuck himself, Reef had swallowed his disgust and followed him up to the second floor, where there were six bedrooms and two baths, then to the third floor, where, because of the sloped ceilings, there were only three bedrooms and one bath. Reef's room was on the third floor and, although it was small, he liked the view from the windows that filled two semicircular areas at both ends.

"The slanted ceilings make it awfully narrow," Alex said, "but you have turrets."

Second rule or no second rule, Reef lost it. "Look, you freak!" he roared. "*You* may have problems but there's nothin' wrong with *me!* I ain't got Tourette's, and I'll kick the shit outta anyone who says different. Including that sonuvabitch Colville downstairs!"

Alex's face flickered through several different reactions, like those flip-books that kids make in school when they're bored, riffling the edges of their looseleaf to make a figure change expressions. Alex's showed surprise, then confusion and, finally, hilarity. Nearly choking with laughter, he managed to gasp, "Oh, Reef honey, are you for *real?*"

Reef's face reflected his own astonishment, and, for the first time in a very long while, he could think of nothing to say.

Chapter 10

"Almost finished," Carly Reynolds said as she inserted Leeza's morning catheter.

Leeza stared at the ceiling and tried not to think about what the nurse was doing. Although her catheter was changed four times daily, she was still mortified by the procedure. Her problem was the reverse of the incontinent residents at Silver Meadows. Because her muscles had been stretched by the accident and during the subsequent surgery that repaired her pelvis, her bladder was unable to empty itself voluntarily. In the weeks ahead, this would be one of many things that physiotherapy would strive to correct. Until then, however, she would continue to be subjected to the indignity of plastic tubes and urine bags.

Carly seemed aware of Leeza's embarrassment and changed the subject. "It's okay if you want to put out some personal items, Leeza. Pictures, knickknacks, things like that. This is going to be your home for several weeks, so feel free to make it look that way. Brett certainly has."

Leeza had already seen the myriad photographs of a good-looking young man pinned to the wall above the other bed and mounted in frames on a table by the window. Sam, of course. But Leeza had no intention of trying to make this place look like home. Her silence said so.

The nurse seemed bent on coaxing her into conversation. "I see from your chart that you had a restless night. The first one's always the hardest," she explained, as she finished the procedure and drew back the privacy curtain, "but believe it or not, you get used to it."

Leeza doubted that. Despite the medication the night nurse had given her, she had woken several times, pulled from sleep by pain that throbbed her to consciousness. Pain like the icy knife drawn up and down her body now, slowing momentarily to jab and twist into a nerve before moving on to another target. But there were other times during the night when she'd been woken by something else, by sounds from down the hall. Eerie, guttural cries that, at first, she thought she'd made herself. Embarrassed, she'd forced the corner of her pillow into her mouth, then listened in surprise as the sounds had continued, rising and falling with siren-like regularity.

"Who's the—?" She stopped, unsure how to phrase the question.

"The screamer?"

Leeza turned her head slightly to see Brett enter, expertly guiding her wheelchair past the nurse's trolley, beds and visitors' chairs that dotted the beige landscape of their room. "Amazing as this may seem to you now," Brett said as she pulled toothpaste and a toothbrush out of a drawer by her bed, "you'll even get used to *him*."

"Who . . . ?" Leeza's voice trailed off. It seemed wrong somehow to be talking this way about a patient she didn't even know.

"Stephen Hayes. Private room three doors down," explained Brett.

Carly popped an electronic thermometer into Leeza's ear. "Stephen has been here over two years. Had an accident with a four-wheeler. Along with other injuries, he received severe trauma to his brain. He's quiet much of the time, but he tends to shout when he gets agitated."

"And not just at night," Brett said as she wheeled herself into the bathroom and closed the door behind her.

"She's right," Carly agreed. "Could be any time." The thermometer beeped, and the nurse pulled it out, read it and made a notation on Leeza's chart.

"T-two years?"

The nurse glanced up from the chart and saw the look of astonishment on the girl's face. "His rehabilitation hasn't taken that long, Leeza. He's only here because we haven't been able to place him. There just isn't an opening in a facility suitable for him to go to. Not yet, anyway."

As if on cue, a low moan from down the hallway rose to a shriek that lasted several seconds before tapering off into silence. "You *do* get used to it," Carly continued. "And at least it's not all the time. We've had other patients do that their whole stay."

At that moment, Leeza bit back a shriek of her own and gasped as the phantom knife slashed at her, leaving her weak and trembling.

Carly glanced at her watch and made another note on the chart. "Almost finished. Then I'll give you a needle for pain. You're just about due for one anyway." She applied a pressure cuff around Leeza's arm and pumped the bulb, listening through her stethoscope and watching the pulse of the silver liquid. "You know, most people hearing Stephen for the first time get this mental picture of someone being tortured by sadistic nurses. It's really not like that. He has a good quality of life. His outbursts are just part of his day." After recording Leeza's blood pressure, she removed the cuff, swabbed her upper arm and then drew some liquid from a vial into a syringe. "This will take the edge off," she said.

She was right. Moments after the injection, Leeza could feel the icy knife grow warm and dull. It was still there in the background, still moving, searching for something vulnerable, but it no longer jabbed and twisted into her. It was like an echo—a muted imitation of the original. Leeza smiled.

"Makes you wonder what you'd get for that stuff on the street, doesn't it?" Brett asked, grinning from the bathroom doorway.

Leeza smiled again. "Mmm," she said, then slept.

When she opened her eyes, her mother was sitting in a chair by her bed reading a magazine. "Hungry?" she asked, getting up.

Leeza was surprised to find that, yes, she *was* hungry. She tried to say so, but her tongue was a wool sock. She nodded.

Her mother pulled her tray table within easy reach, lifted a glass of whole milk and brought a straw to her lips. Leeza grimaced. She hadn't drunk milk since she was in junior high. "Calcium," her mother said. "You need it for your bones."

Leeza drew the liquid into her mouth, nearly gagged on its creaminess, had to force herself to swallow. "N'more," she said.

Her mother shook her head. "Yes, more. There are lots of things on the list you aren't going to like, but you'll have to eat them anyway. They'll help speed up the healing process."

"List?" Leeza asked.

"Aaah, the list. Sounds sinister, doesn't it?" Leeza

and her mother looked up to see a young woman enter the room. "Hi, Leeza. I'm Valerie Harris. Everyone calls me Val. And you must be Mrs. Hemming." She held out her hand and shook Diane's.

"Morrison, actually," said Leeza's mother. "I remarried."

"Oh. Sorry."

"Don't be. I prefer Diane anyway."

"Nice to meet you, Diane." The woman turned to Leeza. "Hope I'm not interrupting anything, but we're on a schedule."

"Are you a volunteer?" asked Leeza's mother.

The young woman grinned at her. "We do have volunteers here, but I'm not one of them. I'm Leeza's physiotherapist."

Leeza was as surprised as her mother now looked. With her small frame, short dark hair and a dusting of freckles on her nose and cheeks, the person standing in front of them looked more like a teenager than a health care worker.

"Oh, I'm very sorry—" Leeza's mother began, but the young woman interrupted her.

"Happens all the time. My husband tells me there'll come a day when I'll be glad I look like a high school student. I'd just settle for not being asked to show my ID at R-rated movies."

Diane returned her smile. "Trust me, your husband's right."

The physiotherapist grinned again, then turned to Leeza. "I'd like to go over your treatment before we get started, if that's okay with you. I know your doctor told you some things already, but I always think it's best if there are no surprises. Surprises sometimes have a way of becoming setbacks."

Leeza nodded, and she and her mother listened as the woman outlined the various forms of therapy she would be receiving, the progression toward full mobility, indicators of improvement such as weight-bearing status and a dozen other aspects of her rehabilitation. Then, when she'd finished, she asked Leeza's mother if she would mind leaving. Seeing Diane's surprised expression, she continued, "Your support is extremely important. In fact, there are some therapies that Leeza's doctor and I will want you to be directly involved with. It's just that the first day can be tough and Leeza will need to focus. That's sometimes easier when no one else is here. Please don't be offended."

"Not at all," Leeza's mother said as she stood up. "I'm sure you know best." She moved to Leeza's bed and leaned down to kiss her. "I'll be back this evening, okay?"

It wasn't okay. Maybe it was hearing about all she'd be going through in the weeks and months ahead. Maybe it was the look of apprehension she'd seen in her mother's eyes. Or maybe it was just the ominous sound of the words "the first day." But Leeza nodded anyway, hoping her mother wouldn't see the fear in her own.

"So," the physiotherapist said when Leeza's mother had left, "are you ready for day one?"

Chapter 11

"Everybody, this is Reef. *Saaaay hiiiiiiii!*" Alex's voice fluttered up and down with his hands, which gestured like those of a game-show girl revealing the prize behind curtain number one. Standing in the kitchen doorway, Reef felt like anything *but* a prize. More like a contestant who'd wandered into a freak show by mistake and couldn't get out without answering a skill-testing question. The only problem was that nobody knew what the question was, just the penalty for losing: The Next Twelve Months Of Your Life.

"Hi, Reef." The combined greetings from the four other people in the kitchen sounded false, like the singsongy welcome a bunch of preschoolers might give someone new at daycare. Three had barely glanced up, while a short kid, who looked like he belonged in daycare himself, ignored him completely. He sat at the kitchen counter staring at the back of a Cheerios box while slowly shoveling spoonful after spoonful of the soggy circles into his mouth, milk dribbling down his chin.

Before coming back downstairs, Reef had unpacked

while Alex had filled him in about the staff—there were two part-timers who came on alternate days— and the other residents, who had already begun heading down to breakfast.

"Don't you mean inmates?" Reef had asked as he'd shoved socks and underwear into the top drawer of a dresser, then put his three T-shirts and two pairs of jeans in the drawers below. He'd hung his jean jacket in the closet and left his toothbrush, comb and razor sitting on the dresser top. He had nothing else.

"Reef honey, you don't *ever* want Frank to catch you using *that* word."

Reef gritted his teeth to keep from shoving Alex's "honey" down his goddamn throat. Once he got the lay of the land, though, he'd be putting that little faggot in his place fast, along with anyone else who thought they could say what they wanted to Reef Kennedy without paying the price.

"Why? Colville have a problem with the truth?"

Alex looked at him and grinned. "You don't know, do you?"

"Know what?"

"Frank's story."

Reef scowled. "I've had more social workers than I can remember, and every one of 'em had a story. Spare me the bleeding heart bullshit."

But Alex didn't. He told Reef how Colville had a rap sheet as long as his arm. Disturbing the peace, assault, breaking and entering, theft, possession of illegal substances. "You name it," Alex said, "Frank did it, and most of it before he was twenty. He did some time in Dorchester."

"So how d'you know all this?"

"They did a write-up on him a while back in some magazine. About how he cleaned himself up, kicked the drug monkey, stuff like that. When he got out of prison, he began an outreach program for kids in trouble, then got together enough money to buy this place. I think he got funding from somewhere to help with fixing it up."

Reef was unimpressed. "Thinks he's the original bad boy, huh?" He snorted, thinking of Rowdy Brewster and his crew. "I know guys who'd eat him for breakfast. Colville don't scare me."

Alex stared at him for a moment. Then, grinning, he struck a classic Hollywood diva pose and breathed, "Hold onto your hats, boys, 'cause it's gonna be a bumpy ride."

Reef smiled in spite of himself. Yeah, it'd be a bumpy ride all right. Until Frank Colville finally figured out who the driver was around here.

Coming downstairs, Alex had given Reef thumbnail sketches of the other guys currently living at North Hills: Gordy Towers, seventeen, multiple substance abuser; Owen White, sixteen, glue-sniffer and chronic runaway; Keith Benjamin, also sixteen, shoplifter extraordinaire; and Jimmy Franz, fourteen, pyromaniac with anger management issues. There had been two other residents until the previous week, but one had broken his contract and got sent back to Riverview, and the other, as Alex put it, had graduated.

"Graduated?"

"You know, came out the other end. Turned citizen."

Reef had no idea what any of that meant, nor did he care. "So what's your story?" he asked as they reached the foyer. He could have guessed, but he was curious what the homo would tell him.

Alex slid a long-sleeved arm around the carved pineapple newel post and batted his eyelashes. "Oh, honey, there's just *soooo* much to tell. You're gonna have to wait for the movie."

Standing in the kitchen now, Reef put faces to the names Alex had given him earlier. It wasn't hard to tell which one was Gordy. The tallest of the group, he looked ghoulish: skin so white it was almost transparent, the blue veins on his arm writhing like snakes as he poured himself a glass of orange juice. The Cheerios kid, the shortest, was obviously Jimmy, and Reef tried to imagine what would motivate someone who couldn't bother to wipe the milk off his mouth to go to the trouble of starting fires. He got the other two wrong. Owen, the glue-sniffer, wasn't the overweight, acne-faced guy with the ring in his nose who was buttering what looked to be a whole loaf of bread. That was Keith. Owen, slicing up a banana, was the most normal-looking one of the bunch—slim, athletic type with short dark hair, square jaw, perfect teeth. The kind of guy you'd expect to see wearing Hilfiger sweats shooting hoops with his buddies while his cheerleader girlfriend watched from her daddy's BMW. Go figure.

Just then, Frank Colville came into the kitchen. "Morning, fellas."

"Morning, Frank," they all chorused, and Reef noticed even Jimmy looked up for that greeting.

"I see everyone's met Reef. Thanks, Alex."

"My *pleasure*, Frank," Alex said, flashing Reef a Colgate smile. Keith turned toward the pair and whistled, and Gordy made loud kissing noises.

Reef felt his neck and cheeks burn. He'd have given anything to knock Alex's smile clear into next year, followed immediately by Keith and Gordy's shit-eating grins.

"Guys, does that sound respectful to you?"
Sudden silence.

Then, "Sorry, Frank," said Keith.

"Me, too," Gordy mumbled.

"I'm not the person you should be apologizing to."

The two turned to Reef and Alex. "Sorry."

Reef shrugged. Their apology meant nothing—he was just surprised they'd given in so quickly. They didn't *look* like pussies.

"You get anything to eat, Reef?" Frank asked.

"I'm not hungry."

"If you change your mind, just help yourself." Frank turned to Owen. "You're on kitchen detail this week, right?"

Owen nodded.

"I'm putting Reef on with you."

"No problem," Owen said.

"Everybody doubles up on jobs here, Reef. There's a list on the wall in my office, and you'll rotate through different duties. You and Owen will be partnered up for the next few days."

Like I fucking care, Reef thought. But he realized Colville was waiting for a response, so he nodded. Noncommittally.

"Part of being accountable involves letting me know where you are at all times. You don't leave without my say-so, and where you go must be approved by me. You call to let me know you got there, and if something comes up and you're going to be late getting back, you call and let me know that, too."

"Right." Like *that*'ll happen. "Anything else?"

"Just that I want you to feel free to come talk about anything at any time."

"Right." *That*'ll happen, too.

Colville studied him for a moment, then nodded toward the back door that opened onto the deck. "Come with me for a minute, okay?"

He led Reef outside, across the deck and through the back yard toward the greenhouse. Close up, Reef could see a number of glass panels were cracked, and here and there some were missing. Colville stopped and turned to Reef. "You're giving me lip service right now. Most new residents do. I expect that."

Reef said nothing.

Colville seemed to expect that, too. "Sooner or later, though, you and I are going to have to come to an understanding. It'd save us both a lot of headaches if it was sooner."

Reef just looked at him.

"See this greenhouse, Reef?"

"I'm not blind."

"It's your responsibility now."

"So what's that mean? I dust every Thursday?"

A muscle twitched in Colville's lower jaw, but he showed no other reaction to Reef's sarcasm. "Those cracked and missing panels need to be replaced. There's a tape measure in the tool drawer in the kitchen. Just ask one of the guys to show you. And there's usually paper and pencils on the counter." He turned and headed back toward the house.

"And those would be for . . . ?" Reef trailed off.

Colville never broke his stride. "You're a smart guy," he called over his shoulder. "I'm sure you'll be able to figure it out for yourself." When he got to the door, he turned. "Oh, and don't forget you're on kitchen detail with Owen." He went inside.

Reef stood looking at the door, anger scrabbling up his throat, its sharp taste souring his mouth. "You prick," he muttered, and his eyes scoured the loose soil around the greenhouse. It took him only seconds to find what he was searching for. He bent down and pried it loose from the ground, brushed the dirt from its rough surface, took several steps back, then threw the rock as hard as he could, shattering one of the greenhouse panels. Reef smiled, suddenly feeling better than he'd felt in weeks.

"One more thing."

He turned to see Colville standing in the open kitchen doorway.

"The other part of being accountable is paying for your mistakes. The money to fix that panel you just broke comes out of your own pocket."

"Fuck you!" Reef said, but Colville had already gone back inside. Reef's face twisted and he ground his teeth, felt a sudden coppery taste in his mouth as he bit the inside of his cheek. He raised his hand to his lips, brought it away red, made fists that clenched and unclenched uselessly there in the back yard.

Chapter 12

No one could have prepared Leeza for the agony she experienced that first day. Lying in bed focusing on the top left sprinkler and waiting for her next shot of morphine was one thing. Being forced to get out of that bed was another entirely. She'd been astonished when Val had told her she'd be going down to the fourth floor to meet "the team."

"What team?" Leeza asked. The morphine in her system made her tongue thick and lethargic and she had to concentrate to form her words.

"The specialists assigned to assist in your recovery. Along with Carly and me, there's your doctor, an occupational therapist, a vocational counselor and a social worker."

"Why so many?" Leeza couldn't have cared less if there'd been two hundred people assigned to her. She was just stalling, hoping Carly would return to explain that clearly a mistake had been made, that there was no way she could be expected to get out of that bed, let alone into a wheelchair. She suddenly realized why

Val had asked her mother to leave. Now Carly was Leeza's only hope.

But when the nurse entered the room moments later, it was only to assist Val in getting her patient up.

"Each person on the team has a different function. You've only heard mine," Val explained, slowly raising the head of Leeza's bed to its maximum incline. The gradual shift in Leeza's center of gravity put new weight on different areas of her body, the flesh around her pin-sites tugging at the fixators and producing brand-new degrees of pain.

"I can't—" Leeza gasped, "—do this!" Even with the morphine in her system, the spasms that accompanied this upright position were unbearable.

"Yes, you can, Leeza."

It took Leeza a moment to realize it was Brett who had said this. She hadn't even been aware her roommate was still in the room. "No! I can't!" she hissed. Her body was trembling uncontrollably, and for a moment she was sure she'd split right down the middle and whatever wasn't pinned or stapled or riveted together would spill out onto the bed. "Make them stop!"

"Leeza," said Brett, "everybody goes through this. I did, too. It's the worst part. But you have to do it."

"No! I don't!" Leeza panted as she spoke, the words coming in short puffs through clenched teeth. "If they need to see me, make them come here!"

"Leeza, take a minute and breathe slowly." Val's

voice was low and even, a soothing contrast to the ratcheting in Leeza's chest. "I want you to listen to me. Focus on the sound of my voice."

Tears slid down Leeza's face. Ashamed, she tried to turn away, but this movement only produced new spasms, and she choked back sobs.

"Leeza, honey," said Val, "you *can* do this. Just focus on my voice. I want you to picture a place in your head."

Leeza sobbed again. "I *can't!*"

Val gently took Leeza's hand and put herself directly in the girl's line of vision. "We're going to do something called imaging. It'll help. Picture a safe place. It can be real or one you imagine. It's a place you can go to in your head when the pain gets too great."

Leeza gulped, ground her teeth, tried to focus.

"Think of somewhere you went when you were younger that made you feel good, made you feel happy. Or picture a place you've always dreamed of going, a place where everything is warm and soft and soothing."

Leeza again tried to focus, tried to empty her head and think of places she had been or wanted to go. Nothing. Another wave of pain surged through her, this one a breaker complete with jagged whitecap, and she cried out.

"Keep trying," Val said. "It'll come." She continued to speak, her tone low and soothing as she urged Leeza to concentrate, to open her mind and allow the images to form.

Leeza let the waves of Val's words wash over her and, in doing this, she remembered a place from her early childhood, a place where she and Ellen had gone with their mother one summer on Nova Scotia's Northumberland Shore. It was the summer of their parents' divorce, and their mother had taken the girls away to give their father time to pack and move out. Diane had rented a cottage at Pictou Lodge, and, soon after they'd unpacked, she'd driven west along the coast looking for a place where the girls could swim. By accident, she'd stumbled on Skinner's Cove, a tiny fishing community that wrapped around a secluded harbor, a sea-grayed wharf separating half a dozen boats on one side from a deserted stretch of sand on the other.

Diane had parked the car and urged the girls out, and they'd trudged after her, listlessly carrying the blanket, water toys and picnic basket over the dune and down to the sea. The previous weeks had been difficult for the girls, the first time they'd come to understand that nothing was forever. They hadn't wanted this trip, had wanted only to stay home, to hold on to whatever fragile permanence they could still find there.

Diane had nearly had to drag them into the water, but once in, all three had delighted in its bath-like temperature. Accustomed to the icy waters of the beaches near Halifax, they later learned that the water of the shallower Northumberland Strait was easily warmed by the sun-heated sand over which it ebbed and flowed. They'd reveled in being able to walk out dozens of yards and still stand only waist-deep in the water. Diane had brought them back to that tiny cove every day of their stay—it was as though the warm waves had a healing effect on all three of them, caressing, rocking, lifting them out of themselves and teaching them how to smile again.

It was the water of Skinner's Cove that Leeza pictured now, imagined herself and Ellen floating in, suspended weightless above the warm sand. Gulls floated lazily above them, their cries distant and muted, much like the pain that ebbed from Leeza now.

"When you think you're ready," Val said softly, "let me know."

A minute passed, then another. Leeza knew she would never be ready, never wanted to leave the moment she'd made in her head, but finally she whispered, "Okay."

Carly positioned a piece of plywood between Leeza's body and a wheelchair by the bed. Varnished to a high gloss, the wood was nearly frictionless as the nurse and physiotherapist eased her down the board and into the chair. The teenager gasped and clenched her teeth during the procedure, but she managed to keep from crying out, focusing instead on the warmth of the water and the sand in her mind. When she was at last sitting in the chair, she glanced up and smiled. It was a fleeting expression, but Val and Carly could see the triumph behind it. So could Brett, who cheered loudly from across the room. "You *go*, girl!" Brett put her fingers between her lips and blew, producing a shrill whistle that echoed down the hallway beyond their room. "You'll be racin' with us wheelers in no time!"

Carly raised her eyes heavenward. "Oh, Lord," she sighed, "what have we done now?"

This time, Leeza's smile lasted longer, and she gave Brett a feeble thumbs-up.

"All set?" Val asked her.

"Never better," she lied.

The rest of the day was no less arduous, and pain was the constant companion who shared Leeza's wheelchair.

The meeting with the specialists was more a chance for Leeza to meet them than an opportunity for any formal assessment of her condition. That would take place in the days ahead as they monitored her progress and responded to her needs, both physical and emotional. Their names were a blur of syllables, and the only one she remembered that morning was the physician assigned to her case. His last name was at least a dozen letters long—Dandenshefsky or Danderhelsky (and quite possibly something entirely different)—but he'd apparently taken pity on patients and staff and now told everyone to call him Dr. Dan.

He began by asking Leeza if she had any questions. There were so many that the words had tumbled over each other in her mind, the throb of each pin-site making coherent speech a challenge. But she managed to make her mouth form the one question that was her most immediate concern: "How . . . how long will I have the catheter?"

"Hopefully," explained the doctor, "not more than a month. Six weeks at the most, depending on how your muscles spring back. Trust me, I don't want you to have it any longer than you do. There's always risk of infection with a catheter, and an infection would slow the healing process."

And it would be quite a process. The team members clarified their roles in Leeza's treatment, giving her specific details so she would know what she could expect of each in the weeks ahead. At times, Leeza was sure they had her mixed up with someone else, someone who could actually *do* the things they described. Besides the several kinds of physiotherapies she would undergo daily, she would eventually cook some simple meals, do her own laundry and take part in a variety of activities designed to reacquaint patients with life in the outside world. They seemed oblivious to the fact that, at that very moment, Leeza wanted nothing more than two minutes without a buzzsaw ripping at every nerve.

Surprisingly, the team had some good news for her.

Initially, the group had been worried that Leeza might experience embolisms, obstructions of blood vessels caused by clots not uncommon after a bad fracture. Fortunately, though, she had experienced no shortness of breath associated with pain, which was the telltale sign of embolismic distress, and because of the length of time that had passed since the accident, Dr. Dan felt it unlikely that she would. In addition, her age was in her favor. He explained that, because teenagers had greater energy and more rapid healing processes, they recovered much faster than older patients. According to the physician, while someone her mother's age or older might take five or six months to heal, Leeza could—depending on her commitment to her rehabilitation—expect to reduce that time to three months. Of course, that would be followed by at least six weeks of outpatient therapy, but she would be home then and able to begin resuming normal activities.

When the meeting ended an hour and a half later, Leeza's body was no longer at the mercy of the buzzsaw. She *was* the buzzsaw, every muscle part of the mechanism that churned and roared in her head. With her one good hand, she brushed at tears that formed in the corners of her eyes, ashamed of her weakness yet unable to make the tears stop.

Val saw her tears, produced a tissue and murmured that it was probably time for Leeza to rest.

Leeza smiled gratefully, but the tears didn't stop until she was again lying in her bed, her second morphine shot of the day cradling her, lifting her, carrying her toward the sand and waves of Skinner's Cove.

"We've increased your dosage," Carly explained when Leeza awoke shortly after noon.

Leeza's head felt fuzzy, and her tongue was, if possible, even thicker than it had been that morning, but the pain was not as insistent. She could still feel it waiting in the background, circling like some long-toothed creature ready to pounce, but each time the creature caught her in its mouth, its teeth slid harmlessly over her. She smiled. "Mmm," she said.

"It takes the doctors a while to find each patient's baseline. Everyone's different. But you should be more comfortable now."

"Mmm," Leeza said again. She sensed the creature's annoyance. Taunted it. *Bite me*, she told it, then smiled at her unintentional pun.

"Lunch came while you were asleep," said Carly. She pointed to the tray in front of her, and Leeza was suddenly aware of her hunger.

"But don't be gettin' used to those meals on wheels," came Brett's voice from the other side of the room. "You only get a few more days of the invalid treatment, you know. By the end of next week you'll be

eating with the rest of us in the lounge down the hall."
She smiled. "Everyone's looking forward to meeting
you."

"Mmm . . . mmeet me?" she asked.

"Yeah, it's quite a group we got here." She began
listing the other patients on the floor, but Leeza wasn't
listening to the names, injuries and character sketches
that Brett reeled off. For the first time, she was thinking about what it would be like to meet people now. In
her present condition. She suddenly thought about all
the times she'd told people in the past that she felt "like
a wreck." She'd been wrong. She'd really had no idea
what a wreck felt like. Or looked like.

But she did now.

She ignored the food Carly uncovered, her appetite
suddenly gone.

"So, I hear you had quite a day," said Leeza's mother.

Quite a day. Three words. Words Leeza had often
used herself when she'd visited Ellen and, later, the
kids at the Children's Hospital. The kind of meaningless comment you make when you really have no idea
what someone has been through. Quite a day, indeed.

Her mother had run into Brett in the hallway. Or,
more accurately, Brett and another wheeler had
almost run into her. Despite what Brett must have told
Diane, though, Leeza could tell her mother really

wasn't prepared for the obvious toll the day's events had taken on her. Nor, in fact, was Leeza, who, following another nap that afternoon, had used a mirror to assess the damage. She looked like the "before" shot in those make-over pictures she often saw in magazines. Her skin, already pale from weeks in a hospital room, now seemed ashen, and her face had a waxen quality that reminded her of the rubber masks her mother used to buy her and Ellen at Hallowe'en. Disney characters with permanent smiles. How many times, she wondered, had she ended up sobbing behind those smiles? The time she fell while walking down a neighbor's front steps, her mask blocking her view. Or the time she'd dropped her whole bag of Hallowe'en candy in a puddle while crossing the street behind Ellen.

As she grew older, of course, she'd learned you didn't need a Disney mask to hide behind. You could paint a pretty convincing mask of your own when you knew how. You just had to get the muscles all pointed in the right direction and then concentrate on holding everything together. Like the day her mother had told them about the divorce. And then when they'd learned their father was marrying the flight attendant he'd had the affair with and was moving with her to Toronto. And again when it became clear Leeza and Ellen weren't his first—or even his fourth or fifth—priority, that weeks without seeing him would become months, and then years.

And, of course, when the doctor had told them about Ellen.

"Yes," she said to her mother now. "I've had quite a day."

Her toneless comment hung in the air, and her mother made no attempt to press her further. "I've been meaning to tell you," she said, reaching into her purse and pulling out a piece of paper. "The school called shortly after the accident. Your teachers agreed to disregard the final exams you missed, and they made up their marks based on your semester's work. I've been carrying your report card around in my purse but I kept forgetting to show it to you. Do you want to see it?"

Leeza made a sound that could have been a yes or a no. Diane rummaged through a purse the size of a beach bag and pulled out a brown envelope. She opened it, took out the report card and held it up for her daughter to see. "Great marks. The lowest was the 88 in chemistry. You beat Jennifer."

Leeza's eyes widened, revealing interest for the first time. "You've seen her? Jen?"

"A while ago," Diane said. "She and Robin brought me the report card."

A while ago. Leeza turned away.

Diane continued brightly, as if unaware of the pall that had settled over them. "I've been meaning to let them know you've been transferred here. But what with the hearing and all—" She stopped suddenly, tried to recover. "I'll give them a call later. I'm sure they'll—"

"Hearing." Leeza repeated the word as if it were foreign to her, as if she were trying it out, seeing how it sounded, how it felt in her mouth. She said it again, remembering. "What happened?"

Diane busied herself putting the report card back into the envelope. "When would you like to see them? Robin and Jennifer."

"What happened at the hearing?"

Diane sighed. "Leezie, honey, there's no point in—"

"What *happened*?"

Diane looked at the envelope in her hands, studied the torn parts where she'd opened it. She looked at Leeza, as though trying not to see *her* torn parts, kept her voice low and even as she explained what had happened that last day at the courthouse. Leeza had heard her use that low and even voice only once before. On the phone with Proule's Funeral Home making arrangements. As though, in the act of accepting the inevitable, she had given up some part of herself.

Neither of them said anything for a while. It was Leeza who finally spoke first. "Why'd he do it?"

"Because . . ." her mother began, then stopped. She took a breath, released it before continuing. "Because he wanted to," she said.

Another silence. Then, "And he just gets . . ." The

words caught in Leeza's throat. She could make no more.

"He gets nothing," her mother finished. She put her arms around Leeza as gently as she could, held her while both of them wept.

Chapter 13

"Your turn, Reef," said Frank Colville.

Everyone in the family room looked at Reef, waiting for him to speak. Reef hated this part more than anything else, but he knew by now that they'd go on waiting until he spoke. One of Colville's rules: *Honor your commitments.* And at North Hills, one of your commitments was spilling your guts in the family room every night at 6:00. "Issue exploration" was Colville's name for it, but what it amounted to was a whine-and-whimper session when everybody got to bitch about something that was bothering him and everyone else got to suggest—what did Colville call it?—"strategies for resolving the problem," or some such bullshit. And somehow the process was supposed to "empower them." Another of Colville's phrases. Right.

It wasn't that Reef didn't have things to complain about. Hell, if he'd *wanted* to, he'd have ranted nonstop about what life the last two weeks had been like. He'd have said how listening to a bunch of losers moan over how misunderstood they were was enough to make him puke. How their infighting and back-stabbing were worse than any group of girls he'd ever seen. How those goddamn "weekly duties" Colville assigned them were a pain in the ass and he'd give anything not to wash another dish, clean another shower or vacuum another rug—unless, of course, it was his *own* dish, shower and rug that he didn't have to share with these dickheads. At the top of his list, though, would be that fucking greenhouse out back. The thing hadn't been used in years, yet for some reason it was Reef's job to repair it, like world food production would rise 10 percent once he managed to replace all those broken panels. He only had to look at the bandages on his fingers to remind himself what Issue Number One was for Reef Kennedy.

But, of course, he didn't say any of those things. Frank Colville was a few bricks short of a load if he thought Reef was going to take part in all that touchy-feely family room sharing shit. So Reef fell back on his old standby: the lack of toilet paper in the third floor bathroom. Although he'd already used that one a few times, he didn't have the energy—or the inclination—to make up something else. And besides, since Alex was still the only other "resident" on the third floor, Reef was pretty sure he could count on the fairy to take offense and launch into his wounded drama queen routine, which was always good for a laugh. That is, if you could forget about rule number two. In the last two weeks, though, Reef had learned how to laugh on the inside without letting anyone know he was busting a gut at their expense.

The room was oddly quiet and he looked up to see everyone staring at him. Even Alex was silent, apparently now impervious to the toilet paper attack. One of Colville's eyebrows was raised, an expression everyone including Reef now recognized as one of impatience. "Somethin' else?" Reef asked.

Colville made a tent with his fingers and he studied them for a moment. Then, turning his gaze on Reef, he sighed and leaned back in his chair. "Why are you wasting everyone's time, Reef?"

Reef returned his stare without blinking. "I wasn't the one who came up with this family room sh—" He paused for just a second, remembering how his profanity had earned him more than a few "extra jobs" since day one. He continued carefully, "—stuff. If you don't wanna hear what's botherin' me, don't ask the question."

Colville's expression did not change. He brought his hands up and pressed his index fingers to his lips, then lowered his hands and folded them in his lap. "I *do* want to hear what's bothering you, Reef. We *all* do. That's why I'm asking the question."

"And I *told* you—"

Colville cut him off. "Don't you ever get tired of playing the part?"

Reef blinked. "What part?"

"The I-don't-need-anybody-tough-guy routine. Doesn't it get old after a while?"

It was Reef's turn to look at his fingers. He tried not to make fists. For one thing, his fingers hurt—he wasn't used to working with a hammer, and its metal head had found his fingers nearly as often as the nails they'd held. But he also didn't want to give Colville the satisfaction of knowing he'd hit home. "I don't need a routine," he said.

Colville leaned forward. "That's where you're wrong, Reef. We all need routines. Most human beings can't handle a life that's always in flux. We'd go crazy if there weren't constants we could depend on. We instinctively look for patterns, and when we don't find them, we create our own. It's our innate need for security, for normalcy."

"But you don't think I'm normal, is that it?" Reef fought the urge to stand up, cross the room and ram his bandage-covered knuckles into Colville's face.

"On the contrary, Reef, I think you're *very* normal. It's just that you've become so good at sustaining the patterns you've created that you can't see a way outside them."

Reef swallowed, the sound in his throat like air bubbling up through ketchup. *Two minutes outside with you alone, you sonuvabitch. With no court ruling, no group home regulations, no "additional duties"—nothing. Just you and me. Then we'd see what patterns I could create, all right. On your fucking face.*

Reef was suddenly conscious of five other pairs of eyes on him, their owners waiting for his response with open-mouthed interest.

"Do me a favor," Colville said.

Reef blinked again. "Favor?"

"Be honest. With me, with us, with yourself. Say one thing you'd like to see happen here that would make a difference to you."

Reef let the moments pile up on each other, let the silence occupy space in that room. Then, "I'd like to see toilet paper in the third-floor bathroom."

"Jeez, man, you sure get off on yankin' Frank's chain." Owen pointed the remote at the television, flicking back and forth between a sitcom and a movie in which Emma Thompson played some bald professor dying of cancer. He flicked so rapidly that at times it seemed as though the laugh track were part of the movie, the chuckles and guffaws an ironic counterpoint to the cancer victim's tragic life. When Reef didn't reply, Owen pressed the "mute" button and turned to face him. "I really thought he was gonna lose it."

Reef dragged his eyes from the television screen to Owen. "You think so?"

"Didn't you?"

Reef grinned. Yeah. There was a moment when he'd thought Colville might actually let his guard down, show them he was human and not just some

psychology-spouting ex-con with a degree in sancti-
monious bullshit. But it hadn't happened. Not yet,
anyway. Maybe soon, though. If Reef kept the pressure on. And he was good at that. After all, he had
plenty of time. He certainly wasn't going anywhere.

In that, however, he was wrong.

"Reef. Got a minute?"

Reef turned to see Colville in the doorway. "What's
up?"

"I need to see you in my office." He turned and
walked down the hallway toward the front of the
house, his solid bulk making the oak floorboards
groan.

"Doesn't sound good," Owen said.

Reef shrugged. What could Colville do to him? He'd
done his work, *technically* followed every one of his
goddamn regulations, hadn't earned an "extra job" in
two days, hadn't had any contact with his friends,
hadn't even left the house except to pick up groceries
when he was on kitchen detail, building materials for
the greenhouse and some personal stuff—Colville
himself had driven him there and back in his pickup.
There were days, of course, when he'd have given his
right arm for a snort or a joint or even a lousy Bud Lite,
but he'd played the game, kept his nose clean. What
could Colville possibly do to him?

"Sit down," Colville said when Reef entered his
office.

Reef slumped into the same chair he'd sat in his first

day at North Hills. Nothing in the office had changed. Same neat rows of binders, same neat piles of papers. *Jesus, Colville*, Reef thought. *And you accuse me of clinging to patterns. You're textbook, man.*

Colville closed the door but didn't go around behind his desk. Instead, he pulled up a chair beside Reef and sat down. In his hands was a folder. "You've got two weeks under your belt, Reef. How would you say things are going?"

Reef thought about the question, wondered if this was going to be one of those empowering self-assessment sessions he'd heard Alex describe. He hoped it wouldn't take too long. He wanted to see if the bald chick croaked. "Okay, I guess," he replied.

Colville's face didn't betray his thoughts. "You've toed the line, all right. Although you're still giving me lip service. I'd hoped that would've eased up a little by now."

Reef thought suddenly about an old Sandra Bullock movie that Alex had watched a few nights ago. Alex was big on Bullock, wanted to *be* Bullock, in fact. The movie was stupid and Reef had left the family room ten minutes after it started. He might have guessed it'd be a turkey with a name like *Hope Floats*. He thought about that title now. Apparently, Colville still thought hope was a good thing. He hadn't learned that hope sinks like a fuckin' stone.

When Reef offered no comment, Colville opened up

the file he was holding. "Now that you've settled in, it's time to start complying with the other conditions of Judge Thomas's ruling."

Reef gave no reaction. Just waited.

"I've registered you for school, which is still a few weeks away." He flipped through some papers in the folder. "Now it's time to get you involved in the rehab volunteer program the judge mentioned. You've got quite a few options, if you'd care to hear—"

"Just pick one." What goddamn difference did it make anyway?

Colville looked at him, let the seconds tick by the way Reef had done earlier in the family room. Then, "Let's go with the first one on the list." He looked down at the file. "There's a contact person listed here that I'll call tonight. They're busy people. I'll try to set up a meeting for sometime next week." He closed the folder and glanced up. "You know, it's a good time to be getting involved in this. Volunteers can be scarce during the summer with people away on vacation. And besides, you'll soon be finished with the repairs to the greenhouse. You've done some good work there."

Reef thought of the days he'd spent crawling over that christly structure in the back yard. Thought of the cuts he'd got on his hands and arms from the sharp edges of the glass panels he'd replaced. He'd cracked two in the process but, surprisingly, Colville hadn't made him pay for those. "There's a difference between an accident and an intentional act," he had said. Reef wasn't so sure about that when the result was pretty much the same, but he'd been glad nonetheless that Colville was only going to deduct from his monthly Social Services check the cost of the panel he had broken his first day.

"Is that all?" he asked, standing up.

"One more thing," Colville said.

"Yeah?"

"You had another call today from that girl."

"Scar," Reef said. It was a statement, not a question.

"Yes. This is probably none of my business, but are you ever going to call her back? You do have phone privileges, you know."

"You're right," Reef said. "It's none of your business."

Reef tilted his head back and drained the can of Coke he'd taken from the fridge. When he'd returned to the family room, Owen had been joined by Keith and Gordy, and the three of them were glued to some monster truck rally on the extreme sports channel. In the past, Reef would have enjoyed watching the mindless destruction such an event offered, but that was before. Before *what*, though? Before coming to North Hills? Or before sitting through the hearing and seeing the picture of the car that girl had been driving? He wasn't sure. Or maybe he *was* sure and didn't want to admit it. Christ! Colville's mind games were fucking up his head. Now he wasn't sure of anything! He left the family room and headed through the kitchen, grabbing a Coke on his way out to the back yard.

He set the empty can down and leaned against the railing, staring at the outline of the greenhouse in the fading summer light. *You've done some good work there.* Good or not, it certainly hadn't been easy. The initial cleanup had been a bitch, since no one had ever bothered to clear out the broken glass. Colville said he hadn't had time to get around to it with all the work he'd been doing on the main house, but Reef suspected he'd just been waiting for free inmate labor. When Reef had asked why some of the others couldn't help out, Colville had just said everybody had jobs to do and this one was Reef's. *Eat shit and die*, Reef had wanted to tell him, but as it turned out, having someone else working with him would have been too awkward, maybe even dangerous. It wasn't a big structure to begin with, and having another body moving around inside would have complicated things. And, truth be told, Reef preferred working alone. That way, only he saw the mistakes he made.

It was an old greenhouse, made of wood rather than vinyl-covered metal like the mock up he'd seen at Kent Building Supplies. That one would have been a lot easier to work on since all you'd have to do was take the screws out of the brackets that held the panels in place, replace the glass and screw the brackets back on. His greenhouse—and he'd surprised himself lately by thinking of it as his—required a lot more work than that. The panels were held in place by strips of cedar that had to be pried away from the glass, no easy feat since the glass offered no leverage to pry up the nails. The first two tries, he'd cracked perfectly good panels when he'd pulled the hammer back, its head bearing down directly on the glass. But he'd figured out how to use pieces of wood so the pressure of the hammerhead was evenly distributed over the frame.

Removing the broken panels was hard enough—installing the new glass was a bitch. Although the guy at Kent had cut the glass to the measurements Reef had written down, Reef had to cut new cedar brackets himself, and getting them the right length wasn't easy. If he cut them too long, there would be no room for the wood to expand in damp weather, and if he cut them too short, water could seep in under the bracket and, over time, rot the wood again. Colville had told him that a couple of the panels had broken simply because the inside brackets had rotted out and the glass had fallen clean through.

The most crucial part of the process was the glazing, applying a thin line of caulking between the wood and the glass to keep everything watertight. Too much and you just made a mess. Too little and you ended up with rot. Nothing, it seemed, was easy.

Like this thing with Scar. She'd called him four or five times already, but each time he'd refused to go to the phone, told whoever had answered it to take a message. He wasn't even sure why he didn't want to talk to her. The first time, he'd been up on the ladder removing one of the cracked roof panels and it didn't make sense to crawl all the way down when he could just call her back later. The next time, though, he'd been watching TV, and the time after that he'd just been eating supper, but something had kept him from going to the phone. He wasn't quite sure what. For a time, he thought the reason was tied up somehow in the greenhouse. Like the bit about the glazing. Scar was the wood and he was the water. There needed to be something between them to keep everything solid and whole. And, for the time being anyway, North Hills was that something.

Reef looked at the Coke can again, picked it up with his right hand and squeezed it. The can collapsed easily into a crude hourglass shape, the words on the side accordioned and illegible. From somewhere in his head he heard, "Goddamn cars are no more'n tin cans," then recalled the moment in a sudden rush of memory.

The old Dodge Dart sat along the edge of some road. It was a Sunday and his grandmother had wanted to take Reef to the beach. He'd never been before and he was excited, but they were late setting out because his grandfather had been drinking. Now the Dart was pulled over to the side, its hood up, motor dead, and his grandfather was everlastingly kicking the shit out of the front fender, driver's door, back door, back fender, working his way around to the trunk, which he'd opened. Taking out the lug wrench, he swung it again and again, first smashing out the taillights, then working his way back around to the front of the car, knocking off the side mirror and bashing in the driver's-side windows.

Reef had slid out of the car just as his grandfather began kicking the front fender, and he'd pleaded with his grandmother, who sat in the front seat, to get out too. But she hadn't. She'd just sat there waiting, staring straight ahead, as if looking down a road different than the one Reef and his grandfather were standing on. A road that held possibility rather than punishment, a future rather than endless nights of fear. When her drunken husband was finally too exhausted to swing the lug wrench any more, she climbed out and put her hand on his shoulder, whispered something Reef couldn't hear. Then she moved to the edge of the road and held out her thumb, flagged down a car that drove them all back to the city.

Goddamn cars are no more'n tin cans.

Reef thought again of that picture in the courtroom, tried to twist and pull the Coke can back into shape. But, of course, it was ruined. He threw it to the ground, jumped on it, flattened it with both feet. Bent down and picked it up, wound his arm back to fling it as far as he could.

But the greenhouse was in his way.

He wanted to cry out, but he did not. He lowered his arm, looked at what remained of the can for a long moment, then turned and dropped it into the recycling bin beside the deck.

Then he went back into the house.

PART TWO

Chapter 14

It looked different than he'd thought it would. Taller, more like an apartment building than a hospital. But, then again, what did he know about hospitals? Weren't they just places people went to die?

Standing at the entrance to the Halifax Rehabilitation Center on that first day of August, Reef felt someone dance on his grave, gooseflesh marching up his back and arms despite the warmth of the morning. He hoped the grave-dancer was his grandfather, hoped he was dancing somewhere hot, red flames licking his toes while the soles of his feet singed and charred, then fell away from his bones in blood-blackened slivers.

"Something wrong?" Colville asked.

"No." Reef moved forward and an electronic sensor opened the door. Colville followed him inside.

A man in his early sixties met them in the foyer. "Hi, I'm Jim Granter! You must be Mr. Colville! We spoke on the phone!"

"Frank," Colville said, shaking his hand. "Pleased to meet you." He turned to Reef. "This is Reef Kennedy."

Jim Granter was the polar opposite of Frank Colville.

Where Colville was tall and trim, Granter was short and fleshy, at least forty pounds overweight; where Colville's hair was thick and dark, Granter's was sparse and threaded with white. But what Granter lacked in physical stature, he more than made up for in exuberance. His voice was filled with music, and every sentence seemed to end with an exclamation point. "Reef, my boy!" he said. "Glad to have you here! We always have room for volunteers!"

"Yeah," Reef mumbled.

Granter took Reef's hand and pumped it four or five times, then clapped him on the shoulder and led him toward the elevator. "This young man will be fine here with me, Frank!" he called over his shoulder. "We'll take good care of him!" He pressed the call button, and the doors of one car immediately slid open. He and Reef stepped inside.

Reef felt as if he'd been hijacked by a sidewalk Santa on speed. He kept his face forward, tried to ignore the heat that was working itself up his neck to his face. Colville was still standing in the foyer, watching him, and even from the elevator, Reef could see a muscle twitch at the corner of his mouth. The sonuvabitch was trying not to laugh. Asshole.

"So, I'll be back around four to pick you up, okay?" said Colville.

"That's just dandy!" Granter enthused. He turned to Reef. "Tons to do, my boy, tons to do! And don't you worry, we'll feed you!" The elevator doors began to close.

"Good luck, Reef," Colville called.

Bite me, you bastard.

When the elevator arrived at the fifth floor, Jim Granter was still talking, and Reef felt like the target of a firing squad, a barrage of words instead of bullets pelting him endlessly. Granter was himself a volunteer. "I'm the greeter!" he'd said. "Granter the Greeter, they call me here!" He'd explained that he came to the rehab at least a couple times a week, and more often when new volunteers were expected.

As they stepped off the elevator at the fifth floor, Granter was outlining for Reef the various levels in the facility: the first floor included the X-ray department and the cafeteria, the second floor contained the physio gym and pool, the third floor was a general recreation area and the fourth floor housed occupational therapy and several doctors' offices. The fifth floor contained more offices and the cardiac rehab program, and the sixth floor was the musculoskeletal trauma unit, which also included beds for patients who had suffered brain injuries. The seventh floor contained beds for patients with spinal cord injuries or who'd had amputations and were coming in for prostheses. The eighth floor, Granter said, was set aside for stroke patients.

Following Granter down a long hallway, Reef was suddenly overwhelmed by the variety of injuries the human body could sustain. His stomach lifted uneasily, and he imagined Judge Thomas somewhere laughing her head off right that moment. He suddenly wished for the opportunity to inflict an injury or two on her. *Bitch*.

"Here we are!" Granter exclaimed. They'd come to the office of Shelly Simpson, the recreation therapist who was in charge of coordinating volunteers. Her door was open, but Granter knocked anyway.

A woman working at a desk looked up and smiled, then got up and came around with her hand extended to Reef. "So you're our newest volunteer," she said as she shook his hand. "I'm Shelly. Very nice to meet you, Reef." In her late thirties, Shelly Simpson was an attractive woman, tall and willowy with soft features and an even softer voice, but her handshake was surprisingly firm. In some weird way, she reminded Reef of a female version of Frank Colville, but he couldn't say why. She certainly didn't seem like an asshole. At least, not yet. But give her time. All any of them needed was a little time.

Reef finished shaking her hand. Stood there awkwardly, unsure what to say.

"I've got more people to meet, so I'll just leave you in Shelly's capable hands!" Granter all but shouted. "You take care, Reef!" And he was off.

The office was suddenly silent, and Reef could hear

a slight ringing in his ears. He shook his head and Shelly smiled.

"Jim is one of the most effervescent people you'll ever meet," she said, pulling up a chair for Reef to sit in. She sat in one beside it.

"If that means loud, you're right," he said, glancing around the room as he sat down. Its neatness and organization reminded him of Colville too. Even the frames on the wall, two of which held photographs of children while a third contained a certificate of some kind, seemed perfectly parallel to the floor and each other.

Shelly laughed softly. "Jim's been helping us out here ever since he retired. Ten years before that, he was one of our patients, which is what makes him such a terrific volunteer. He knows firsthand what goes on in our facility, knows what the patients are experiencing even before they do."

Granter a patient? "What'd he break?"

"He was helping a friend build a garage and he fell from the roof to the concrete footing. He broke his back."

"Fuck," Reef muttered, then noticed the immediate disapproval on the woman's face. "Sorry," he said.

She nodded. "You'll have to watch the language here, Reef."

"Yeah," he said, thinking of Colville's extra jobs. "I been tryin'. You just surprised me. I thought a broken back meant you were paralyzed for life."

"Fortunately, Jim's spinal cord wasn't severed, but his injuries required months of extensive physiotherapy."

Must be quite the place, he thought, then realized he'd said the comment aloud.

She smiled. "We're very proud of the work we do here. And we're very grateful for the work our volunteers do, too."

Reef frowned. Looking down at his hands, he said, "You should probably know—"

She interrupted him. "I know you were assigned here by a court order. I don't know any of the particulars and I really don't care to know them."

Reef looked at her closely to see if she was telling the truth. Couldn't.

"The only thing I *do* need to know," she continued, "is that you're ready and willing to help out. Our staff is far too busy to babysit someone who doesn't want to be here in the first place." She paused, clearly waiting for an answer to the question she had not asked.

If it were up to him, Reef thought, he'd be heading toward the elevator right now. No, he did *not* want to be here. Or anywhere *like* it. But it *wasn't* up to him, was it? And, he thought, if he had to be somewhere, it might as well be this place. The sooner he got started with this shit, the sooner it'd be over.

The woman obviously mistook his hesitation for uncertainty. "If it's any help, Reef," she said quietly, "you're not the first person the court has assigned here. In fact, some of them have turned out to be our best volunteers."

Reef wasn't looking to win Volunteer of the Year at this place or anywhere else, just do his time and get out. But there was no need to tell her that. She could think he was Saint fucking Christopher if she wanted to. As long as she kept off his back, they'd get along fine.

"I'm ready," he said.

Shelly spent the next half hour explaining the various ways that volunteers helped out. They were not permitted, of course, to assist with any kind of medical or therapeutic procedures, since these could be performed only by qualified personnel. But there were many other duties that focused on improving the quality of life for patients at the facility. "Some volunteers," she explained, "are more comfortable doing one-on-one work, visiting with patients who don't have families close by, for example. People like that really appreciate having someone to talk to or to play cards with, and in the good weather volunteers often take them outside for walks or just sit with them for a bit in the sun." She went on to explain that others preferred to work with groups of patients. "We have volunteers who do things like get a group of people together and show a movie downstairs on the third floor, make popcorn, things like that. Then there are volunteers who do programs in the evening—bingo, for example—and sometimes they bring in people they know who can demonstrate activities like painting, craft design, you name it." Shelly smiled. "We even had someone do archery with one group."

Besides their involvement with individual patients and organized activities, volunteers also assisted the staff directly. "They help set up barbecues, accompany patients from one part of the hospital to another, help them get their food and so on. The list is endless. At least you won't have to worry about the time being long. The staff will keep you hopping."

When she had finished, she asked if Reef had any preferences regarding how he might help out. His preference, of course, was to put as much distance as he could between himself and every gimp in this place, but he thought for a moment. "I don't see myself doin' things with a group," he said. "Maybe one on one with somebody. Or I could just help out the staff doin' some of the things you told me."

"I'm sure Jim filled you in already on the different kinds of injuries this facility treats. Any particular floor you think you'd be more comfortable working on?"

Reef had long forgotten which floor was which, but he knew what he *didn't* want to do. "I don't wanna work with stroke patients."

"What makes you say that?"

Reef paused, wasn't sure how to continue. Then, "My grandfather had a stroke. It's what killed him."

"Oh, I see."

He was sure, of course, that she didn't see. *Couldn't* see. He'd actually been grateful for the stroke. Had, in fact, once wished it had come sooner. It was the one thing that had finally stopped the drinking, the rages, the flood of empty threats he'd never stood up to, never challenged. Wished he could have but never did. If he'd believed in God, he'd have thought the stroke was an answer to an unspoken prayer. But he knew it wasn't. Not when he saw what it did to his grandmother. He'd hated watching her look for any sign of improvement, any reason to hope. She'd held her husband's hand for days in the hospital, rubbing it softly, all the while talking to him, telling him over and over that everything was going to be all right. But it wasn't. Not then. Not ever. Even then, the cancer was growing inside her. It just hadn't told anyone yet.

"I don't assign new volunteers to the eighth floor anyway," Shelly continued. "Or the seventh, for that matter. Patients who've had strokes or lost limbs often require a level of patience and compassion that even professionals take a while to develop. Over time, though—"

"That's all right," Reef said. "What about the mus . . ." He'd forgotten the term.

"Musculoskeletal. That's on the sixth floor. How about we put you there to start?"

Reef would have preferred she put him on a bus back

to North Hills, but that wasn't going to happen. The judge had made sure of that. "Fine with me," he lied.

After giving him a quick overview of the sixth floor and introducing him to the medical personnel in the musculoskeletal unit, Shelly Simpson had left him with a nurse named Carly Reynolds, who put him to work almost immediately. "We can always use another body around here to help out," she said. She glanced at her watch. "In fact, I've got a job for you right now. You're on traffic control."

He waited for an explanation.

"In the next few minutes, that elevator door is going to open and two wheelchairs are going to come out full tilt." She seemed to notice the surprise in his eyes and laughed. "No, I'm not clairvoyant. It's just that two of my patients usually come up from physio at the same time, and if someone isn't here to stop them, this hallway turns into the Indianapolis 500."

As if on cue, the elevator binged and the doors opened, revealing two people—a young woman and a man about Carly's age—in wheelchairs, each jockeying to be first off.

"Hold it!" Carly ordered, sticking her hand out like a crossing guard.

The two looked up and grinned sheepishly. "Busted," the young woman said.

"Reef," said the nurse, "meet the bane of my existence,

Brett Turner. And this is her partner in crime, Ron Sheffield. Guys, this is Reef Kennedy. Hall cop." She punched out the last two words for emphasis. "Reef here is going to help me make sure everyone observes the speed limit." She leaned toward Reef and murmured, "Whatever you do, don't get your feet in front of them."

Turning to her partner, the young woman groaned. "Looks like the hall Nazi has reinforcements. We're screwed."

Her partner laughed. So did the nurse.

Reef moved forward, keeping an eye on his feet.

It turned out that Brett was as much help as she was hindrance. She gave Reef a tour of some of the other floors, including the second and third, where, she said, the "real action" was.

It was when he saw the physio gym that Reef began to wonder if he'd be able to handle this volunteering thing after all; the patients he saw there were a far cry from Brett Turner. An old man sat hunched over in his wheelchair pulling on a rope attached to a weight, and, despite the encouragement he was getting from the therapist working with him (and despite the fact that the weight couldn't have been more than a couple of pounds), it was all he could do to pull the rope a few inches. To his right, a middle-aged woman was attempting to walk between two parallel bars but had managed little more than a halting, snail-pace shuffle.

At the far end of the gym, a man in his late twenties or early thirties was trying to walk up a ramp whose incline was minimal, but even from the door Reef could hear him groaning with exertion. Across from him on the far wall was a basketball net, and Reef thought whoever'd hung it had one christly sick sense of humor. It was obvious that no one here would be using it.

The third floor, which contained the general recreation area, was much less depressing. Many of the walls found on the other floors were absent here, allowing for a large, open area beyond the elevators that served as an entertainment center. The room contained three large sofas and several armchairs and recliners, separated here and there by tables covered with books and magazines. Off to the left were higher tables on which lay a chess set, cribbage board and assorted games. To the right was a large-screen projection TV with VCR and DVD player, and near the windows at the far end stood a regulation-size pool table. He thought briefly about Jink and Bigger and knew they'd have a ball on the third floor, momentarily pictured them hanging out there, then shook his head to clear that image. Those two would level the place.

He also thought about Scar. Brett reminded him of her, and not because of her hair—where Scar's was the red of kids' crayons, Brett's was much lighter, more blond than red. No, their similarity lay more in their manner: completely genuine. What you saw was what you got.

During the tour, Brett introduced Reef to a number of patients, most of whose names he forgot the minute she said them, so focused was he on their various physical limitations. It was like a freak show, only free. Many were missing something—an arm or a leg; others had all the parts but these seemed to have a life of their own. Or no life at all. Most of the time he looked away, but not from any courtesy on his part. They creeped him out. And every one of them knew Brett.

"She's a wild one," warned a bald man with a handlebar mustache who was slowly pushing a metal walker down the hallway. "Nearly knocked me down twice this week already."

"Yeah, well, next time signal when you're turning," Brett retorted impishly.

Reef was surprised people weren't pissed off at her. If *he* said the kind of things she did, he'd be sure to get a dirty look—or worse—but everyone she met seemed to enjoy her comments and many stopped to chat. Watching her carrying on with the other patients, he wondered what had brought her to the rehab. Shelly Simpson hadn't told him he couldn't ask.

"So," he said later as he rolled her wheelchair toward the elevator for the ride back up to the sixth floor, "you fall down some stairs or something?"

Brett turned to look at him and grinned. "You're not real subtle, are you?"

Reef reddened, unsure if he'd offended her. "Look, uh—"

"Or something," Brett said.

"Huh?"

"You asked if I fell down some stairs or something."

Reef was surprised. "Off a roof?" he asked.

"Out of an airplane," she said.

"Yeah. Right."

"No, really. I did."

"You fell out of an airplane." He waited for the punchline.

"Well, actually, I jumped."

"Look," Reef said, not bothering to mask his annoyance, "if you don't wanna tell me—"

"I was skydiving. My parachute didn't open."

"You're shittin' me." It was out of his mouth before he realized he'd said it. "I mean—"

Brett laughed. "No, I'm not shitting you. Actually, it was my first time skydiving. Sam, that's my guy, he warned me not to but I'd always wanted to try it, so I paid to take a course. On the last day everybody got one jump. Some luck, eh? My only jump and the chute doesn't open."

Reef remembered something he'd seen in a movie. "Ain't there another parachute?" he asked.

"The reserve, yeah. It got tangled in my lines."

Reef shook his head slowly, stopped pushing the wheelchair and moved around in front of the girl. "Christ," he breathed. "What was it like?"

"The falling or the landing?"

Jesus! "Well, uh, both."

"At first I thought, 'This isn't happening to me.' You know, like those nightmares you have and you wake up drenched in sweat?"

Reef nodded. He'd had lots of nightmares like that when he was younger. And a few since the hearing. Since seeing those pictures.

"Then I panicked. Forgot *everything* I learned in the course."

"No shit."

"I almost did that, too. Which, when you think of it, might actually have made for a softer landing."

Reef grinned. The chick had balls. Big ones. "Then what?" he asked.

"Then I got myself under control and started trying all the things we'd been taught. Which didn't work." She shrugged. "I found out later that what happened to me was just fluky. The main chute almost always works. And on the off chance it doesn't, the reserve takes over with no problem. It was just a weird combination of events. But hey, I guess when you jump out of an airplane you should be *ready* for weird, right?"

"Fuckin' right!" he exclaimed, then remembered where he was.

It was nearly noon when Reef returned Brett to the sixth floor. They found Carly, who thanked him for "keeping the Turner Terror occupied and making the hallways safe for the rest of us." She gave him a lunch voucher and told him to grab a bite to eat in the cafeteria. "You know where that is?" she asked.

"First floor, right?"

Carly smiled. "You learn fast. You're gonna work out just fine here, Reef."

Reef flushed. That was the third time that morning he'd turned red for some reason or other. Wouldn't Scar have loved to see that, he thought, then realized that was the second time she had come to mind that day. For a moment he wondered where Scar was, what she was doing.

"Well, Reef," said Brett. "I was looking forward to seeing more of you, but there's little chance of that now."

He looked at her. "Why not?"

She nodded at the lunch voucher. "Carly's sending you to the cafeteria. Clearly the woman is trying to kill you."

The nurse raised her clipboard threateningly and Brett wheeled around and sped down the hall. "Nice meetin' you, Reef," she called over her shoulder before disappearing into her room.

"So, how was your first day?" Colville asked when Reef opened the door and slid into the truck.

Reef didn't answer right away. Finally, "Okay."

Colville pulled the truck out onto Winter Street, came to the lights on Spring Garden Road and turned right, heading down toward the harbor. "What you expected?" he asked.

"You want a play-by-play?" asked Reef. "You think maybe I should take a video camera next time and tape it for the sharin' sessions?"

Colville didn't say anything for a bit. Satisfied, Reef watched the city slide by. Warm air rushed through the open windows, and mingled with the traffic fumes were the undeniable smells of midsummer. Reef thought about Bigger and Jink, wondered what they were doing on such a nice day. Not wheelin' gimps around, that was for damned sure. Or reading to vegetables, which was how he'd spent the afternoon.

"You have some visitors coming later," Colville said.

Reef turned. "Whaddya mean, visitors?"

"Friends of yours. Jim, Scar and . . . Bigger?"

"Jink."

"What?"

Reef breathed a loud, derisive sigh. "Not Jim. *Jink.*"

"Oh."

They drove in silence, and before long Colville's truck pulled onto the span of the Murray MacKay Bridge. He could have taken the MacDonald Bridge, but once on the Dartmouth side of the Murray MacKay, it was only a couple minutes to the 118 and then a straight haul to Waverley. In a moment they were high above the water, and Reef could see dozens of sailboats dotting the Bedford Basin to the west and, beyond that, outbound vehicles lined up on

Magazine Hill. People playing, working, living their lives.

"Thought I wasn't allowed to have visitors," he said finally.

Traffic on the span was heavy and a blue Grand Am cut in ahead of them, forcing Colville to brake hard to keep from rear-ending it. To Reef's surprise, Colville showed no impatience, didn't even honk his horn.

"Not at the beginning," Colville agreed. "And no unsupervised visits for the first six months. But I thought it might be good for you to see them. I talked to your social worker about it and he agreed."

Reef mulled that over, knew somehow that his continued refusal to join in the nightly whine-and-whimper was part of this. As if bringing his friends in would get him to open up, make him—how did Colville put it?—more likely to "disclose." Such bullshit.

"Anyway, Greg offered to bring them over this evening for a bit. I told him I thought you'd earned it." When Reef snorted disdainfully, Colville continued, "Look, if you don't want to see them, just say the word."

Reef turned away, looked east down the harbor past the shipyards, the MacDonald Bridge, MacNab's and George's Islands, the Atlantic Ocean beyond them all. Even now, he could see the bank of offshore fog moving in. "S'okay," he said.

The truth was, though, it didn't *feel* okay, though he wouldn't let Colville know that. For some reason, the idea of seeing his friends again suddenly made him uneasy. Maybe it was because he hadn't returned Scar's calls. Yeah. That was probably it.

He drummed his fingers on the door frame, watched as the water beneath them fell away and became land.

Chapter 15

Leeza could hear Brett drumming her fingers on the arm of her wheelchair. Then again, louder this time.

Her eyes closed, Leeza ignored her, concentrated on riding out a spasm without grinding her teeth. Val had told her that sometimes patients respond to pain by clenching their jaws together, which just creates more problems later on. Leeza hadn't realized she'd been doing it until Val pointed it out. Now she had to break herself of the habit.

Brett began to hum. Something between a nursery rhyme and the national anthem. Badly.

"If you're doing that to get on my nerves, it's working," Leeza said.

"Sorry." Brett rolled her chair over beside Leeza's bed. "You asleep?"

"Certainly not *now*," Leeza said dryly. "Exactly what is it about the concept of resting that you don't understand?"

"Meeeowwwww," said Brett. "Aren't *we* in a great mood."

Leeza sighed and opened her eyes. "We can't all be as bubbly as you, now can we?"

It was Brett's turn to sigh. "Cripes, Leeza. After three weeks, you'd think you'd get tired of the 'poor me' routine."

Leeza closed her eyes again, but not to shut out her roommate, as Brett probably thought. Squeezing her eyelids tight was the only way she could keep the tears from slipping out. Tears that had become more and more frequent in the last few days. Brett had been at the rehab several weeks before Leeza arrived, so she'd had more time to get used to it all. Waking up to the pain every day, enduring the agony of physio, coping with the loss of freedom to move around the way she once had, even putting up with the humiliation of the damn catheter—all these were bad enough. But for Leeza, these weren't even the worst of it. It was seeing every day the wreckage that had once been her body.

Of course, that part was difficult for anyone, but as Dr. Dan had pointed out to her earlier that week, it was even harder for young people. "Body image is many times more important to a teenager than to someone my age," he'd told her during an examination. Leeza had been crying when he'd arrived, and he'd explained that everything she was feeling was perfectly normal. "Teenagers who've had debilitating injuries worry about how strangers will react to them. They worry about not being accepted by their peers, about not being attractive to the opposite sex."

He'd waited a moment, allowing his acknowledgement of her fears to register before continuing. "And this psychological trauma is compounded even more by the fact that young people don't have the same life experiences they can draw on to put their injuries into perspective." At this, Leeza had sobbed even louder. "I know you've had a rough time this past year, Leeza. The loss of your sister was a terrible thing, and I'm not trying to diminish that." He'd given her a moment to realize this was true. Then, "Do you remember that first day when I said your youth was an advantage, that you would heal faster than an older person?" Not waiting for an answer, he'd continued, "Youth can be a double-edged sword. Yes, you'll heal faster. But for young people, injuries like yours seem more traumatic and long-lasting than they would for an older person. The advantage of age is that older people have been through so much more in their lives. They realize that, although this is terrible, it's not as devastating as this thing that happened ten years ago or that thing that happened twenty years ago."

All of this made sense to Leeza, but it was, nonetheless, difficult not seeing the improvement she saw in those around her. The doctor had told her there would be periods during her rehabilitation when she would plateau, but these periods would eventually pass. She just had to be patient. Understanding that and accepting it, however, were two different things. As the days turned into weeks, she'd found herself becoming more withdrawn, less willing to involve herself with life on the sixth floor. Every free moment she seemed to spend napping. Even visits with Jen and Robin weren't enough to pull her out of her funk. They had come by a few times after her mother had called them, but they hadn't stayed long. And Leeza could understand why—it was painful trying to make conversation when they had nothing in common. Leeza's days were one therapy after another and trying to cope with pain. Theirs were filled with summer jobs, shopping, afternoons at the beach, new boyfriends.

Of course, her parents still came every day. That is, her mother did, sometimes even twice, despite the fact that it took time away from the decorating work she contracted. Being self-employed made it easier for her to get away, unlike Jack, whose work, she said, was the reason he hadn't visited much. It seemed important to her that Leeza believe the lie, so she pretended for a while that she did. Now, even pretending seemed like too much effort. What was the point?

"So, you wanna know my news?"

Leeza opened her eyes again to see Brett still parked by her bed. "You finally killed someone with that wheelchair of yours," she said humorlessly.

"No, even better."

"You're sick."

"And you're a pissant, but I'm not holding that against you. C'mon, Guess."

Leeza automatically clenched her teeth, then forced them apart as she rode another spasm to its end. "I don't feel like guessing."

Brett sighed, then moved even closer to the bed. "Okay, you dragged it out of me. Fresh meat," she said.

Leeza stared at her blankly. "You want to talk to me about *food*?"

"No, stupid. We had a *male* on the floor today."

"How old? Eighty? Ninety?"

"I said *fresh* meat, didn't I? He's about your age, I think."

"Another patient?"

"No, that's the best part. He's a volunteer. Non-gimp. Has the use of all his extremities. And," she narrowed her eyes, "mighty fine-looking extremities they are, too."

Now it was Leeza's eyes that widened. "Aren't you almost a married woman? How'd you like Sam to find out you've been checkin' out other guys?" She'd met Brett's boyfriend the weekend before, and Brett had shown nearly everyone in the hospital the engagement ring Sam had given her. "He proposed in the cafeteria," she'd gushed to Carly and Leeza later. "Got down on his knee and everything." Sam had wanted to set the date right then, but Brett wasn't making any plans until she got back on her feet. "I'm *walkin'* down that aisle," she'd told them. Carly, of course, had said she was relieved to hear it: "I wouldn't want to read in the wedding announcements about a bunch of brides-maids being mowed down by a wheelchair."

Brett made a face now at Leeza. "It's not me I was checkin' him out for, stupid. It's *you*!"

Leeza suddenly felt like someone had sucked all the air out of the room. She lowered her eyes. "That's not funny."

"Who's tryin' to be funny? He's cute. Got kind of a moody bad-boy thing goin' on but I think that's all show. Seemed nice enough."

Leeza turned her head toward the wall. Or tried to turn it. Made the pretense of doing so.

"And the best thing is he's coming back."

No response.

"I think you'll like him. Really."

Nothing.

"Look, he beats the hell outta naptime."

Still nothing.

"Okay. Jeez. Sorry I brought it up." Brett returned to her side of the room, and Leeza could hear her rummaging in her locker for a chocolate bar. Moments later she left, and Leeza knew where she was headed: first to the pop machine for a Pepsi and then to the third-floor big-screen TV and her favorite soap. Brett was so predictable.

She was also a good friend to everyone on the floor, even the screamer, whose room she dropped into a couple times each day. Although Stephen could not respond to her, he seemed to know she was there, seemed to enjoy listening to her chatter about nothing and everything, keeping him up-to-date on all that happened in the building. Including the Big Proposal.

Brett was being a friend to Leeza, too. She knew

that. What Brett didn't know, though, was that guys were the *last* thing she wanted in her life right now. Leeza had never been really comfortable with guys. Sure, she'd dated, but there'd never been anyone who'd asked her out more than two or three times. Which was probably *her* fault: the overachiever thing. Ellen had often told her she was far too serious. "You need to loosen up," her sister would say. "Let yourself have *fun*." But there was always schoolwork to do, committees to serve on, plenty to keep her busy. And then Ellen's illness.

So, even under different circumstances, Leeza would have felt uncomfortable about meeting some guy. Throw in the bandages, the fixators, the wheelchair and all the rest of it and you had some fairly solid reasons for not getting excited over meeting a male.

Besides, any teenager who'd spend his free time volunteering at a rehab center had to have *something* wrong with him.

Chapter 16

Reef was nervous. More nervous, in fact, than when he'd gone to the rehab that morning. He had no reason to be. Hell, he'd known Bigger and Jink since eighth grade and Scar for two years. And except for Scar, who often had those errands to run for her old man, there wasn't a day when they hadn't got together for at least an hour or so. And it had only been three weeks since he'd seen them.

But three weeks was a long time when you were used to seeing someone every day.

And, of course, there was the bit about not returning Scar's calls. He didn't know himself why he hadn't, so it was probably gonna be weird trying to explain that to her.

Bigger and Jink hadn't called, but that was no surprise. He couldn't remember the last time he'd spoken on the phone to either of them. Maybe ten seconds to find out where they were getting together, but not just to talk. Girls talked on phones, not guys.

Probably, though, his unease had a lot to do with

giving up smoking. Colville didn't allow it, and the man practically had a dog's sense of smell when it came to sniffing out anyone who was stupid enough to try it. Reef had earned himself two "extra jobs" earlier that week before he'd finally given up and tossed what was left of his last pack. It had been rough, though. He'd chewed gum till his jaws ached, and the last couple nights he'd even dreamt about smoking, woke up with the phantom taste of a cigarette in his mouth. He'd caved only once and bought one from Keith, but that acne-faced asshole charged four bucks a pop and Reef didn't have cash like that to burn. He'd spent a pretty good chunk of his Social Services check paying off the glass panel he'd broken that first day.

He walked to the end of the veranda and stood looking at the traffic, then pulled up a wicker chair and sat down. Longed for a cigarette.

"Not here yet?"

Reef glanced around at Alex, who was standing just inside the screen door. Despite the heat, he was wearing one of his many long-sleeved shirts, this one a glaring color somewhere between orange and olive green.

"Nothin' gets by *you*," Reef said.

"You *know* it, honey," said Alex as he turned and headed toward the family room.

There was that, too, of course: Alex's "honey." He could just imagine Jink and Bigger's reaction to the resident fairy. In the last three weeks, he'd almost

grown used to all the posing and prancing and prat-
tling. That last word was Alex's. Reef had never heard
it before, hadn't even known what it meant when Alex
had said one night, "Oh, just listen to me prattle on."
Reef and Owen had been finishing the supper dishes
when Alex waltzed in with news of a new Cher CD, yet
another Greatest Hits compilation. He already owned
everything the singer had recorded, but he'd just seen
this latest one—some godawful remix, Reef imagined—advertised on MuchMusic and he absolutely
had to have it. "She's the *quintessential* performer,"
he'd gushed, then launched into his own breathy version of "A Different Kind of Love Song" that cracked up
both Reef and Owen. No one could accuse Alex of not
being different.

Funny, Reef thought, about what you could get
used to. It wasn't too long ago that, under different circumstances, he'd have "cleaned Alex's clock," something his grandfather used to say. Alex's being a fag
still disgusted him, but it didn't get to him like it did
before. Still, he was glad his friends were coming during back-to-back episodes of "I Dream of Jeannie."
Alex loved watching reruns of the old show on the
comedy network, squealing each time the genie left
the bottle in a puff of smoke. "Every good queer knows
that sequence is a visual metaphor for coming out,"
he'd crowed. Grinning, Reef and the others had
shaken their heads, glad they had no personal knowledge of fag metaphors or fairy filmmaking.

He heard the car a good minute or two before it rounded the corner. Clearly, Greg Matheson had yet to get the Escort repaired. If anything, the knocking was louder than ever, and the blue smoke that trailed the car now seemed like an accessory, a third bumper or a fifth wheel. Reef sucked in a deep breath and stood up to greet them.

Scar, sitting in front beside Matheson, was out of the Escort even before it stopped, darting up the steps and flinging her arms around Reef's neck. "Good to see you, baby," she said, planting her lips squarely on Reef's and grinding her body against his.

It took Jink and Bigger considerably longer to get out. Pulling away from Scar, Reef grinned as he watched them unfold their long legs and climb out. They bent and rubbed their knees, reminding Reef of the old man he'd seen in the physio gym that morning, and his mind did a sudden flash-forward: they, too, would be old one day. It was the first time he'd ever been conscious of his friends'—and, therefore, his own—mortality. It was suddenly sobering.

"Hey, asshole, how're ya doin'?" This from Bigger, whose face split in a huge grin.

Reef came down the steps and Bigger punched him in the arm.

Jink slapped him on the back. "You look good, man! Place must be agreein' with you."

"He's right," Matheson said, coming around the car and shaking Reef's hand. Although he called every couple days, he'd seen Reef only twice since bringing him here, and that had been during the first week. "You've put on a little weight. And that's quite the tan you got goin' there."

Reef was embarrassed by the attention but pleased by the comments. He, too, had noticed the changes in his body. He'd always been wiry and strong without an ounce of fat on him, but the combination of Colville's rigid meal requirements—the guys assigned to do the grocery shopping on any given week knew *Canada's Food Guide* by heart—and the lifting and lugging Reef had been doing on the greenhouse had bulked up his arms and chest. As a result, he'd had to buy some new T-shirts, and the black one he wore now accentuated the extra muscle he carried.

"I'm gonna go see Frank for a bit and give you guys a chance to visit," Matheson said.

"He's out back on the deck," Reef told him.

Matheson nodded and disappeared around the side of the house.

"So, whadda you guys been up to?" Reef asked, leading his friends up the steps to the chairs on the veranda.

"Up to or *in* to?" Bigger chuckled, settling himself on a wicker loveseat that seemed just wide enough but far too flimsy for him. It creaked ominously.

"We missed you, man," said Jink. "Things ain't been the same without you."

"Where've you been?" Scar asked. "I called. Lots of times. Didn't you get my messages?"

Reef nodded. "Yeah, I got 'em. Thanks. I just been real busy."

"Doin' what?" Bigger asked.

Reef was grateful for the question, glad for there not to be a silence after his answer.

"Workin' on a greenhouse out back. Replacin' broken glass panels and wood that's rotted. Turned out to be a bigger job than I thought."

"Part of your sentence?" Bigger asked.

Scar kicked his foot.

"What?" Bigger demanded. "What'd I say? He ain't here on vacation, ya know."

"No," Reef said. "Just somethin' the guy who runs this place wants me to do."

"Free labor, right?" Jink muttered scornfully.

Reef nodded, simply because that was the easiest explanation. Lately, though, he'd been wondering how accurate that explanation was. Sure, he was saving Colville a pile of money by fixing the greenhouse, and there were still times when he'd be pulling out another splinter or bandaging another cut that he'd curse Colville long and loud in his head, the words piling up like cars bottlenecking a merge lane. But then there were other times. Times when he finally figured out how to do something he'd been puzzling over, determined not to ask Colville for his goddamn help. And times when he did something just right, like when a bracket fit perfectly or a panel slipped exactly into place, and he'd step back and admire for a moment what he was doing. It was times like those that the reason behind why he was doing it just didn't seem to matter as much. But he doubted that would make sense to his friends. Especially when it didn't even really make sense to him.

"What about the other . . . you know, the other thing . . ." Bigger stumbled.

"Started that today. Volunteering at the Halifax Rehab."

"What's that?" Jink asked.

Reef ran a hand through his dark hair. The muscles in his upper arm and shoulder bunched and relaxed, and he noticed Scar staring at him, checking him out. He felt a rush of heat and wondered again why he hadn't returned her calls. He suddenly wished she had come alone.

"What's that?" Jink repeated. "The rab."

"*Rehab*. Kinda like a hospital," he began, "except people stay a long time. Months."

"*Christ*. Months in a hospital, man," Bigger murmured. "Fuckin' depressing."

"What d'you do there?" Scar asked.

Reef looked at her again. It was a warm evening, and he noticed a sheen of perspiration at the base of her neck that extended down between her breasts. The white halter top she wore contrasted dramatically with her deep tan, and her long red hair lay in soft waves on her bare shoulders. He had difficulty concentrating on her question, putting words together to answer it. "I only been there once," he said.

"Do you wash floors and stuff?" Bigger asked. "Like a janitor?"

Reef shook his head. "I help out the nurses. Today I spent time with some patients."

"Like who?" asked Jink.

"Most of the morning I was with a woman, and the afternoon I was with a man. Visitin'. Keepin' 'em company."

"A woman?"

Reef and the others could hear the irritation in Scar's voice, and the three guys grinned at each other.

"She's engaged," Reef said. Brett had told him all about the Big Proposal on the ride back up to the sixth floor. Cafeteria, bended knee, ring. Sounded ridiculous, but he didn't tell her that.

"Why's she there?" Bigger asked.

Reef told them about the skydiving accident, and all three were suitably impressed.

"Wonder if she bounced," growled Jink, and Bigger guffawed. Longer and louder, Reef thought, than the joke warranted.

Then he told them about the man he'd spent the afternoon with. "Guy named Stephen. In his early twenties. Got banged up pretty bad ridin' a four-wheeler. Hit by a car when he was crossin' a highway."

Jink whistled. "*That's* gotta hurt."

Reef nodded. "Lotta brain damage, too. He screams a lot, especially when he gets upset, so they get people to read to 'im. Helps calm 'im down."

"Fuck," breathed Bigger. "He'd give me the creeps."

"Did me, too, at first," agreed Reef. "Especially the droolin'."

"Oh, man," moaned Jink, "you're freakin' me out here."

"You pussy," said Scar. "Try looking in the mirror next time you eat tacos. Now *that's* disgusting."

"Ooooh, man, she got you!" Bigger crowed as he high-fived Scar.

Reef looked at his friends, knew they didn't understand. For some reason, he wanted them to know what it was really like. When all the catcalling had died down, he continued. "Wasn't so bad after I got used to it. Someone'd left a newspaper in the room, and I just read to him. Don't know if he understood any of it, but it kept him quiet." He shrugged. "First time I ever read a paper from front to back. There's a lotta shit goin' on I never knew about."

"Speakin' 'a things goin' on," said Jink, "you heard about The Pit?"

Reef nodded. "About the store they're puttin' up? I seen it in the paper." He'd read Stephen an article about a sports equipment outlet that was supposed to revitalize the downtown core.

"For yuppie faggots," Bigger snickered.

"Hey," interrupted Jink, "you know what you call two queers wearin' Spandex?"

"No, what *do* you call two queers wearing Spandex, honey?"

They all glanced up to see Alex glide out onto the veranda and lean against the railing in what had to be his most dramatic pose. Reef groaned inside. Somewhere a phone rang, but the sound was muffled by the sudden roaring in his ears.

Jink stared at Alex as if seeing proof of extraterrestrial life, but his expression paled in comparison with Bigger's, whose face suddenly looked like the can Reef had crumpled a few nights ago, his eyes narrowed to slits and his lips twisted into a diagonal sneer. Only Scar revealed no physical reaction to Alex's presence.

"Aren't you going to introduce me to your friends, Reef?" Alex asked elaborately. He tossed his head like those women in shampoo commercials, his long blond hair cascading over his face.

Reef stood up awkwardly, and so did the others. "Guys, this is Alex. Alex, this is Scar, Jink and Bigger."

"You certainly *are*," Alex said, his words an exaggerated lisp as he dangled his hand toward Bigger. Bigger didn't move, simply stared at the hand as though it were a separate living thing that had crawled out from under some rock and now floated disembodied in the air.

Reef's face burned. Leave it to Alex to put on a fuckin' performance.

"Nice to meet you, Alex."

Reef was grateful for Scar, who took Alex's hand and shook it. Jink watched the exchange as if mesmerized, then gave Reef a hard, questioning stare.

At that moment, Greg Matheson came around from the back of the house. "Guys, sorry to cut this short, but my wife just called. My six year old fell off her bike and chowdered her chin. I'm gonna run you home on my way to Outpatients."

Reef released the breath he hadn't known he was holding.

Jink was still staring at Reef when he said, "S'okay. We was about finished here anyway."

"Yeah," Bigger agreed. Quickly.

"Glad you could make it, guys," Reef said. His comment sounded ridiculous even to him. Something out of "I Dream of Jeannie."

They nodded, then went down the steps two at a time and folded themselves into the back seat of Matheson's car. Scar gave him a quick kiss and said, "Next time, call me." Turning, she hurried down the steps, then looked back as she was getting into the car. "Nice to meet you, Alex," she said.

The Escort seemed to churn as it started, backfired twice, emitted a plume of blue-black smoke and then coughed down the driveway. This time Reef didn't watch it go, instead opening the door and heading into the house.

"I really don't think your friends liked me," Alex called after him, his voice theatrically melodious.

Reef said nothing, just climbed the stairs toward his room. But every footstep on the oak treads conveyed an unmistakable *Fuck you!*

Chapter 17

"So when?" Leeza asked.

Dr. Dan grunted unintelligibly to acknowledge he'd heard her, but he continued examining her without comment.

"Well?" Leeza said again a moment later, her impatience getting the better of her.

Her mother clucked her tongue softly. *Don't be so difficult*, her eyes said.

Leeza frowned, turned again to the doctor. "Well?" she repeated.

"We'll see," he said finally.

"That's what you said *yesterday*!" she snapped, resenting the whine that had crept into her voice yet unable to dispel it. "And the day before that." He had told her during her first week at the rehab that her fixators would stay in for at least a month to ensure her fractures knit together correctly, and it was the phrase "at least" that she worried about now. She knew it was necessary, but the network of metal pins and rods was excruciating, limiting Leeza's range of motion and preventing her from getting into a comfortable position no matter what she tried. And if she did happen to find a position that was less painful than others, the small relief was short-lived because nurses came in several times a day to change the dressings around her pin-sites to keep them free of infection. "Come on," she pleaded, "you must have *some* idea." When he didn't respond, she continued, "Then what about my catheter? Can you tell me that much?"

Concluding his examination, the doctor turned to her. "Leeza, there are no guarantees. Every patient is different. You can't rush your rehabilitation. Any shortcuts now would only complicate matters later on. We just have to take it one day at a time."

Don't rush your rehab. Now *there's* a bumper sticker, Leeza thought sarcastically, the familiar wave of dread settling over her once more. Getting the cast off her arm a few days after she'd arrived at the center had given her an emotional boost, but that had soon faded. The only thing that managed to push back the depression constantly weighing on her now was her anticipation that perhaps today, tomorrow, even the next day would be her last wearing her fixators. But Dr. Dan refused to give her any assurance that his at-least-a-month timeline might not extend to five weeks. Or six. She squeezed her eyelids shut, trying to keep her disappointment from spilling out.

Her mother leaned over and put a hand on hers. "Now, Leeza, like the doctor says, you don't want to rush things."

No, that's where you're wrong, Leeza wanted to scream. *I do want to rush things. I'm tired of fixators. I'm tired of physio. I'm tired of this bed, this room, my wheel-chair. I'm tired of eating food I hate. I'm tired of every god-damn part of every goddamn day in this place! But most of all, I'm tired of pretending to be strong. I did that enough for Ellen. I can't do it for you, too!*

But, of course, she didn't say any of those things. Instead, she just nodded, smiled, forced back the tears and allowed herself to slide deeper into melancholy.

"You did a great job with Stephen the other day, Reef," said Carly. "He doesn't always respond as well to strangers as he did with you. In fact, some of the patients in the unit commented on how quiet he was that afternoon."

Reef nodded noncommittally. He certainly wasn't there because he wanted to be. But each day was one day closer to the end of this shit. If nothing else, there was *that* to celebrate.

"I've got another patient I'd like you to meet," the nurse explained.

Reef shrugged. "Whatever," he said. He had, in fact, hoped he'd be assigned to the vegetable again. It was weird being in the same room with an adult who drooled and pissed his pants, but he actually preferred that to having to make conversation with someone he didn't know. That Brett person hadn't been hard to talk to, but she certainly wasn't like the rest of the patients in this place. His skin crawled as he watched them lurch and stagger down the hall like zombies from *Night of the Living Dead*, one of those old movies he'd seen on late-night cable when he was living with the Barkers.

"We've got a girl here about the same age as you who's been having a rough time of it. I thought I'd get you to visit with her for a bit."

Reef grimaced. "Don't she have family or friends to do that?"

"Her mother is in every day, but there aren't many young people who come. A couple friends came at first, but they haven't been around for a while. That happens sometimes. Young people find this a difficult place to be."

No shit, Reef thought. "So what happened to her?"

"Car accident," the nurse explained.

Reef's mind suddenly conjured the mangled Subaru he'd seen in the courtroom photo. "What's her name?" he asked uneasily, thinking again of the girl he'd read about in the newspapers following the accident. Elizabeth Something. He didn't recall her last name. In fact, he'd tried not to think about the accident since the hearing, deliberately turning his mind away from the event and the emotions it stirred in him. Keeping busy on the greenhouse had helped during the day, but in the evening, when things quieted down, it was easier for the memories to return.

Sometimes they came when he was watching TV, a car crash or a courtroom scene invoking recollections that bloomed suddenly in his head. Sometimes they came in dreams, nightmares that left him sitting on the side of the bed dripping sweat. Elizabeth Something. He'd never seen a picture of her, but he didn't need a photo of her parents to remember *them*, to remember the way her mother had pointed at him outside the courthouse, cursing the judge's ruling, then cursing him. Suddenly the newspaper photo of the girl's parents swam into memory, their name printed beneath their angry faces. Morrison. Elizabeth Morrison.

"Leeza Hemming," said the nurse. "I think you'll like her."

"I need to leave early today, Leeza," Diane said. "I have a new client who's opening up an office downtown. Wants a completely new look, and I told him I'd meet him there this afternoon with some preliminary sketches." She gathered her things and leaned over to kiss her daughter's forehead.

Leeza smiled, feeling none of the warmth she pretended. She was glad her mother was getting back into her work. Glad she'd be busier. Leeza was tired of the false front she had to wear when her mother came. At least with Brett she could be herself. Her mother, on the other hand, was always looking for reassurance.

Sleeping well? Eating more? Feeling better? And, of course, her favorite: *Is it getting any easier?* Like any of this could ever get easier. Leeza smiled—and slipped more deeply into depression each day.

Her mother continued brightly, "You should see how the previous leaseholder decorated the place. Lots of wall coverings and area rugs with zigzag patterns, but then there's this weird lace hanging everywhere."

"Sounds like a cross between Santa Fe and Victoria's Secret," Brett commented from the other side of the room.

Diane laughed aloud, and Leeza could tell she was glad her daughter had such an exuberant roommate. *What fun she must think we have when everyone's gone*, Leeza thought. *A couple of goddamn Girl Guides sharing campfire stories. Christ.* She forced another smile, grimaced when she found herself grinding her teeth.

"That's really more accurate than you think, Brett," Diane explained. "The business was supposed to offer investment counseling. Turns out the owner was running an escort service."

"Seems like a good combination," Brett observed wryly. "I imagine an escort could suggest some pretty interesting places to put someone's money."

Diane laughed again. "Good point. But the police didn't feel the same way. The owner goes on trial sometime this fall. Meanwhile, the man who's leasing the place now wants a complete overhaul." She turned to Leeza. "It's going to be a huge job, honey. I'll really be busy the next couple weeks."

There was a moment's silence as Leeza, caught off guard, stared blankly at her mother. She'd been thinking about her next morphine shot, calculating in her head how much time before it arrived, imagined its numb embrace. "That's good," she said, wondering without caring what could possibly be good.

"Your mother's a neat person," Brett said after Diane had left. When Leeza didn't respond, she continued, "You ever help her with her decorating?"

A moment passed. "No."

"Ever think you'd like to try it?"

Another moment passed. "No."

"Ever wanna try the escort business?"

If Brett expected a reaction—a laugh maybe, or even a grin—she was disappointed. Leeza ignored her, returned to counting minutes. Seconds. Was both surprised and pleased when she willed Carly to appear in the doorway.

"Hello, you two," the nurse said. "You've got company."

Leeza heard Brett chuckle. "Just what the doctor ordered," her roommate said.

Chapter 18

Leeza could have killed Carly.

It was bad enough that she had to endure the embarrassment of having her catheter changed four times a day, the agony of the impossible tasks Val asked her to perform during physio, the continued ambiguity of Dr. Dan's assessment of her progress, her roommate's bubbly "Cheer-up-it-could-be-worse" attitude and absolutely everything else in this godforsaken place. But this. This was too much.

"Reef," said Carly, "this is Leeza Hemming. Leeza, meet Reef Kennedy. He's our newest volunteer."

Leeza's face was on fire. Lying in her bed, she was sure she couldn't possibly look worse. Her hair was a mess, despite her mother's efforts to brush it. She hadn't worn makeup since the day of the accident, having found it too painful to apply it herself and too humiliating to allow anyone else to put it on for her. The nightgown she wore—at her mother's insistence, because Leeza saw no reason to put herself through the agony of dressing—was at least two years old and covered with ridiculous images of cuddly bears dancing on puffy white clouds. And, of course, there were her fixators, which she'd left uncovered when Dr. Dan had finished examining her leg.

"Hi," she mumbled.

"Hi, Reef," Brett chirped. "Back again, I see. Glutton for punishment."

Reef looked as awkward as he sounded. "I guess," he said.

"Reef's agreed to help out in the unit, Leeza," Carly explained. "I was wondering if you could show him around a bit."

Leeza tried to freeze the nurse with her glacial stare. "I thought Brett already did that."

"Only *part* of it," Brett said. "He spent most of the time keeping the sixth floor safe from wheelchair jockeys."

"Full-time job," Leeza muttered.

The nurse laughed. "You *know* it," she agreed. "So what's it gonna be, Leeza? Care to help Reef here complete his orientation?"

There was, of course, no way she could refuse. Doing so would have been rude, and although Leeza hadn't been a slave to courtesy these past few weeks—Brett could certainly attest to that—there was something in the guy's face that suggested he was as unhappy as she was to be there, which made her warm to him a bit.

"I'll need some help getting up," she said.

"Sure," Carly said. "Reef, could you wait in the hall for a minute?"

"No problem." He sauntered out.

It took, of course, much longer than a minute for Leeza to get up and mobile. She had become adept at maneuvering her body down the plywood slide into her wheelchair, but the pain that caught her whenever she moved still took the wind out of her, made her pause to catch her breath and brace for the next onslaught. Dr. Dan had begun to decrease her dosage of morphine, and the result of this was never more apparent than when she transferred herself from bed to wheelchair or back again. She was trembling when she'd finally completed the process.

"Glad you could do this for me," Carly said. "You're a lifesaver. I have too much to do to add tour guide to my duties."

"I'm just sorry I have physio now," Brett said elaborately, "or I'd be more than happy to take him off your hands."

"I'm sure," Leeza said as she absently adjusted her robe, her response clearly suggesting that even physio was preferable to this new task that awaited her.

"Look at it this way," Brett said. "How often do good-lookin' guys come round askin' to take you for a spin?"

Leeza shot her roommate the most malevolent glare she could muster, and Brett's grin vanished. "Hey, don't blame *me*," she continued. "*I* wasn't the one who brought him here."

Somehow Leeza wasn't so sure of that. A look had passed between Brett and Carly that suggested Brett might have been more instrumental in Reef's appearance than she let on.

Well, if they thought she was going to put on a happy face for some stranger who'd clearly been coerced into taking her off their hands, they had another think coming.

"So you're Reef," Leeza said after Carly had pushed her out into the hallway and then disappeared into another room.

"Mmm," he said. He leaned against the wall, one foot crossed in front of the other and his thumbs hooked casually into the belt loops of his jeans. "And you're Leeza."

They both turned to watch a nurse roll a cart filled with medications down the hallway, the clink of containers providing an almost musical counterpoint to their awkward silence. When the nurse turned the corner and the unintentional rhythm of the cart had vanished, the two teenagers turned to each other again.

Surprisingly, Leeza found she shared Brett's assessment of the volunteer. Wearing a T-shirt, he was, indeed, a "good-lookin' guy." His upper arms rippled into broad shoulders, and his chiseled face and dark coloring reminded her of the young Greek men whose pictures filled the decorating magazine her mother had brought by earlier that week. The theme of the issue had been the neo-Mediterranean style that was currently the rage in the homes of the rich and famous, but Leeza was sure the women who bought the magazine were more impressed by the male Mediterranean models than the furniture they sat on. She suddenly felt even more frumpy than she looked, and she shifted nervously in her wheelchair.

"So, uh . . ." she began, then faltered, regretting she'd ever agreed to this. "What do you want me to show you?"

The young man blinked. "I don't, uh . . ." Now he seemed to be the one faltering. "I ain't sure." He ran his fingers through his hair, the dark curls rearranging themselves as soon as he removed his hand. "What do you wanna show me?"

Leeza raised an eyebrow. "Depends on what you haven't seen yet, doesn't it?"

The young man's eyes widened and, clearing his throat, he glanced around the hallway. "Well, I, uh . . . I've seen plenty already."

Leeza looked down, horrified to find that her robe had parted, revealing not only her fixators but also an unobstructed view of her crotch and her catheter, which were no longer covered by cuddly bears and puffy clouds. Her slide on the varnished plywood had hiked her nightgown nearly to her waist, something neither she nor Carly had noticed when she'd tugged her robe around her. And because of her fixators, she was not wearing panties.

If her face was on fire before, it was positively volcanic now. "Oh. My. God," she moaned, yanking the edges of her robe together, then burying her face in her hands.

"There's one thing," the young man said after a moment.

Ears ringing with embarrassment, Leeza did not look up. "Obviously," she muttered into her now-covered lap.

"No," he said, and he made a noise that was somewhere between a gasp and a gargle. "That's not what I meant."

Peering through her fingers, Leeza could see he was trying hard not to laugh.

"Not that," he said, and he made the noise again. "The lounge."

She had no idea what he meant. "Lounge?"

"Yeah. Brett said somethin' about each floor havin' one." His eyes shifted from Leeza to the wall behind her and back, and she could tell he was being careful not to look in her eyes. "I ain't seen yours yet," he said.

Maybe it was the way the left side of his face quivered, as though he were biting the inside of his cheek. Or maybe it was the way his eyebrows knitted together in a portrait of strained concentration. Or maybe it was just because she really had nothing left to lose. Whatever the reason, she said the first thing that came to her mind: "Oh, I think you have."

Then they were both laughing, loud gusty whoops that echoed up and down the hallway. And they continued laughing, Leeza gulping back sobs, Reef wiping his nose, both of them gripping their sides, and before long curious patients and nurses were drawn into doorways to see what had caused such uncommon hilarity.

"Quite a view," Reef said as he looked out across Winter Street and Aberdeen Road. Far below, pedestrians in shorts and sunglasses were enjoying the August sunshine. In the distance, a patch of harbor glinted beyond office towers in the downtown core.

Leeza rolled her wheelchair over to the window. There was no one else in the lounge, which was fine with her. "Certainly prettier than the one you had earlier," she said, and then the two were laughing again.

Leeza struggled to remember the last time she had laughed as hard, really laughed with no holding back, and a memory surfaced of Ellen on the day Leeza passed her driver's test. In her excitement to show her sister her new Registry of Motor Vehicles license, she'd pulled quickly into the driveway and, pressing the gas instead of the brake, rammed her mother's Subaru into the garage door. Diane had been livid and was well into a full-volume lecture about motor vehicle safety when Ellen had appeared. Seeing her, Leeza had held up her license and shouted, "Look! I can drive!" and the irony of the moment struck both sisters at the same time, sending them into simultaneous gales of laughter. Even Diane, in the midst of her tirade, had begun to smile, then chuckle, then burst into wheezy gasps. All three had laughed hysterically for several minutes, clutching each other weakly for support. It was the last time Ellen had had anything to laugh about. She'd been diagnosed with cancer the following week.

Before she knew it, Leeza was sobbing. Images of Ellen in the driveway laughing and Ellen in the hospital dying alternately blurred and focused in her memory. It was like looking at those 3-D pictures hidden in two-dimensional drawings—it was only when you stopped trying to see them that they rose off the page, sudden and surreal.

The young man turned from the window. "Uh, look, uh . . ." he began when he saw she was crying. He shifted awkwardly, obviously unsure what he should do. "I, uh, I'm sorry if I, uh . . ." He trailed off.

She shook her head. "No, it's nothing," she choked. Then she sobbed even harder. Dr. Dan had warned her there would be times like this, times during her rehabilitation when the physical damage to her body would unexpectedly trigger a release of raw emotion. It was like wires crossing, he'd told her—two completely unrelated things would suddenly connect and the floodgates would open. Leeza had thought he'd been speaking metaphorically at the time, but, trying now to wipe away her tears with the sleeve of her robe, she was no longer sure that was true.

A tissue appeared under her nose. She looked up and saw the young man holding a Kleenex box he'd taken from the table by the window. "Here," he said, and something about the gesture, the contrast of the soft tissue in his large, rough hands, touched her.

"Thanks," she said.

"So, how'd today go?" Colville asked when Reef climbed into the truck.

Jesus. Was every day gonna be like this? Two seconds in the truck and already the third degree. Reef hated the thought of taking the bus back and forth, but it beat being grilled each afternoon by Constable Colville. He sighed, slumped back in the seat. "Okay," he said finally.

"Just okay?"

Christ Almighty. Reef ignored him and stared out the window. Cyclists and skateboarders were out in full force, their lithe bodies sweeping past them in the heavy traffic. Reef thought about bikes, thought about never having had one of his own. He'd stolen a few over the years, of course, ridden them a day or two before ditching them. But it wasn't something you could enjoy. You always had to be watching for cops, could never just forget everything and pedal, the wind tugging at you, pulling everything out and away.

Colville steered the pickup expertly through traffic, stopping at a crosswalk to let two small children and a woman pushing a stroller cross the street.

Reef watched as the woman maneuvered the stroller down off the sidewalk. The two children with her each placed a hand on the stroller, one on either side, and the procession moved slowly but purposefully across in front of them. When they reached the other side, the woman knelt down and said something to the children, then kissed both of them, and Reef remembered how he had knelt by the wheelchair in the sixth floor lounge.

It had been weird how, in the middle of all that laughing, the girl had started to cry. And not just a few sniffles. Once she'd got started, the sniffles had become sobs, her shoulders shaking like branches on a windy day, and he'd wanted to leave her there, call the nurse to come deal with that shit, tell her it wasn't his job to babysit loonies who belly-laughed one moment and then bawled the next.

But he hadn't. Had, instead, found the Kleenex and given it to her, listened to her apologize over and over. And then, out of nowhere, begin to talk. About her sister. She'd cried even harder then, telling between sobs what it was like to watch the cancer eat her sister alive. And he'd said, without even thinking, wasn't it more like watching someone burn up, watching the flame become a flicker then go out altogether? And she'd looked at him and nodded, asked him how he knew, and he'd begun talking about Nan, about what she'd been like before, about the first signs that something wasn't right, about the doctors and the drugs and the hospitals. And the funeral home.

She'd *known* that funeral home. Proule's on Pinehurst. Had sat in the same "slumber room" with her sister. Had watched people come in and go out, get on with their lives, while she'd left so much of hers behind.

He'd told her about the service, how it was all words and nothing at all like his grandmother. And she'd told him how the music had been the only comfort, Ellen's favorite songs piped through a PA system from a portable CD player. And he'd told her about the gravesite, the casket suspended by straps over a gaping hole. And she'd told him about how wrong it all was, how they'd made all the mud look clean, the bright green of the fake-grass carpet hiding the dirt that would seal her sister in. And he'd told her about the feel of that dirt in his hand, how he'd ground it under his fingernails before dropping it into the hole, needing somehow to have even this much of his grandmother left behind. And she'd told him how she had done the same, had refused to let it all slip from her fingers, had carried some back with her in the car.

They had talked all afternoon.

And when Carly had come to collect him, they'd still been talking.

He looked now at the young mother bent over the stroller, turned to watch as the scene slid by. Still looking out the window, he surprised himself by saying, "It was a *good* day."

Thankfully, Colville said nothing. Let the moment be what it was.

Chapter 19

The person who rolled into the room and greeted Brett was not the one who had rolled out earlier that day. She was a total mess, her face covered with what looked like tear-tracks, her hair bunching out in all directions. Nothing unusual about those. It was the ear-to-ear smile on Leeza's face that clearly astonished her.

"Okay, who stole my roomie and replaced her with you?" Brett asked.

Leeza's grin became, if possible, even wider. She guided her wheelchair into the bathroom and ran warm water over a facecloth, emerging a few moments later with her hair combed and face freshly washed. She gasped as she bent toward her locker, but hummed as she rummaged through it, pulling out various articles of clothing and looking them over. "I thought you had physio this afternoon," Leeza said brightly as she sorted through her things.

"I did. I went and came back while you were gone."

"Mm-hmm," Leeza replied.

"Like I *said*," Brett repeated, "I went and came back while you were *gone*."

"I heard you."

"And then I was *here* while you were *gone*," Brett said slowly, as if giving dictation.

"Mm-hmm."

A slipper sailed across the room and bounced harmlessly off the locker above Leeza's head.

She turned. "Something you want, Brett?"

"Only every last *detail*!"

"So. Sounds like you had an interesting afternoon," her mother said. Even over the telephone, her voice revealed her pleasure at the obvious improvement in her daughter's spirits.

Dressed for bed, Leeza leaned back against the pillow, barely aware that the morphine injection Carly had given her was somewhat weaker in strength than her last. "Yeah," she said, "I did."

"I'm glad. This Reef sounds like a nice person."

"He is," Leeza said. "I can't believe how long we talked."

"Losing his grandmother like that," Diane offered, "he knows how you feel, knows what you went through with Ellen."

"What we *all* went through," Leeza said softly.

The silence on the other end of the line spoke louder

than any words her mother might have said. Leeza heard a sound, knew her mother was swallowing, forcing back the tears that were just beneath the surface of any moment. She waited.

Her mother cleared her throat, then continued. "So, Leeza, why's this Reef volunteering at the rehab?"

"He didn't say. Because he wants to, I guess. Maybe because of his grandmother. Why else would anyone spend time in this place if they didn't have to?"

"Gotta point there, honey. Speaking of spending time there, sorry I can't make it tonight. I think I'm in over my head with this office I'm doing."

Leeza smiled. Whenever her mother said she was in over her head on a decorating job, Leeza knew she was having a great time. It had everything to do with challenge and her mother's Type A personality. If a job went smoothly, chances were her mother was bored. The more overwhelming a job was, the more passionate she became in exploring options, experimenting with different solutions, discarding everything and returning to the drawing board yet again. Her mother was having fun.

And it was about time. Leeza knew the situation at home was not good. Although Diane had never mentioned it, Leeza knew things hadn't been great lately between her mother and Jack. Part of the reason Leeza knew this had to do with how carefully her mother avoided talking about him. Leeza liked Jack, and so had her sister. He was, after all, the only father they had known in the last nine years. Except for birthday and Christmas cards containing checks—always the same amount—they almost never heard from their real father. He had a new family. Three sons, two of them twins.

But liking Jack and understanding him were two different things. Leeza knew that Ellen's illness had put considerable strain on her mother's and Jack's marriage, and she couldn't ignore the fact that her car accident and hospitalization had caused even more stress between them. Jack Morrison feared illness. His obsession with health and fitness grew out of a childhood filled with illnesses of his own—besides the usual things like chicken pox, measles and mumps, Jack had developed diabetes and renal disease, and doctors had had to remove one of his kidneys when he was nineteen. What followed was an almost manic preoccupation with diet and exercise, and when their mother met and fell in love with him two years after her divorce, she had no idea that this tall, powerfully built man who worked out at the gym twice a week quavered at the sound of a cough, left the room when someone sneezed and paled at even the thought of entering a hospital. Despite this idiosyncrasy, he'd been a good parent, caring and thoughtful. But the last year had taken its toll on the in-sickness-and-in-health part of his marriage vows.

Suddenly things were clearer to Leeza than they'd been in a long time. "I'm glad you can't make it tonight," she said.

"What?"

"You're here too much anyway."

"Leeza, honey—"

"No. I mean it." Leeza took a deep breath. Plunged ahead. "You're here all the time. You need to focus on that job you're doing. And Jack, too. When's the last time the two of you went out to dinner or to see a movie?"

"Sweetheart, there's plenty of time for that. Once you get out of rehab—"

"Look, I'll be here for at least two more months. Probably longer. Are you going to put everything on hold until then?"

"You're my daughter, Leeza. I don't mind."

"But I do. You need your life back. So does Jack." She paused. "And so do I."

She could hear her mother's sudden intake of breath. "What's *that* supposed to mean? When have I ever done anything but try to help you?"

It was Leeza's turn to swallow. Hard. "I know. But I think now it's time I tried to help myself."

There was a long moment when neither of them said anything. Then, "You can't keep me from visiting you, you know."

Leeza smiled at the hint of compliance that had crept into her mother's voice. "I'm not trying to. I think I just need to see a bit less of you."

There was another silence, this one shorter than before. "Well, can I still call you?"

Leeza looked at the phone, imagined her mother on the other end of the line, saw her as someone much younger, a child asking permission of an adult. "Of course you can call me. Any time. And you can visit, too. Just not for a while, okay?"

She heard a sigh. "Okay." Then, "I love you, Leeza."

"I love you, too, Mom." Leeza yawned, suddenly very tired. "I'll talk to you tomorrow. Say hi to Jack for me, okay?"

"I will, dear." But her mother didn't hang up. "Leeza?"

"Yes, Mom?"

"This Reef person. Did he have anything to do with this?"

The question surprised her, made her think. "Not directly, no."

"But indirectly?"

Leeza's mind went back to that afternoon in the lounge, the stories Reef and she had shared. "He made me remember something I'd forgotten."

"What was that?"

"That I can be strong too."

"Honey, you didn't need a stranger to show you that."

Leeza looked up at her sprinkler and smiled. "I think maybe I did."

Chapter 20

"Back again," Carly said. "You're getting to be a permanent fixture around here."

"Yeah," mumbled Reef. He wasn't sure what to say. Didn't feel like replaying the explanation he'd given Colville for why he needed to return today when he wasn't scheduled to show up at the rehab again until next week. "I didn't finish everything yesterday," he'd said. Which wasn't exactly a lie. But he was afraid the nurse would see right through him.

There was something in the way Carly had looked at him as he was leaving the day before that made him think she'd seen what had happened in the sixth-floor lounge, had maybe even set the whole thing up. Whether that was true or not, he hadn't been able to get Leeza out of his head, had lain awake half the night thinking about her. Reef had never felt like this before. Sure, he'd had more than his share of girls over the years. There had always been plenty on the periphery, girls who skipped classes with him, smoked and drank, did whatever drugs were available for the taking. Girls who liked the rush of breaking rules.

And then, of course, there was Scar. But it was different with her. With Scar, whatever fun he had was always diminished somehow by guilt. Like he was keeping her from being more than she was, making her less than she could be. Those other girls used him as much as he used them. Scar, however, used no one. She only gave. And in giving, she'd made it more and more difficult for Reef to take. She had too much to offer to waste it on him. Or anyone like him. It had taken him a while to see all that, to understand. Maybe it was being away from her for so long. His grandmother was fond of saying how sometimes you couldn't see the forest for the trees. He'd never really understood what she meant. But he thought he did now.

"So," Carly said, "how about reading to Stephen again? He's been pretty agitated this morning."

"Okay," said Reef. But, of course, it wasn't really okay. Stephen wasn't the patient he wanted to see.

And Carly seemed to know that. Her smile said so. "Leeza's down having physio. She won't be back on the floor until noon. I imagine you'll be wanting a break by then, won't you?"

Reef smiled, the expression on his face hot and clumsy. Even the roots of his hair felt red. "Could be," he said.

The morning unwound like thick yarn. Every few moments, Reef found his eyes drawn to the clock on

Stephen's table, surprised to see that the minute hand hadn't advanced much farther than the last time he'd looked. He'd picked up a *Reader's Digest* that someone had left behind and begun reading aloud some of the "Life's Like That" submissions, but he didn't find the anecdotes amusing. Nor, apparently, did Stephen, who moaned and thrashed about continually in his bed. Someone had put him in restraints before Reef arrived, and Reef didn't like seeing his wrists in those straps, didn't like hearing the restraints ring against the metal side rails each time Stephen flailed about.

So Reef put down the magazine and reached for a Halifax newspaper, yesterday's *Chronicle-Herald*. Reading the paper aloud had seemed to calm Stephen the last time Reef was with him, and he thought maybe it had something to do with the news. As he moved through the paper, though, he discovered it wasn't what he read but the way he read it that Stephen responded to. News items dealing with business developments on the world scene—in which Reef had zero interest—elicited considerable thrashing on Stephen's part, while items about events closer to home—to which Reef paid much more attention—seemed to calm him.

There was one article that silenced both Stephen and Reef, a local item about Rowdy Brewster that left Reef mute in mid-sentence. He thought about calling Jink and telling him to watch his back, but he knew what Jink would say, knew how he'd laugh at Reef for being such a pussy. Or maybe he wouldn't laugh. Maybe he wouldn't even talk to Reef at all. Things hadn't gone great when they'd visited him at North Hills. Jink and Bigger couldn't have got out of there any faster.

But he couldn't help worrying all the same, couldn't help remembering Bigger's words that day at the courthouse: *I wouldn't want Rowdy and his goons lookin' for me.* It wasn't until Stephen began to moan and tug on the restraints again that Reef remembered where he was, could turn the paper over and continue.

"Carly said I'd find you here," whispered Leeza.

Reef swiveled in his chair and saw her in the doorway. Stephen had fallen asleep a while earlier, but Reef hadn't wanted to take the chance of disturbing him by leaving the room. He'd sat quietly, watching the sheet over Stephen's chest rise and fall, rise and fall. There was something about that movement, repetitive and endless, that made him think about the events of the last few weeks, made him wonder if everything was automatic or if a person could actually change things, could make a difference somehow.

He was still mulling over that question when Leeza arrived.

He carefully lifted the newspaper from his lap and laid it on Stephen's table, then eased himself up from the chair. The vinyl seatpad made an embarrassing sucking sound as he peeled himself off it. He colored, shrugged his shoulders in an it-wasn't-me motion, and moved quietly to the door.

Out in the hall, he felt suddenly awkward, unsure what to say, the events of the previous afternoon suddenly a lifetime ago. What did he know about talking to girls like her? He looked over her head for signs of Carly or Brett, saw none. Cleared his throat. "Hi," he said finally. Like he was twelve.

"Hi."

He could tell she felt the same awkwardness, and it made him think about Bigger's dog, Ripper, the ugliest mutt on the planet. Reef had never had a pet, didn't know what everyone else knew about dogs, and the first time he'd seen Ripper, he'd made the mistake of patting him right away. Hadn't waited for the dog to sniff him first, look him over. Since then, Reef hadn't been able to drop by Bigger's house without the animal snarling at him, then slinking off when Bigger told him to shut the fuck up. The dog didn't trust him.

He wondered if people could be like that. Wondered if too much too soon made a difference, if maybe Leeza was wary of him now.

Then again, she was no dog. Not by a long shot.

"So." They'd both said it. At exactly the same time. Then they were laughing, and Reef felt the easiness of the previous day settle around them.

"Had lunch yet?" Leeza asked.

Reef shook his head. "What time is it?"

"Almost noon."

Reef looked at the hall clock over her head to confirm what she'd said. He'd lost all track of time. Probably because of that article in the paper.

"You want to grab a bite in the cafeteria?" she asked.

He thought about Bigger's dog again, wondered if maybe he was making a mistake. *Fuck it*, he thought. "How'd you like some real food?" he asked.

Carly had made them promise to be back by two o'clock, but Reef had called from a pay phone and asked for an extension—he'd taken Leeza to the Public Gardens and time had seemed to melt there in the hot August sun.

Despite her mother's encouragement, Leeza hadn't been outside the rehab once; now she regretted all the time she'd spent indoors. The ride wasn't comfortable, her wheelchair on the pathways joggled her uncomfortably from side to side, but Reef was very careful. It took a lot out of her, but not nearly as much as it would have if Val hadn't been driving her so hard in physio. And besides, she loved seeing all the flowers in bloom, grass and hedges neatly trimmed, kids feeding the ducks bits of bread, street artists' sketches and paintings pinned on lines strung along the fence around the gardens. By the time they left, both of their stomachs were complaining loudly.

Reef had some trouble maneuvering her chair across the busy intersection at Spring Garden and South Park.

The "Walk" sign flashed for only a few moments, and they were barely halfway across when the hand lit up, making it necessary for Reef to push the wheelchair faster, jiggling Leeza painfully. Getting the chair up onto the sidewalk and in through the Dairy Queen entrance was even trickier—Reef had expected people to be more polite, but several had rushed past them before a woman stopped and held the door open so they could enter. Reef seethed at the idiots who ignored them. Then suddenly remembered how he'd looked away from the patients Brett had introduced him to. Pretended they weren't there. He shrugged the thought away. *You think too much*, he told himself.

"You sure you want to do this?" asked Leeza as she scanned the menu on the wall behind the counter. The pain in her pelvis and leg had begun to talk to her, reminding her it was still there, stretching its claws under the morphine. Waiting. Just so she knew: it wasn't going anywhere.

Business at the Dairy Queen on Spring Garden Road was brisk, and there were several people in the line in front of them. A few of them turned to glance at Leeza, her wheelchair, the blanket that bulged over her fixators, but meeting Reef's dark scowl was enough to turn them face forward again. Fast.

"Yeah," Reef said. He still had money left over from his Social Services check, even after paying for the glass panel he'd broken, and DQ had to be a whole lot better than tuna sandwiches in the rehab cafeteria.

"What're you having?" she asked.

"Two cheeseburgers," Reef said. His stomach warbled in agreement. "Maybe three if this line don't move any faster," he said.

Leeza stared up at the pictures on the menu with something resembling reverence on her face. "Fast food never looked so good," she said. "I think I'll have one too." Then added, "With fries."

"Anything to drink?"

"D'you suppose the milkshakes here are as healthy as the ones at the rehab?"

Reef smiled. "Prob'ly better we don't know."

They'd wanted to eat outside, but it would have been difficult for Leeza to balance food on her lap so they ate in the restaurant looking out at the people walking past. Reef watched as another person in a wheelchair—this one a young man by himself—crossed the busy intersection and rolled up onto the sidewalk. He thought suddenly about that girl, Elizabeth Morrison, and couldn't help wondering where she was, what she was doing. More thoughts. He pushed them aside, chewed on his second cheeseburger.

"Mmm," Leeza said. "I forgot how good this stuff tasted."

"Beats Alex's cooking," said Reef without thinking. When she asked who Alex was, he told her briefly about North Hills, about it being a home for teenaged boys. She didn't press him for more, and somehow he knew she believed he lived there because he had no family. He hadn't lied. But it was the first time he'd been bothered by not telling the whole truth.

He told her, though, how duties at North Hills were divided up, how Alex was in charge of meals that week and Reef had grown tired of trying to identify the concoctions he had been serving them lately. *Haute cuisine* Alex called his dishes, but some of them might just as well have been fried hat. The evening before, Alex had experienced what he called a Martha Stewart Moment and flounced into the dining room carrying a large tray of canapés. Except Reef thought he'd said "canopies" and was sure Alex had served up bits of the old awning that hung over the back deck. When he made a comment to that effect, even Colville laughed, breaking his own "Respect others" rule. He suspended punishment for everyone's infraction that night and took them all out to McDonald's. Of course, Reef left out the part about what happened later.

"This Alex sounds like quite the character," Leeza said.

"He's one of a kind, all right," Reef said, his voice toneless. He turned away, saw the menu on the back wall and thought again of that meal at McDonald's. Over their supersized meals, they'd all started laughing again about Alex's cooking. Reef had asked Alex if he felt another Martha Moment coming on as he was scarfing down his Big Mac. Owen had nearly choked on a McNugget, which set everyone off again, and

Alex had responded by batting his eyes and asking Reef—in his breathiest diva voice—if his Quarter Pounder needed some of Alex's extra special sauce. The guys howled, all of them except Reef, who jumped up, grabbed Alex by the collar and roared, "You can shove your goddamn special sauce up your faggot ass." Which pretty much ended the meal.

This one was over too. Reef could tell Leeza was tired and, judging from the lines on her forehead, in a fair amount of pain. He picked up their empty food containers and napkins and put them into the appropriate bins. Returning to Leeza, he unlocked the brakes on her wheelchair and rolled her toward the exit. This time, a kid about seven years old jumped up and held the door open for them.

Once outside, Leeza thanked Reef for the meal. "No problem," he said, and she smiled at him, the kind of smile you saw on lottery billboards. Reef felt something let go inside.

"Jeez, that intersection," she said, looking at the cars waiting for the green.

Reef was glad she'd spoken. Otherwise he wouldn't have moved, would have continued to stand there like an idiot. "You wanna try crossin' the street on your own this time?" he asked. It was a ridiculous question, but the only thing he could think of to say.

She shook her head. "Maybe we'll save that for another day."

Another day. Reef liked the sound of that. Liked it a lot.

He reached for the handles on the back of the wheelchair and eased her forward.

"I was beginning to think I should send out a search party for you two," said Brett. She was lying on her bed reading a magazine when Reef rolled Leeza into the room. Leeza, however, knew she was only pretending to read. Her favorite soap was on at that moment, and any other weekday she'd have been planted in front of the third-floor big-screen TV. Brett obviously had been waiting. For more details.

"Hi, Brett," Reef said.

"Hi, Reef. I hear you finally got the vampire here out in the sunshine. And it didn't kill her after all."

He grinned self-consciously. "No, it didn't."

Leeza looked up at him. "You want to sit for a bit?" she asked, then grimaced.

"I'd like to, but my ride'll be here in a minute," Reef said. He'd noticed the hall clock and was amazed at how much time had passed. "Thanks anyway. I'll see you, okay?"

Leeza smiled at him. "Okay."

"See you, Brett." And he was gone.

"*You want to sit for a bit?*" Brett echoed teasingly. "Could you have sounded *more* like a senior citizen, girl?"

Leeza's face was pained, and not just from the lateness

of her morphine shot. "I know, I know," she groaned, tapping her forehead with the palm of her hand. "Shoot me now."

Brett pulled herself up onto her elbow. "You had a good time?"

Leeza nodded. "The best. He doesn't talk a lot, but he's a great listener. And the funny thing is, I don't think he even knows it."

They listened for a moment themselves as Stephen began to wail, the sound threading itself through the rooms along the hall until, unexpectedly, he fell silent.

"Did Reef tell you why he was volunteering here?"

"I didn't ask, but I think it's because of some program at this place where he lives." Leeza told Brett about North Hills.

"Jeez. An orphan," Brett breathed. "Rough. I can see why you didn't ask."

Leeza nodded.

"Did you talk to him about your accident?"

"You know, I was going to. He asked me about it, but I thought if I told him he might think I was some weird media freak. All that stuff in the paper." She shook her head. "Besides, I suddenly realized that I've spent the last three weeks thinking about nothing else. I want to put it behind me and move on. No sense dwelling on something you can't change, is there?"

"Wow," Brett said.

"What?"

"I can't believe what I'm hearing. Someone should've

taken you outside *weeks* ago. Did you a world of good, girl." She grinned. "You know, I'd have pushed you out myself if I coulda got one of these windows open."

"Gee, thanks," said Leeza.

"Hey, I'd have given you my parachute."

"That's what I was afraid of."

Stephen began to wail again, but this time his cries were drowned out by Brett and Leeza's laughter.

Chapter 21

"You trying to get all your volunteer time done this summer?" Colville asked as he eased the truck to a stop in front of the rehab. "This is your fifth time this week."

Reef pulled up on the handle and swung the door open. "That a problem?" he asked as he got out. His face had that hard-edged look, like the rim of a mirror, one you'd only hang on the back of a door.

"That's not what I meant," Colville said.

The door thunked shut. "I can take the bus."

"It was a joke, Reef."

"Yeah. Whatever." Reef heard Colville begin to say something else but he kept walking, triggered the automatic sliding doors and went inside.

"You're cheating!" Leeza shouted, reaching across the table and checking the pile of discards.

Brett was laughing so hard she was holding her sides, but looking at Reef's expression of wide-eyed innocence only made things worse. "Busted, buddy," she managed to gasp.

"Look, I can't help it if you two play poker like ol' ladies." Reef reached out and pulled the tangle of toothpicks toward him, adding them to the already considerable pile on his side of the table. "A full house beats two pair every time."

He hadn't been cheating, which was a first for Reef, since he was so good at it. Had, in fact, cheated in nearly every game he'd played with Bigger and Jink, often just using the simple double-up, sandwiching extra cards into his hand. It took nimble fingers to do it, and more than a little nerve when you were playing with Jink. Reef liked to win.

But he hadn't been cheating here. Hadn't, in fact, even thought to. For the first time in a very long while—since he'd played cards with his grand-mother—Reef found himself just enjoying the game. Winning wasn't the thing that kept him sitting at the table. Nor were his assigned hours bringing him back to the rehab day after day. It was being with Leeza. There was something about her that he couldn't get enough of. There wasn't a moment when he didn't find her on his mind. Couldn't do anything without wondering what she'd think about it. Like the green-house. It was finished now, and he'd thought that week about how he'd like to show it to her, how he'd like her to see what he'd done. Wondered if it might be possible. Sometime.

But it wasn't just the greenhouse. It was stupid stuff, too. He'd be doing the dishes at North Hills, or vacuuming, and he'd catch himself wondering if this was the way she'd dry silverware, or if that was the way she'd use the Hoover on stairs. Like any of that shit really mattered.

But somehow it *did* matter. Everything about her mattered to him. He wondered about what she'd been like as a kid, what her favorite things were, what she liked to do when she was alone. And afraid. He'd never known he could ask so many questions. And she'd answered all of them. All but one. What had brought her here.

He hadn't pressed her about it. The more time he spent with her, the less he wanted to think about what had brought *him* here.

Of course, in the last few days she'd had questions of her own, and he'd told her some of what his life had been like, the foster homes, the moving around. About Bigger and Jink, about some of the trouble they'd gotten into. Mostly, though, it was just stuff that made her laugh. He'd left out things she'd never understand, things that maybe even he didn't understand completely now.

So yeah, he could accept it if there were one or two things she didn't want to share. He'd considered asking somebody about her accident—Brett, maybe, or one of the nurses—but somehow it didn't seem right, that if Loozu wanted him to know she'd tell him in her own time. Like his being at the rehab. She'd just assumed that volunteering was something people at

North Hills did, and he hadn't told her any different. Didn't know how he could, if it came to that. Shuddered at what she'd think if she knew.

Because she did something to him. Made him want to be better somehow. Made him think, maybe, that he *was* better. Better than he'd been, anyway.

He'd tried to tell Owen about her a couple nights ago, tried to tell him who she was, what she was like. But Owen had looked at him like he'd suddenly grown an extra head, and he'd felt like a moron even bringing it up. Changed the subject. Because he really didn't understand it himself. Had never felt like this before.

It wasn't like he was in love, or anything like that. Who fell in love any more, anyway? Love was for soap operas and "I Dream of Jeannie" episodes. And deaf girls who got knocked up and left behind.

But he liked being with her. Liked the sound of her voice, how her eyes traveled over his face when he talked, the way her nose crinkled when she pretended to be mad. Like right now.

"Okay," Leeza said, as she stopped riffling through the discards, "I give up. What's your secret?"

"Reef, can I have a word with you?"

All three turned to see Shelly Simpson, the volunteer coordinator, standing in the doorway of the sixth-floor lounge. She wasn't wearing her usual smile, and the grin on Reef's face evaporated. "Right now?" he asked.

"Yes, please," she said. She stepped back into the hall.

Reef looked at Brett and Leeza. "Don't anyone touch my toothpicks," he warned them as he stood up. "I'll be back in a minute."

But it would be more than a minute before he saw them again. Much more.

Chapter 22

"Do they know any details?" Reef asked. He was pacing back and forth in Colville's office, his hands clenching and unclenching as he moved. Shelly Simpson had phoned for a taxi even before coming to find him and delivering Colville's message to return to North Hills. He'd jumped out even before the taxi had pulled to a complete stop, then raced up the steps, knowing what had happened. Hoping it wasn't true, but still knowing.

Colville sat in a chair across from the one Reef had been sitting in a few moments earlier. "Just what I told you. They found him down near the waterfront this morning."

"Near Rowdy's, right?" Reef's voice was low and even, but he was sure Colville could hear the tremor beneath the words. He cursed himself in his head. Colville, too.

"A couple blocks from there. But the police haven't established a connection—"

Reef's snort cut him off. "Connection my ass. That was payback. Rowdy has a long memory," he said, referring to the liquor license the city had revoked. He knew he should have called Jink the day he saw that news article. But he was sure Jink knew—how could he not? And what could he have said? Told him to be careful? Right. Only pussies and queers needed to be careful. Jink was invincible.

Except he wasn't.

"He's stable," Colville said quietly.

"When'll he be outta the hospital?"

Colville didn't answer right away and Reef stopped pacing. Stood in front of the seated man, waiting.

"I'm not sure," Colville finally replied. "I doubt if anyone knows at this point." When Reef resumed pacing, he continued, "Look, I know Jink is like family to you. Greg knows too, which is why he's arranged to take you to the hospital. But you need to be prepared for whatever—"

Just then the office phone rang. Colville reached for it. "North Hills. Colville here." He listened briefly. "Just a minute," he said, then turned to Reef. "It's for you. I'll give you some privacy." He handed Reef the receiver and left the office, closing the door behind him.

"Hello?" Reef said.

"Jesus, Reef, isn't it awful?" Scar's voice was too small for the room, for the receiver in Reef's hand. In the background, he heard Bigger's voice. He wasn't making words, just sounds, like syllables in a blender, their ends clipped off, each one running into the next. He was drunk. And he was crying.

"I just heard," Reef said. "You there with him now?"

"We were," she said. "They asked us to leave when Bigger wouldn't settle down."

"How is he?"

"Oh, Reef, if you saw him you wouldn't recognize him. His face is all . . ." And then she was crying, too.

There was another wail in the background, followed by a new stream of syllables that Reef could tell was a threat. Or a promise.

"I wish you were here, Reef."

"I will be. Matheson's comin' to get me."

As if on cue, Matheson's Escort turned into the driveway. Miraculously, it wasn't much louder than the other cars that passed by on the street, but blue smoke still plumed behind it like a peacock in full fan.

"He's here now," Reef said. "I'll see you in a few minutes." He dropped the receiver without waiting for a reply.

Scar and Bigger met him at the hospital entrance.

"The bitches won't let me *in*!" Bigger wailed, his huge voice drawing the attention of everyone entering and leaving.

Greg Matheson tried to put an arm around Bigger's shoulder but gave up because of the teenager's bulk and guided him to a chair just inside the entrance. Matheson looked up at Reef. "I'll take care of him. You and Scar go see about Jink."

Reef nodded, took Scar's hand and pulled her toward the bank of elevators ahead of them. "Which floor?" he asked, pushing both the *up* and *down* buttons.

"Seventh," she said. She'd let go of his hand and was hugging her arms around her.

Two of the elevators opened at the same time. They stepped into the one closer to them and Reef pushed 7, then realized it was going down. "Fuck!" he said, and two women already in the elevator exchanged looks, moved slightly away from him.

The elevator went down one floor, the women got off, and then it headed back up, only to stop again on the main level, where three more people got on. Each person was going to a different floor, none higher than the fifth. By the time the elevator reached the seventh floor, Reef was ready to kick the control panel off the goddamn wall.

They hurried down the hallway, Scar leading the way to the Intensive Care Unit. When they got there, a woman behind the nurses' station came around to meet them. "Can I help you?" she asked, but Reef could see in her eyes something more than a desire to help. Suspicion, maybe. And fear.

"We're here to see Jink," Reef said.

Scar spoke up. "Stanley Eisner. I was here before."

The nurse nodded. "I remember you. Is your friend—?"

"No," she said quickly. "He's downstairs. He won't cause any more trouble."

"Like I told you and your friend before," the nurse continued, "only members of the immediate family can see patients in ICU."

"I'm family," Reef said. "I'm his brother."

The nurse gave him a long look. "Brother you say?" She reached behind her and pulled a chart from the carousel on the counter, flipped through it, looked up. "His mother was here earlier. She didn't say anything about a brother."

Reef leaned toward her. "I'm his brother," he repeated slowly, then turned to Scar. "And she's his half-sister. On his father's side."

The nurse looked at them both, seemed about to say something, then shrugged. "Five minutes, that's all. And if there's even the *hint* of a disturbance, I'm calling Security."

"Thank you," Scar whispered.

The nurse led them through a sliding glass door into a room with four beds. Only two of them were occupied; the one containing Jink was set against the far wall. Tubes entered his body at various places including his mouth and nose. At least, Reef assumed they were his mouth and nose. His face was a swollen purple mass that bore no resemblance to Jink's real features, and Reef could see that the bruises and swelling extended to other parts of his body, many of them covered in bandages. A monitor beside the bed beeped at regular intervals, and a bag of clear liquid drained down a tube into Jink's arm.

"*Christ*," Reef said when the nurse had left them alone.

Scar choked back sobs. "I saw him through the glass before," she said, her voice a strangled gulp, "but up close . . ." She began to cry.

Reef took her hand and squeezed it. "Just think what the *other* guys must look like," he said.

They both tried to force a smile but failed. Stood there listening to the beep of the monitor, tried not to see the snarl of tubes their friend had become.

Colville met Reef on the veranda. "How is he?"

"You were right. No one knows anything for sure. Not yet, anyway." Reef went inside and headed for the stairs.

Colville followed him. "How're *you* doing?" he asked softly.

Reef just looked at him.

"Everyone's in the family room," Colville continued. "Come on in."

"Look," Reef said, "give me a break."

Colville paused, seemed about to say something, then nodded. "If you change your m—"

"Right," Reef interrupted, taking the stairs two at a time.

He got to his room and sat on the edge of the bed, his feet tracing the pattern of the oval rug over and over. He got up and moved to one of the turrets, stood

looking out the window, his fingers tugging unconsciously at the curtains. He ran a hand over his forehead, rubbed his eyes, put both hands in his pockets,
took them out and crossed his arms.

"Can I come in?"

Reef turned to see Alex in the doorway. *Christ*, he
thought, turned again to the window. "Whadda *you*
want?"

"Sorry to hear about your friend," Alex offered.
"So's everyone else."

Reef just nodded.

Alex entered the room and sat on the edge of the
bed. "You want to talk about it?"

"No. I don't."

"Are you sure?"

His back to Alex, Reef made a sound that could have
been a snort or a cough or a clearing of the throat.
Then, "I'm skippin' the family room sharin' shit tonight,
okay?"

"You know, it helps to say what you're fee—"

"Look, you may like all that garbage, but I don't."

"Why not?" asked Alex.

Reef swung around to face him. "Because it's
nobody's goddamn business, *that's* why!"

"What are you afraid of?"

Reef took the three steps from the window to the
bed, his face dark and twisted. "I ain't afraid 'a *nothin*'!
You *got* that, you little freak?"

"That's denial, Reef," Alex replied calmly. "Naming it's the first step in facing it."

Reef leaned down so his mouth was inches from Alex's ear. "What makes you think I gotta *face* anything?" he shouted. "I'm fine! You hear me? *Better* than fine. I'm fuckin' *fantastic*!"

"Honey," Alex said, pushing up his sleeves and holding out his wrists, palms turned upward, "that's exactly what I said the night I gave myself these." Thick, worm-like scars extended from his wrists up the insides of both arms.

Reef gaped at the angry red furrows that stretched nearly to his elbows. Along both sides of each were indentations where surgical thread had pierced the flesh, stitching the edges together. One furrow was raised and darker in color near the center, as though whatever had carved it had met resistance before plunging on.

Reef stared at the scars for what seemed a long time, then slumped onto a chair at the foot of the bed.

Alex waited, gave Reef time to find the words.

When he'd finally found the first one, the second, and then the third, the others just seemed to find the way on their own.

Chapter 23

The doctor wasn't much more help than the nurse had been the night before. "He's still stable," he said. "That's something."

"But is he gonna get better?" Bigger asked.

Reef knew Bigger was being as polite and respectful as he could—no way were they gonna throw him out like yesterday—but there was no hiding the impatience in his voice. His face folded into something like a smile, probably to show everyone he wasn't mad, but it was too quick, too phony, more like a grimace than a grin.

Reef knew how he felt. He hated the way everyone pussyfooted around, never giving a straight answer. And the doctor's face was unreadable, his expression almost detached. He was clearly a man with many things on his mind, and Jink was only one of them. He sighed. "Like I said before, he's got a lot going for him. He's strong—"

"Like an ox," Bigger interjected. Too loudly.

The doctor blinked. "Yes," he said. "And he's young, which is an important factor in any case that involves injuries as extensive as his."

Reef recalled one of his conversations with Leeza, remembered her saying that her doctor had told her the same thing. He thought of all the times he'd wished he were older so he could be out on his own, in charge of his own life with no one to answer to. Funny how something like your age could be a disadvantage one day and a bonus the next.

"When will you know for sure?" Marlene Eisner asked. She had let Reef, Bigger and Scar remain in the ICU waiting room when the doctor came to see her. But she'd made Bigger promise to be on his best behavior.

"The first forty-eight hours are crucial," the doctor replied. "We're monitoring him closely. Besides the obvious threat of brain damage—"

"*Christ!*" Bigger breathed. Scar shot him a look and he immediately apologized.

"—our greatest concerns," the doctor continued, "are his kidneys and liver. He experienced severe trauma to his back and midsection."

"Bastards!" Bigger said, then realized his mistake. "Look, I'm just gonna wait outside till you're done, okay?" Everyone in the room nodded, and he stepped outside the door.

"So you won't know anything for sure until tomorrow," Scar said.

"And maybe not even then," said the doctor. "So much depends on Stanley. Once he regains consciousness we'll know more. *If* he regains consciousness."

"*Fuck!*" came Bigger's voice from the hallway.

"I tol' him and tol' him," Marlene Eisner said, absently stirring her coffee as they sat in the hospital cafeteria. "I sez to him, 'Stanley,' I sez, 'you gonna get the shit kicked outta you if you keep spendin' time with the likes 'a Rowdy Brewster.' 'But Ma,' he sez, 'I kin take care 'a myself,' he sez." She took a sip of the black liquid, grimaced, then went on, "But when did that boy ever listen t' me?"

Reef and Scar sat across the table from her, having left Bigger upstairs in ICU. Bigger had said he wasn't hungry, which should have been cause for Reef to phone the Channel 9 news team, but they all knew he was worried sick about Jink. He'd have slept last night in the waiting room if Security hadn't made him leave.

Reef looked at Jink's mother and resisted the urge to shake her. It wasn't enough that Jink was lying upstairs looking like meat gone bad. She had to make it all about *her*. If only Jink had listened to *her*, done what *she'd* told him, been the good boy *she* knew he could be. Right. Like she'd actually *had* all those heart-to-hearts with Jink. Like she'd been *home* every night instead of over at the waterfront casino feeding her welfare check into the slot machines for hours at a time. Up five dollars and down ten. Up twenty and down a hundred. She couldn't even walk by a Lotto 6/49 booth without buying an Insta Pik. "Sooner or later, I *gotta* win," she'd say, as though the only difference between her and Bill

Gates was a run of good luck. Marlene Eisner: Mother of the Fucking Year.

But Scar pretended she was speaking gospel. Let her go and on, kept giving her the nod and the smile and the shake of the head that she needed. That was one way of helping out, Reef supposed, but it wasn't his way.

He pushed his chair away from the table.

"You going back up already?" Scar asked.

"No," he said, standing up.

"Then where?"

"Somethin' I gotta do," he said.

"You sure about this?" Bigger asked. The bus was nearly full, and he'd had to squeeze himself into the last seat, his legs triangled up against the one in front of him.

Reef looked at him, turned away in disgust.

"Shit, man," Bigger said, "of *course* I wanna give Rowdy some payback. But I'm not talkin' 'bout *me*. What if that judge finds out? She could screw you big time."

"Fuck her," Reef snarled.

"I'm just sayin'—"

"Fuck you, too!"

A middle-aged man sitting in the seat ahead turned around. "Hey, you guys wanna clean it up back there?"

"Fuck off, asshole!" hissed Reef.

The man gave him a hard stare, opened his mouth to say something, then seemed to notice Bigger for the first time. He faced front.

"Man, you know *me*," Bigger said. "After what they did to Jink, there's nothin' I wanna do more than make sidewalk salami outta Rowdy Brewster 'n' his boys. But we're goin' off half-cocked. We ain't got a plan or nothin'. You think Rowdy's just gonna let us waltz in and kick the shit outta him?"

Reef said nothing. He didn't want to think. He wanted to *do*. Something. Anything. He crossed his arms, unfolded them, crossed them again. He looked across the aisle and noticed a woman sitting with two kids. Boys, no more than four and five, and both were staring at him with open mouths. The mother saw Reef looking, leaned down and whispered something to both of them, and the younger one turned away. The older one, though, continued to stare at Reef, his eyes like spoons.

Reef looked at the back of the guy's head in front of him. His neck was bright red, and he guessed the guy's face was probably the same color. The man hadn't been looking to bother anybody, just asked them to quit the cursing. There were kids there. Little kids. Reef looked across the aisle again. The older kid grinned at Reef and silently formed a word with his mouth. Reef didn't need to hear it to know what it was.

He thought about words. Thought about which ones got said and which ones didn't. Like the words he wished he'd said to his grandfather. All those times he'd bitten them back. He'd told Alex some of those words the night before. He hadn't planned to. They'd just come. And Alex had told him some of his own words. Words like *faggot* and *fudgepacker*, *fruit* and *queer*, words his own father had used against him. Words that had piled up, gathered strength and volume until finally, one night when he was alone, he'd lashed out against those words, trashed the home where he'd heard them shouted. But the lashing out hadn't muted the words in his head, words that dug a well inside him that couldn't be filled up, words that ripped and tore, echoed and echoed until it seemed the only way to silence them was to find the bottom of that well. He'd looked for it with a razor. Had almost found it.

Reef thought about other words. The ones his grandmother used. And the ones he wished he'd said to her. He'd tried to say them at Proule's, standing over the casket. But even then they wouldn't come. The only ones his mouth would form were his grandfather's words. Like the one the kid across the aisle had just learned.

The bus pulled over and Reef stood up.

"This ain't the stop," Bigger said.

Reef had no more words. He moved toward the front. Bigger looked at him, baffled, then hauled himself to his feet and followed.

•   •   •

Colville's truck pulled up to the curb and the two
teenagers climbed in, Reef sandwiched between the
two larger bodies. Colville looked at him and smiled.
"I'm glad you called," he said. Then he put his left signal light on and waited for a break in traffic. "I'm
proud of you, Reef."

Reef didn't say anything. Couldn't. Those were his
grandmother's words. The last ones the cancer had let
her say.

Chapter 24

"Hey!" Carly said when the elevator doors opened and Reef stepped out. "Look who's here!"

Reef didn't know what to say. Despite the nurse's continued warmth, he still hadn't got used to being welcomed when he walked into a room. It felt good. Weird, but good.

"Funny?" she asked.

"What?"

"The joke you just heard. I haven't seen you smile like that."

"No joke," he said to his feet. What was it about this place? Six seconds inside and his face was as red as salsa. As hot, too.

"We've missed you this past week," she said. "Been having a good time?"

Yeah. If you could call spending your days in another hospital a good time. But things were definitely looking up. Jink had regained consciousness shortly after Reef and Bigger's bus ride to nowhere, and the results of his preliminary tests were "promising"—the doctor's word, not his. Since then, however,

Jink had astonished both the doctor and his friends, improving faster than anyone would have thought possible. Much of this the doctor attributed to his patient's considerable physical strength, but Bigger had another explanation: "He's havin' a ball hasslin' all those nurses." Which, Reef had to admit, was painfully obvious. He'd laughed more than once at the lengths Jink had gone to to get a rise out of the hospital staff. Like getting Bigger to bring in those cans of apple juice that he poured into his bedpan, confounding the nurses keeping track of his fluid input and output. Reef didn't need to hear the doctor's prognosis to know Jink was on the mend. The constant fuming at the nurses' station on Jink's floor was enough.

And then, of course, there'd been the call he'd received that morning. Bigger had phoned to tell him two cops had arrived at the hospital with news about Jink's assault: Rowdy Brewster and two other men had been formally charged as a result of a witness who'd come forward with an account of the attack. Bigger'd been so wound up he was practically hollering into the receiver, but he'd settled down long enough to tell Reef that the men were being held without bail, and the case against all three looked solid.

Reef shrugged. "Just some good things been happenin' lately," he said.

The nurse smiled. "Glad to hear it. We've had a few good things happen around here, too," she said.

"Like what?"

"I'll let Leeza tell you."

"She got her catheter out!"

Reef turned and just had time to leap out of the way of Brett's oncoming wheelchair. "Darn," she muttered. "Teenagers are worth ten points. From now on, no more advance warning."

Reef grinned. "That's good news about the catheter. I know how much she hated that thing."

"That's not the best part, though," said Brett.

"Maybe we should let Leeza tell him," Carly repeated. Turning to Reef, she continued, "She's been wondering when you were coming back."

"I been tied up," said Reef. "A buddy 'a mine was in the hospital."

"We know," Brett said. "Shelly told us."

"He's doin' okay now."

"So's Leeza," said Brett, almost bubbling. "In fact, *better* than okay. She's improved so much that she's getting her fixators off tomorrow."

Carly sighed. "I thought we were going to let Leeza tell him."

"So sue me."

"That's great!" said Reef. "But I thought they weren't supposed to come off for a couple more weeks."

"They weren't," said Carly. "But that was before you showed up. She's been a different person since then— eating better, putting a hundred percent into her physio, really taking control of her recovery. Her change in attitude made a world of difference. And you made that happen, Reef. We're all very grateful to you."

"So's her Mom," Brett said. "I think she's in the room with Leeza now if you'd like to meet her. I know she really wants to meet you."

Reef looked at his feet. "Uh . . . I'm not much for meetin'—"

"She's really nice. You'll like her, I promise." Brett turned her wheelchair and rolled down the hallway. "Come on."

Reef continued to stare at his feet, his face revealing the agony of his sudden self-consciousness.

Carly put her hand on his shoulder. "You did a really good thing, Reef. You need to let people tell you how they feel about what you did."

He looked up and she smiled. "Go on," she said.

Chapter 25

The silence in the family room was a solid thing. Colville studied the faces of the young men as they sat in the circle, waiting. All but one of them, from Alex on his left to Owen on his right, wore the same look. Haunted. Helpless. All but Reef. Reef's face was empty, as though everything in it had been wrung out. A dishcloth in a dry sink.

Everyone waited.

The boys had been there that morning when the call came. Had seen Colville run to the truck and tear out of the driveway, then return later with Reef. Or someone who looked like Reef. The person who sat in the circle with them now. But surely not the person who'd sat there every other evening, his eyes barely masking the bored sneer behind them. This was a different Reef. Hollow. Depleted. A body that breathed.

Everyone waited.

The boys knew some of it, had heard him shouting up on the third floor. Not shouting, really, which would have implied the manufacture of words. More like sounds than speech. Patternless. Without form or function. Yet threaded throughout had been Frank Colville's low tones, his comments stitching meaning into the torn fabric of that morning.

Everyone waited.

The sounds had lasted a long time, and then Colville had come downstairs alone. He shook his head when Alex offered to go up. "Give him some time," he'd said. And they had. They all had. Morning had become noon, then afternoon, and afternoon had stretched into night. And then Reef had come down. Not the Reef they knew, though. Some other Reef.

Everyone waited.

And then they didn't have to wait any longer.

This other Reef drew a breath, the sound ragged and shallow. Then he spoke.

Even before they neared her room, Reef heard evidence of Leeza's good news: she was singing. Her voice was terrible—someone more charitable might have called it "untrained"—and yet oddly beautiful, in the way that storm clouds have beauty, their tattered edges like dark lace against the lighter sky behind them. She was humming an old Bruce Springsteen song, every few seconds breaking into remembered words and phrases so the effect was like hearing one side of a conversation. A dialogue between Leeza-then and Leeza-now.

When they reached the doorway, Brett grinned at him broadly and then sped off. Standing there, Reef could see Leeza in her wheelchair by her locker, putting something into the lower compartment. She was bending at the waist, and a gasp momentarily interrupted her singing as her position put strain on the flesh around her metal pins, but then she continued, Springsteen's lyrics accompanying her task once more.

Something else was different. On Leeza's bedside table were framed photographs that had not been there during Reef's earlier visits. Some of them were photographs of Leeza and another girl, and some were pictures of the girl alone. The girl looked much like Leeza, her hair the same shade of blond, her smile the same crooked line that suggested an effort to keep from laughing, probably at the antics of the photographer. *Ellen*, thought Reef.

"Hi," he said.

"Ow!" He'd startled her and, turning quickly, she'd bumped her head on the open locker door. But she smiled when she saw the person in the doorway. "Reef!" she said.

"What're you doin'?" he asked.

"Housecleaning. Or locker cleaning, actually. Making room for some more things." She beamed. "I'm getting these off tomorrow!" She pointed at the metal on her leg. "I'll actually be able to wear clothes again!"

He entered the room and stood by the end of her bed. "Brett told me. Must be a relief, huh?"

"You have no idea!" Leeza trilled. "And," she continued more softly, "everyone agrees that I have *you* to thank for that."

Reef felt his cheeks burn. Hotter than salsa this time. Stove-hot. "I didn't do anything," he said. He picked up one of the photographs. "You look like her," he said gently.

"We both took after our mom," Leeza explained. "Which is another reason why I'm glad you're here. My mother wants to meet you." When Reef glanced around the room, Leeza added, "She went down to the cafeteria to get me another milkshake." She shrugged. "It's a mother thing. She hasn't been here for a while, and she thinks she has to make up for lost time." She made a face. "I've drunk enough milk and eaten enough foods with milk in them to last me a lifetime! When I get out of this place, the first thing I'm going to do is drop-kick a carton of 2 percent as far as I can."

As if choreographed, a strawberry milkshake carton fell to the floor in the doorway, a plastic straw oozing pink liquid onto the tiles.

Leeza turned to see her mother standing above it, Diane's face as white as the cotton blouse she wore. She looked as though someone had struck her in the stomach, her mouth working oddly yet forming no words.

"Mom?" Leeza asked. "What's wrong?"

But her mother just stared, unable or unwilling to speak.

"Mom, are you going to be sick?"

Clearly this was a possibility, as something resembling revulsion flickered back and forth across her mother's face. "You!" she cried.

Leeza turned in the direction her mother was looking and saw Reef, his face a darker mirror of her
mother's wide-eyed astonishment.

"You *bastard*!" her mother shouted. "What are *you*
doing here?"

Reef recoiled as if slapped, the backward motion
bringing him up against Brett's bed. He dropped
heavily onto it.

"What's wrong?" Leeza cried. "Do you know each
other?"

Diane turned to her, her voice shrill and insistent.
"Don't you know who this is?" She swung back to
Reef. "What are you doing with my daughter? Haven't
you hurt her enough? Is this some kind of sick joke?"

Footsteps hurried down the hallway and Carly
Reynolds appeared in the doorway behind Diane.
"Mrs. Morrison, is something—"

At the mention of her name, Reef groaned.

"Mom," Leeza sobbed, "this is Reef! The one I was
telling you about, the one who helped—"

Her mother shook her head violently. "No!" she
shouted, and Leeza could hear in her mother's voice
an emotion she'd heard only once before. Diane's
hands shook as she pointed at Reef. "This is . . ." and
then her voice cracked and she could not speak.

"Mrs. Morrison," said Carly. "What's wrong? Is
there something I can do?"

Diane turned, as if only now aware of the nurse
behind her. Her voice was little more than a croak:

"You can get that goddamn son of a bitch out of my daughter's room!"

Carly turned to Reef, who had managed to pull himself to his feet, his shoulders hunched, drawn in toward his body. He looked unsteady, unsure if his legs would support his weight. "Reef?" Carly asked.

"Mom, what have you *done*?" Leeza cried.

Her mother reacted as if she'd been slapped. "What have *I* done?" she managed to ask. "It's what *he's* done! That," and she paused, groping for words, "that *monster* is the one who *put* you here!"

Leeza looked at Reef. "What's she saying?" she choked. "What does she mean?"

"Leeza . . ." Reef began. And then he ran.

". . . and then I ran," Reef said. His voice was little more than a whisper, and the others had to strain to hear him. "I didn't even know where I was going, what I was doing. I didn't wait for the elevator. Just ran down the stairs. Six flights," he said softly, his eyes aimed at some point between his feet as he spoke.

The others in the room somehow knew he hadn't finished, wasn't through the telling yet. They waited for him to go on.

"I kept running. All the way down. I almost fell twice. Wished for a second I *would* fall." He stopped, swallowed audibly. Took a breath. "And when I got to the lobby, I ran into the guy who greets people.

Slammed right into him. Knocked him clear off his feet." He dragged a hand through his hair, down the back of his neck. "I stopped to help him up." He paused, managed to continue. "But . . . but he helped *me*. Called the person in charge, Shelly. Who called here." His voice, like an intermittent radio signal, trailed off, became stronger. "I put her in that place. Me. Like Rowdy did to Jink. Except Rowdy used his hands. Looked Jink in the face while he did it." He drew another ragged breath. There was nothing more to say.

But, of course, there *was* more. Far more.

"What are you gonna do?" Alex asked quietly.

Reef did not look up. He did the only thing he *could* do. He wept.

PART THREE

PART THREE

Chapter 26

No one in the classroom said a word for a moment. A few looked at each other self-consciously and one or two squirmed slightly in their seats. Reef was used to those reactions. He gave them a few more seconds. Then he asked, "Anyone have any questions?"

Several hands shot up.

"Yes?" said Reef, nodding at a boy near the front.

"How much money d'ya make doin' this?" the boy asked.

"Robbie!" Mr. Brighton admonished, silencing several students in mid-laugh. "Didn't we talk beforehand about appropriate questions? Maybe you need to see me tomorrow at noon hour so I can refresh your memory."

"No, that's okay," Reef said to the teacher. "Actually, it's a good question." He turned to the boy. "I don't get a cent for doin' this, Robbie. It was one of the requirements of my probation."

"Probation?" Robbie asked.

"One of the things I had to do to keep from goin' to jail."

That comment elevated a dozen eyebrows, and several other hands waved in the air.

"Yes?" He pointed to a girl sitting near the back.

"Did someone get in trouble for puttin' you in the same place as that girl?"

Reef looked at the teacher and smiled. "Another good question," he said. He turned to the class. "It was no single person's fault. The judge just said I had to volunteer at a rehabilitation center. I'm a young offender, so the facilities didn't know who I was or what I'd done. It was just a fluke that I ended up where I did. A one-in-a-million chance," he said, and he thought briefly of Marlene Eisner feeding coin after coin into those casino slot machines. She'd never understood odds like those. Never would.

"Yes?" he said, nodding toward another girl, this one with long red hair. Almost the same color as Scar's.

"Can she walk now?"

"Yes," Reef replied, quickly pointing to another hand.

"How do you feel about havin' to tell your story to people like us?" asked a boy near the front. He spoke quietly, as if unaccustomed to asking questions. He had a soft voice, and he reminded Reef of Alex. It had been a long time since Reef had seen him, and he wondered if things were better than the last time they'd spoken.

"I haven't told you everything. There's too much for one hour." Reef took a deep breath. "But even tellin' this much is hard." He smiled ruefully. "Imagine havin' to go to a place like this and tell total strangers what a jerk you been, the idiot things you done. Tough, huh?"

There was a murmur of assent.

"When the judge made that part of my probation, I hated even the *thought* of doin' it. I figured it was a power trip, her havin' fun at my expense." He looked around the room. "But she was a lot smarter than I gave her credit for. Now I'm glad she did it."

"Why?" asked the boy with the soft voice.

Reef nodded toward Mr. Brighton. "Do your teachers ever get you to think back over things you done in class? Maybe ask you to write about what you learned?"

Someone else spoke up. "They call it 'reflecting.'"

Reef smiled. "That's one word for it. I'm not sure it's the best one, though. When I think of reflectin', I think of a mirror. The thing you see in a mirror is always the same as the thing in front of it, only the reverse." He leaned back against the teacher's desk. "When *I* think back over things . . ." He glanced around the room. "I mean *really* think them through, like I have to do when I'm tellin' others about 'em, like today—you know what I mean?"

Several students nodded.

"When I do that, I usually find out they *aren't* the same as I first thought." He looked down at his hands, at the object he'd been holding throughout his talk, that he'd held during every talk he'd given. "You know, the very first time I told my story to a class like yours, I realized somethin' about what happened that I didn't know before."

The red-haired girl spoke up. "What was that?"

Reef smiled, but there was no humor in it. "I realized I was *afraid* the day I went to see my buddy in the hospital." He stood up, looked for a moment out the window at the empty soccer field and the buildings beyond, then turned to face them. "I know that doesn't sound like much, but to me it was important. Before I told my story that day, I thought I was just *worried* about Jink. And I *was* worried. But I was afraid, too."

"Afraid of what?" the girl asked.

"That he'd look as bad as some of the people I'd seen in rehab. Or worse." He gripped the object tightly in his fingers. "Until then, I had no idea how bad a body could be broken." He shook his head. "You know all those movies you see where somebody gets totally clobbered but then he hauls himself up 'n' runs after the bad guys?"

She nodded. So did several others.

"That only happens in the movies," Reef said. "Believe me."

"So did you learn anything different today?" the soft-voiced boy asked.

Reef smiled at him. "I learn somethin' new every time," he said, and slipped the object into his pocket. He glanced at his watch. "And speakin' 'a time, we're just about out of it. But before I go, there's one more thing I'd like to say." He cleared his throat. This was always the hardest part: trying not to sound preachy. "There's another reason I'm glad the judge ordered me to do this. It's because I hope what I have to say to people will make a difference. I'm only a few years older 'n you are, but that's plenty 'a time to make mistakes. Big ones. Most of the things I regret in my life I did because I was afraid. I used to think it was because I was angry. Anger is a hard thing to deal with. But I think fear is harder. It makes you feel more alone. If there's somethin' botherin' you, there are people who can help. I'm gonna leave some cards with your teacher, and if you think you'd like to talk to someone sometime, call the number on the card, okay?"

Mr. Brighton stood up and moved to the front of the room. "I'd like to take this opportunity," he said, "to thank you for coming in to talk to us. You can tell from the questions that everyone was very interested in what you had to say today." He turned to the class. "Let's show Mr. Kennedy our appreciation, okay?"

Everyone clapped, including Robbie. When the bell rang and the class was filing out, he said to Reef, "I *still* think you should be gettin' money for this."

Reef grinned and turned to collect his jacket, which he'd hung over the teacher's chair.

"Great presentation," Mr. Brighton said, smiling. "Really. I wish they paid as much attention to *me*."

Reef flushed. "Thanks."

"You ever think of making a career of this?" the teacher asked.

Reef nodded. "I've been thinkin' about that quite a lot lately."

"You're a natural. I'd give it some more thought if I were you. What are you doing now?"

"I'm in my final year 'a school. I get time off to give these talks."

"How many more do you have left to do?"

"Technically," Reef replied, slipping on his jacket, "I'm all done. Finished last semester."

The teacher cocked an eyebrow. "And today?"

Reef shrugged. "Hard to explain. People keep callin' and askin' and I keep sayin' yes. Just somethin' I still need to do, I guess."

Brighton held out his hand. "Well, I'm certainly glad you're doing it." He shook Reef's hand firmly.

"Mr. Kennedy?"

Reef turned to see the red-haired girl standing by the teacher's desk. She was the last of the students to leave. "Call me Reef," he said. "The 'Mr. Kennedy' stuff is hard to get used to."

"There was something else I wanted to ask you."

"What's that?"

"Did you ever see that girl again?"

He'd hoped he would make it through at least one of these presentations without someone asking that question. It was the one he dreaded most. "There's not a short answer to that," he said.

"Yes or no seems pretty short to me."

"Kelly," said Mr. Brighton, disapproval in his tone,

"maybe that's something Reef doesn't want to talk about."

"That's part of it," Reef said, "but the more important part is because yes or no doesn't really tell you anything. Actually, the answer is kind of both."

Kelly just looked at him.

Reef turned to the teacher. "Is there anybody coming in here now?"

Mr. Brighton shook his head. "This is my prep period. What class do you have now, Kelly?"

"Gym."

The teacher looked at Reef. "You're welcome to stay here and chat longer if you want."

"Fine with me if it's okay with Kelly," Reef said. He thought of the times he'd done this before, had lost track of how many.

The teacher walked over to the door and pressed a button on the wall. In a moment, a secretary's voice came over the classroom speaker. "Yes?"

"This is Paul Brighton. Would you please tell Mr. Marshall in the gym that Kelly Bradshaw will be in my classroom a while longer? If that's a problem, he can let me know."

"I'll tell him," the voice said.

"Thank you." The teacher turned to Reef. "Do you mind if I stay? I'd like to hear the answer to that question myself."

Reef pointed to the chairs. "We may as well sit down. This'll take a while."

Chapter 27

Leeza sat at her desk looking at the pages of neatly written script, her eyes now and then drifting to the newspaper clipping included along with all the color photos she'd pulled from the fat envelope. She was, yet again, surprised by Brett Turner, who was now Brett Hollister. She and Sam had got married in March, and the letter was filled with details about their honeymoon. To Leeza, however, it sounded more like an Iron Man endurance test, because, in typical Brett fashion, they had gone white-water rafting in British Columbia, had helicoptered into the Interior to hike on a glacier, and then whale-watched a pod of Orcas off the Queen Charlotte Islands from the dubious safety of a rubber dinghy. Brett complained in her letter about having to work overtime now at Home Hardware to help pay off their Visa bill ("our Rocky Mountain of debt," as she called it), but from both her account of their adventures and the pictures she had sent, it was clear she and Sam had enjoyed every minute of it. It would take more than falling from an airplane to slow Brett down.

"What're you looking at, sweetheart?"

Leeza jumped, turned to see her mother in her bedroom doorway. "Brett sent me some pictures of her honeymoon."

"Really? May I see?"

Leeza casually slid Brett's letter over top of the clipping as her mother entered the room. She picked up the pictures and moved to the bed, spreading them out for her mother and herself to examine.

"Oh, my," said Diane. "Who do you suppose was brave enough to take this one?" She held up what looked to be a shot of Brett and Sam standing on the edge of a gigantic sheet of ice that dropped away dramatically behind them.

Leeza grinned. "Had to be someone almost as crazy as Brett."

The two laughed quietly as they pored over the remaining photos. Then Diane stood up. "Okay if I read her letter?" she asked, moving toward the desk.

Leeza got up quickly, gritting her teeth to conceal the twinge in her left leg that caught her momentarily. She scooped up the letter and envelope. "As soon as I finish with it," she said with forced nonchalance. "I'm only halfway through."

"Okay," Diane said. "Jack's taking us out to dinner tonight, so I'll be on the deck with my novel while it's still warm. Bring the letter down when you finish."

Leeza listened to her mother go downstairs but waited until she heard the patio door slide open before closing her bedroom door and returning to her desk. She pulled the newspaper clipping out from under the pages of Brett's letter, looked at the black-and-white photo and read again the four words Brett had penciled on the edge: "A person can change."

She absently rubbed her thigh, easing the cramp that had caught her, and looked out the window over her desk. She remembered hearing those same words spoken to her at the rehab the day she'd had her fixators removed.

"I'm not going to lie to you, Leeza," said Dr. Dan. "This will hurt."

Is there anything that doesn't? she'd wanted to ask as she stared at the ceiling, but she was afraid she'd just start crying again. The way she had cried the night before. Despite having jammed the corner of her pillow into her mouth, she'd made noises that had even blocked out the sounds Stephen made. Or maybe Stephen had lain awake listening to *her* for a change.

"I'm going to give you some local freezing first, okay?" explained the doctor. "That will dull the pain somewhat. It won't stop it, but it should make it more bearable."

That's what she needed, Leeza thought. Something to dull the pain. She could have used it yesterday. *You bastard! What are you doing here?* She made a straight line with her lips, tried once again to keep from crying. *Don't you know who this is?*

"If it starts to hurt too much, you just squeeze real tight, okay sweetheart?" Diane said. She gripped Leeza's right hand while Jack, his face pale but determined, held her left.

"That's what my husband told me the night I gave birth to our first son," a nurse offered as she passed the doctor the needle.

"Did it work?" he asked.

The nurse laughed softly. "I nearly broke his hand," she said.

Leeza tried to let their small talk do its job, get her mind off things. Not the medical procedure they were involved in—removing her fixators—but the drama that had unfolded before her the previous day. *Is this some kind of sick joke?* Wanted to forget the shock, the deception, the betrayal. *That monster is the one who put you here!*

"Everything okay?" the doctor asked.

Leeza nodded. *Get that goddamn son of a bitch out of my daughter's room!* "Everything's wonderful," she lied.

The procedure took less time than Leeza would have expected. Of course, she had no idea just what to expect any more. She'd learned you really couldn't depend on anything. Or anyone.

"All finished," the doctor said as he placed the last of the metal pins on the tray. "Sheila here is going to dress the pin-sites again. You're going to notice quite a difference in the healing process once the holes begin to close over."

Leeza would think of those words often the rest of that morning, think about holes that weren't drilled through skin and bone. Holes you could see and holes you couldn't. Holes you didn't think could ever close over. Would, instead, remain red and raw, would ooze pus and grow leathery tissue around the edges that would only crumble and decay. Perhaps there *were* things you could depend on after all. Death and decay. And disappointment.

When she was returned to her room and Jack and her mother stepped out for lunch, she finally allowed the tears to come. And they kept coming, gulping sobs clawing at her throat, making her shudder. She was reaching for yet another tissue to dry her eyes and blow her nose when one was handed to her. She looked up.

"I'm sorry, Leeza," Reef whispered hoarsely. If anything, he looked worse than she did. As if he'd had something of his own surgically removed.

"Go *away*," she moaned, turning her face toward the window.

"Leeza." It was Brett's voice. "You need to hear him out. He's been calling. He was downstairs with me all morning. He really didn't know who you were. Honest."

Leeza stared at the window across the room, her

back an iron bar. "Does that even matter?" she asked. "He did this to me!" And then she was sobbing.

"Yes, I did that to you." Something seemed to clutch at the voice behind her, and the rest came out sounding strained. "I'm so sorry. You gotta believe me." The voice caught again and there was silence for a moment before it continued. "But the guy who did that isn't the guy who's here now. A person can change."

"What in HELL do you think you're DOING?"

Leeza turned to see her mother enter the room. Except that "enter" didn't describe her movement. She advanced into the room, *took* the room like a general would take an enemy camp. Thrusting herself between her daughter and Reef, she lowered her voice, but the intensity of emotion was the same as if she'd shouted the words: "You get out of this room and you *stay* out or I'll call the police."

"Please—" Reef began.

"And if I *ever* see you near my daughter again, or if you ever try to *contact* her, I'll make sure you end up where you should have gone in the first place. *Do you hear me?*"

"I just want to—"

"No one *wants* you here!" she screamed. "Is that clear?" She picked up the phone on Leeza's bedside table and began pressing numbers. "You've done all the damage to this family you're *ever* going to do." She spoke into the phone. "I'd like the police. I want to report—"

"Fine!" he shouted. "I'm outta here!" He was at the doorway when he turned again. "Leeza—"

"*GET OUT!*"

And he was gone.

There was a terrible silence in the room, a silence so palpable that the air seemed thick with it. Brett was the first to puncture it. "He just wanted to say he was sorry."

Diane tore her eyes from the empty doorway and stared at Brett. "How could he think saying he was sorry would make up for what he did?"

"I don't believe," Brett said softly, "that he thought that."

"I don't care what he thought or didn't think. I'll see him in jail before I see him anywhere near Leeza again."

And that's how it ended. Leeza later learned from her mother that a judge had issued a court order preventing Reef from contacting her again. And she learned from Carly that Reef was reassigned to the Victoria General Hospital to complete his volunteer service.

And she learned from Brett, who had called North Hills and spoken to someone named Alex, that the Reef they knew really wasn't the person Leeza had seen standing on the overpass that afternoon a lifetime ago. That person had never known his father, a boy not much older than himself who had gotten a deaf girl pregnant and then run off. Nor had that person known his mother, whose world of silence had kept her prisoner within herself until the boy's attentions had drawn her out and then betrayed her. She'd wasted away, barely pushing the scrawny baby out of her body before leaving it herself. That baby became the focus of his grandfather's anger: the reason for their poverty, the justification for every drink, the root of every rage. That baby became the frightened, angry boy who lost his grandmother to a disease he couldn't see, the boy who was then shunted from one foster home to another, one school to another. That was the person on the overpass. Not the person who had sat with her, taken her for walks, taught her how to play poker, reminded her it shouldn't hurt to laugh again.

There had been times during the rest of her rehab when she'd considered calling him herself. There'd even been times after she'd returned home that she'd picked up the telephone book and turned to the Ns to find the North Hills number.

But something had stopped her, some part of her that couldn't forget the rock and the windshield and the cars that slammed into her, the sounds that she still heard sometimes at night, still made when the nightmares came too close, got too real.

She could not forget that. Would not excuse what had happened to her. What was still happening to her.

And then last Sunday her mother had convinced her to go to church with her and Jack, the first time she'd attended since Ellen's funeral. She'd sat there, bored as usual, seeking a distraction to get her mind off the hard pew that cut off the circulation in her legs and made the left one throb. Her eyes were drawn to the stained-glass windows, drawn to the thousands of fragments, the shards of color that combined to form scenes and symbols and words. And it was at that moment that she heard the words of the minister as he preached about forgiveness from the Book of John: "And when the scribes and the Pharisees dragged the adulterer to the temple to be punished, Jesus said, 'Let the person who is without sin cast the first stone.'"

Leeza picked up the clipping again, looked at the black-and-white photo and those four pencilled words one more time.

Chapter 28

"Sorry, Frank," Reef said as he climbed into the pickup. He was almost thirty minutes late coming out of the school, and the April air had turned cool.

"You got the question again, right?" Colville asked.

Reef nodded.

Colville pulled the truck out into traffic, then glanced at Reef. "Doesn't get any easier, does it?"

Reef shook his head. "Some parts do," he said. "But not that one."

They rode in silence for a few blocks. A light up ahead turned red and Colville geared down, eased the truck to a stop beside a Mustang convertible. Despite the cool air, the top was down and two girls sat in the front bucket seats, laughing and talking above the tortured wail of the stereo. The driver looked over at Reef, said something to her passenger, and they both waved at him and smiled. Then the light turned green and they were gone.

Reef stared ahead as Colville eased into the left lane, waited for oncoming traffic to pass so he could turn. "Frank . . ." Reef began.

Colville didn't need to look at Reef to know the question on his mind. "You know you can't."

"Why not?"

"Because of the injunction." Colville sighed. "We've been through all this before, Reef. If you try to contact her, a judge could rule that you broke the terms of your probation. You know what happened before. Next time you won't be so lucky. And you've come too far to throw it all away now."

The traffic passed and Colville swung left, then straightened out the wheel. It took a moment before Reef realized where they were. Birmingham Avenue, heading west toward the Park Street overpass. He looked up, saw the overpass approaching, saw the chain-link fencing that now made it impossible for anyone to throw objects into the traffic below. *Because of me*, he thought. *That's because of me.*

There were times when it seemed like the events of that day on the overpass had happened to someone else, some other Reef Kennedy, a Reef Kennedy who thought that life could be summed up in stupid lessons like *Shit happens*. Shit didn't just happen. He knew that now. Shit got made. And the worst shit is the shit we make for ourselves.

He looked up, watched the Park Street overpass slide over them, then grow smaller in the truck's side mirror as they left it behind. He had, he realized, left so many things behind during the past year. Some of them he'd worked hard at leaving. Like the anger and fear he'd spoken about to those students today. Some things, though, had just happened. Like friends. One of them was Alex, who had moved back in with his parents. The last time they'd spoken, Alex had cranked up his Hollywood diva act five notches and drawn numerous stares as they'd sat talking in the food court at the Halifax Shopping Center. He'd told Reef that things at home were "absolutely *fabulous*, honey," but Reef had sensed the opposite was true. He'd thought of the Robert Frost poem they'd read in English class that week, thought of the part about home:

> *Home is the place where, when you have to go there,*
> *They have to take you in.*

Reef wondered if that was what home was for Alex. Hoped it wasn't true. But he couldn't get those words out of his head when he and Alex said goodbye for the last time.

Others had drifted out of his life too. Like Scar, who had always been smarter than any of them and had proven it in January when she'd completed her grade twelve at the end of the first semester. On the recommendation of her principal, a guidance counselor and Glen Whidden, she'd been accepted into Business at Queen's University in Kingston, Ontario, and was admitted to courses that were already in session. Although her outstanding performance in her advanced high school courses didn't guarantee her success, everyone was confident she could make the transition. The principal had even managed to get her some scholarship and bursary money, and he'd put her in touch with a friend in Kingston, who'd offered her a part-time job to help with living expenses.

Scar had been embarrassed when she'd told them the news. "It's not like I *have* to go, guys," she'd said. "I don't even know if I *want* to—"

But Bigger hadn't let her finish. "You'd *better* want to!" he'd bellowed, grabbing her and tossing her into the air like a three year old. "You turn down a chance like this and I'll kick your ass!"

Jink had been less enthusiastic. "You probably won't even wanna *talk* to goons like us any more," he'd sulked, but he'd agreed with Bigger that she'd be crazy not to go. And so had Reef. Anything that got her away from her old man was a good thing, and education was the only thing that could deliver any of them from the hardscrabble existence their families had known.

So she had gone. They'd seen her off at the train station, her two bags like orphans on the crowded platform. Her father, of course, hadn't come, and her mother left the station long before the train did. But Jink and Bigger made so much commotion that bystanders thought there were twenty people seeing her off. She hugged them all goodbye, including Reef. She didn't kiss him, and he was grateful for that. He was even happier to get her second letter, the one telling about the guy she'd met in her Financial Accounting class. If anyone deserved a new life, a decent life, it was Scar. He'd traced his fingers slowly over her signature, lingering over the second syllable she'd finally chosen to use.

It was weird to think of her in Ontario, but he'd already gotten used to not seeing her much after starting at his new school in September. The same was true of Jink and Bigger. They'd called a few times, and he got together with them once in a while, but he was busy trying to keep his marks up and fulfilling the other conditions of his probation. Like extracurriculars. Judge Thomas was wrong about one thing—he was lousy at track and field. But he surprised himself by turning out to be a better-than-average soccer player and, more recently, an excellent volleyball player. He'd led the volleyball team in points all season, and he'd even scored the tie-breaking and match points that had earned the Bonavista Bruvehearts the provincial title the previous weekend. The team's picture appeared in the newspaper, and the guys at North Hills made a big deal about it, buying a dozen copies of the paper and putting the picture up everywhere. Reef was pleased, but for another reason, too. He hoped that Leeza would see the photo and maybe call to congratulate him. But, of course, he was just kidding himself.

His ability to kick and volley a ball with almost unerring accuracy confounded both his coaches, who found it difficult to believe he hadn't played either of their sports before. Although he didn't share it with them, Reef attributed his success to the considerable target practise he'd got throwing rocks over the years. Yes, the mechanics of kicking and volleying were different than those involved in throwing, but an instinct for distance and direction was crucial in both sports. In rock-throwing, too.

He reached into his pocket and pulled out the object he'd carried with him to each of his presentations. He'd found it the day before school started, when Bigger had borrowed his brother's car and driven all four of them out to Crystal Crescent Beach to celebrate the last day of summer vacation. It hadn't turned out to be much of a celebration, though. Jink's injuries were still healing, and all that walking over rocks and sand had turned out to be an ordeal for him. To make matters worse, Bigger had decided it would be fun to harass nude sunbathers, and before Reef and Scar could stop him, he'd grabbed some clothes and strewn them all along the beach—only to discover that the clothing belonged to a young swimsuit-wearing family who were playing in the surf. It was a windy day, and it had taken the four friends nearly an hour to recover everything.

While retrieving a lost sandal, Reef had spied something near the water's edge and thought for a moment that he was seeing a single black eye. The stone was almost perfectly round, its edges polished smooth by waves and wind, and it fit perfectly in the palm of his hand. He hefted it, saw in his mind's eye the smooth arc it would make when he launched it out over the waves, and then slipped it into his pocket.

The Park Street overpass was still visible in the mirror as he curled his fingers around the stone. That afternoon at Crystal Crescent Beach on the last day of summer, he hadn't known why he'd chosen to keep it. He *still* didn't know. All that mattered now was that he had. It was the first stone he'd found since his grandmother had died that he hadn't flung as far as he could. Hadn't wanted to. Hadn't needed to. He held it tight in his hand as he watched the road unfurl toward home.

Author's Note

Every piece of fiction I've ever written—whether novel or short story—has grown out of something that has bothered me, kept me awake at night, wouldn't leave me alone. As I was mulling over ideas for a third novel, the daughter of a friend was killed when a stolen vehicle, driven by a teenager trying to evade police in a high-speed chase, struck her car. Following this tragedy, I couldn't stop wondering how that teenager might cope with the knowledge that his recklessness had cost a life and irrevocably altered the lives of many others. Before long, I had a character in mind, a teenager with absolutely no regard for the well-being of others who commits an act that results in the death of an innocent bystander. As I continued to think about him, though, I began to see other possibilities for the story and to wonder how my character would handle having to deal firsthand with the results of his actions, actually having to face the person he has hurt—not killed—and to try to make restitution. It was at this point that I knew I had my story.

Although the seeds of *The First Stone* are real, this

book is fiction. To allow my story to unfold within a workable time frame, I took liberties with the judicial system. As well, the people and most of the places in the novel live only in my mind, which is why you'll find references to streets and buildings in Halifax that do not exist. My apologies to the people of this wonderful city for altering its landscape.